JOURNEY
with me

Enjoy the Journey

Catherine Campbell

Isaiah 40:31

Also by Catherine Campbell

God Knows Your Name (Monarch Books, 2010)
Broken Works Best (Monarch Books, 2012; 10Publishing, 2018)
Under the Rainbow (Monarch Books, 2013)
Rainbows for Rainy Days (Monarch Books, 2013)
When We Can't, God Can (Monarch Books, 2015)
Chasing the Dawn (Monarch Books, 2016)

JOURNEY
with me

365 daily devotions

Catherine Campbell

INTER-VARSITY PRESS
36 Causton Street, London SW1P 4ST, England
Email: ivp@ivpbooks.com
Website: www.ivpbooks.com

First published 2018

British Library Cataloguing-in-Publication Data
A catalogue record for this book is available from the British Library.

ISBN: 978–1–78359–726–0
eBook ISBN: 978–1–78359–727–7

Set in Adobe Caslon 10/13pt
Typeset in Great Britain by CRB Associates, Potterhanworth, Lincolnshire
Printed in Great Britain by Ashford Colour Press Ltd, Gosport, Hampshire

Inter-Varsity Press publishes Christian books that are true to the Bible and that communicate the gospel, develop discipleship and strengthen the church for its mission in the world.

IVP originated within the Inter-Varsity Fellowship, now the Universities and Colleges Christian Fellowship, a student movement connecting Christian Unions in universities and colleges throughout Great Britain, and a member movement of the International Fellowship of Evangelical Students. Website: www.uccf.org.uk. That historic association is maintained, and all senior IVP staff and committee members subscribe to the UCCF Basis of Faith.

Dedicated
to
Dad,
who completed his final journey during the writing of this book

and
also to
the church family of Coleraine Congregational Church,
who have allowed my husband and me to walk with you through
your joys and sorrows for the past eighteen years.
As a new journey begins for both of us may we
each experience God's leading and continued blessing,
remembering that 'He is faithful!'

Acknowledgments

I am deeply indebted for the wisdom of those more learned than myself. My research has included the writings of many biblical scholars both from commentaries (mostly from my husband's bookshelves!) and from trusted online sources. As my husband always says, 'Milk many cows, but churn your own butter.' So I have been churning away with what I have milked from God's Word and the intellect of others, in an attempt to make some of the more difficult concepts readable, and the simple ones profound!

Where I have quoted directly, I have made every attempt to acknowledge the source accurately. Apologies if I have missed any along the way.

I am also extremely thankful to the many friends and family who pray regularly for my writing and speaking ministry. Your partnership is an incredible blessing. I couldn't do this without you, and already know that you will pray with me for God to use *Journey with Me* powerfully in hearts and lives.

To my husband, Philip, your patience, support and love strengthen my life, making it possible for me to stretch beyond what at times I think I cannot do. Thank you for releasing me to accomplish what God directs, not only in my writing but also in all of life's current challenges.

And to God, who journeys with me day by day with unchangeable grace, thank You for sticking with Your unworthy servant. My heart is Yours.

Introduction

The message in my inbox made me smile. Owing to a slip of the tongue, the editorial team found themselves discussing the possibility of my writing a year-long devotional – a 'mistake' they decided was worth following up. Having already two forty-day devotionals under my belt, I instantly warmed to their enquiry. I even had a working title. *Journey with Me* suited the idea I had of inviting readers to walk with me in the devotional sense. I'd take a year to write it and simply let others in on what God was teaching me along the way.

Sometimes you get it right, and sometimes you get it so wrong. I hadn't realized how arrogant the idea of inviting others to 'journey with me' was until I hit an emotional rough patch. Feeling a bit like 'Pilgrim', I entered the 'Slough of Despond' feeling totally discouraged, and with my writing sinking despairingly. Only then did I sense God say, 'Catherine, don't you think it would be better if your readers "Journeyed with Me", instead of with you?'

The 'I did it my way' attitude was not working, so with focus redirected, I decided to do it His way instead. The end result you now hold in your hands. For more than a year I've been listening, learning and journeying with the One who knows the path He wanted you and me to follow together all along. As with most journeys, my year of writing was filled with unexpected twists that brought many challenges of both the physical and the emotional variety.

My own personal journey with Jesus started when I was a teenager – full of life and exuberance – and only ever expecting 'good stuff' from the Lord. I never anticipated how high the mountains or how low the valleys would be that God would lead me through. The journey certainly delivered more than I could have imagined, including the deaths of two of my children. However, the biggest and best surprise I received was how deeply I would get to know the God who created heaven, earth and me. If I have any ambition at all for this book, it would be that some who make this journey at God's invitation would come to know Him as I have. At fourteen years of age I gave Him my sin, and in return He gave me everything I needed to complete this convoluted journey called life. I think I was the winner in that 'great exchange'!

So in *Journey with Me* we examine the big themes of life, the seasons and the church year. But most of all we consider God Himself – His Word, the lives of people He has changed, the enormity and wonder of His character, and the love He has shown us as members of His family, through His Son.

It's a privilege for me to be published for the first time by IVP, although that transition has been made easier by working once more with the inimitable Tony

ix

Collins. Thank you Tony for your trust in my writing for seven books now, and for your wisdom in this particular journey – my longest to date!

Special thanks go once more to my two invaluable proofreaders, my husband Philip and my friend Liz Young. I'm sure IVP, and especially the professional editorial team, will be as thankful for your expertise as I am!

Two weeks before finishing this book my dear dad passed on to glory. He'd spoken for some time about the 'journey' he felt was overdue, while looking forward to his 'plane' taking off and reaching his final destination. I'm glad his last painful steps have finally transported him into God's presence, but I miss him dearly. His encouragement and prayers for my writing, but most of all his devoted love throughout my life, are irreplaceable.

Finally, let me say how much I am looking forward to walking with you this year as we journey with God through the days and weeks ahead. May my words pale into insignificance as you experience His divine presence with you along both pleasant paths and steep mountain cliffs.

Catherine Campbell

Catherine would love to hear from you.
You can contact her via:
Facebook <www.facebook.com/catherinecampbellauthor>
or her website <www.catherine-campbell.com>

January

1 January

You crown the year with Your goodness,
And Your paths drip with abundance.

Psalm 65:11

Reading: Psalm 65

Queen Elizabeth pronounced the year 1992 as her 'Annus Horribilis'. Virtually every month of that year had produced personal heartache for the monarch. The marriages of three of her children had crashed publicly. Millions viewed her personal sadness on television as Windsor Castle was badly damaged by fire. And on top of it all the press grumbled words of falling appreciation for the monarchy, which would culminate in further disaster for Her Majesty's popularity following Diana's death five short years later.

How would you sum up the year you have just left behind?

Was it one of the best yet? Did you marry, have a baby, start a new job, move house, retire, come into money? Was it simply all round great? And to add the icing to your happy-year-cake you sensed God's presence and experienced His pleasure. Wow! It's been quite a year. Be thankful.

Or would your summation of the past 365 days be that you are glad to see the back of them? All they've succeeded in doing is to cause pain, loneliness and confusion? Perhaps even a sense of abandonment by God, or at best less awareness of His presence. Might you go as far as to call the old year your 'Annus Horribilis'?

Today we stand at an annual change point. We have no idea what lies ahead for the next 365 days. Yet each of us will undoubtedly desire that happiness will come built into those days. Life gives us no such guarantees.

Conversely, God promises to 'crown', or top off, the year with His goodness. The paths we will walk will 'drip', or overflow, with the abundance of all He has for us. However, happy circumstances may not be God's choice of delivery, but He will come up with the goods. He always does.

Heavenly Father, I choose to leave behind what is past, and journey into this New Year with You, excited to experience the fulfilment of Your promises. Amen.

2 January

Enter into His gates with thanksgiving,
and into His courts with praise.
Be thankful to Him, and bless His name.

Psalm 100:4

Reading: Psalm 100

Who doesn't remember the childhood excitement of exploring what mysteries might be lurking behind some old gate we'd discovered? Thoughts of secret gardens, hidden delights and heroic challenges drew us into the unknown back then. Nowadays, entering a new year can rekindle a similar sense of anticipation for what lies just beyond our view.

In Minnie Louise Haskin's poem 'God Knows' ('The Gate of the Year'), she asks for a light to guide her safely into the unknown of the coming year. Instead she is told to put her hand into God's hand, which is better than any familiar path.

In Bible times, city gates were extremely significant, with particular emphasis placed on the importance of entering, rather than leaving, through them. They were defence structures, providing protection from enemy attack, remaining open during the day and firmly shut during the hours of darkness. Wise town elders ensured they were overlaid with metal to prevent them being destroyed by fire, as poorly constructed gates could lead to disaster. Public meetings, judgments, markets and community issues were also discussed and settled in the courtyards just inside the city gates.

The gates the psalmist speaks of here are not made with hands, yet they provide unrivalled protection from danger, and from enemies who would seek to damage or destroy our lives. And within God's gates lie the wisdom and guidance we need for all that lies ahead in the remaining 364 days of this year. Is it any wonder that we are encouraged to enter through them with thanksgiving!

As we meditate on what it means to dwell continually in His presence, and therefore under His protection, let's give Him our fears and walk into the unknown with our hand securely held in His.

Lord, I give You praise for what it means to dwell within Your gates, and that my hand firmly held in Yours is better than walking a safe way alone. Amen.

4

3 January

Blessed is the man who trusts in the LORD,
and whose hope is in the LORD.

Jeremiah 17:7

Reading: Genesis 8:15–19

You only have to look at Noah to understand what it's really like to go out into the unknown!

He'd been on that huge vessel for a whole year. When the earth eventually dried up, the door opened on a totally new world for Noah, his family and the other living creatures that had journeyed with them. The very geography of the planet had been changed by the ferocity of the flood.

Where had the ark transported them to? Was this new world a safe place to live in? What would they eat? Would the floods return?

Everything they had previously known was gone. Everything!

Noah did more than step into new territory; he stepped into a new year and a new life. The only thing familiar to him was the group of people he'd spent the previous year with, working on that boat. But wait, Noah hadn't simply set off on some great adventure and built a boat to get away from all the trouble around him. No, his architectural feat had been under the direction of God Himself. God had plans, only some of which He had revealed to Noah before the rain fell.

For Noah, there were no unknowns as far as God was concerned. He knew exactly what was next for the one described in Genesis 6:9 as the man who 'walked with God'. Noah had chosen to trust God, in spite of looking foolish during the many years that it took to build the ark. His hope for what lay ahead was in the One who had already proven Himself as faithful to the old builder who walked with Him day by day. That's why Noah was able to leave the place of safety and walk confidently into the unknown. God hadn't changed!

Lord, new beginnings can be scary, but help me to realize today that there are no 'unknowns' with you. May I, like Noah, walk with You, in whom my hope lies. Amen.

5

4 January

You must make allowance for each other's faults
and forgive the person who offends you. Remember,
the Lord forgave you, so you must forgive others.
Colossians 3:13, NLT

Reading: Colossians 3:12–15

Hollywood has long been fascinated with stories of time travel. The idea that you could travel back in time and fix some wrong, or save the planet by making a change or righting an error, might make for fun escapism, but it is far from reality. Life isn't that simple.

Last year is over; its days cannot be reclaimed. Yet too often we drag last year's issues with us into the New Year. Unkind words said, hurts experienced, broken relationships, festering grudges, arguments and love betrayed continue to cause pain and therefore influence our daily lives in what should be a fresh start – a new year.

In this letter to the Christians at Colossae, Paul is explaining the importance of living the new life given to them by Christ. This concept was totally foreign to them in a world where getting your own back was the way to deal with those who had wronged you. Remarkably, we're told today, 'Don't get mad; get even.' But Paul explains that this is not the way of the cross.

Amid all the resolutions of sorting out our body shape and fitness levels, we rarely purpose to make changes to the things unseen that have such a detrimental effect in our lives. A psychiatrist friend once told me that much physical illness is caused by unwillingness to forgive the wrongs done to us.

We are only four days into this New Year. Why not purpose to forgive someone who has wronged you? Refuse to drag the old into the new. It will be harder than dieting, or training for that marathon, but the rewards will be greater than you imagine. Remember, God carries no grudges against us.

Lord, this is hard, but I don't want to live this year like last. You know who I am thinking about right now. Give me the grace to forgive and the strength to forget. Thank You for forgiving me. Amen.

5 January

'Yes,' Jesus replied, 'and I assure you, everyone who has given up house or wife or brothers or parents or children, for the sake of the Kingdom of God, will be repaid many times over.'

Luke 18:29–30a, NLT

Reading: Genesis 12:1–3

Are you a planner? Do you like to set yourself goals? I usually like to have a Plan B to fall back on in case things don't quite turn out right.

Abram had no Plan B when he left the wealth and security of probably the most advanced city on the planet around 2000 BC. In fact, Abram didn't even have a Plan A. Instead, he chose to trust in the plan of the God he had only recently come to know. Even that didn't seem like much to go on!

> Now the LORD had said to Abram:
> 'Get out of your country,
> From your family
> And from your father's house,
> To a land that I will show you.'
> (Genesis 12:1)

What did the son of an idol-maker do when he heard this? How did the man who had lived all his life worshipping the moon god respond? He got up and went! With no idea of where he was going, and only scanty knowledge of the God who had called him, Abram started on a journey. This journey was about more than covering miles, more than distancing himself from a comfortable life in an advanced city. His was to be a journey of developing friendship with the one true God.

Today there is a stress scale that measures how 'life changes' affect our mental health. Abram would have blown the scale when he left Ur! Everything was about to change. Yet we read of no anxiety on his part, because Abram cultivated that seed of faith in his heart and allowed himself to believe that God would make good on His promises.

Lord, that first step of faith is always the hardest; help me today to step out like Abram, believing that Your Plan A can be trusted wholeheartedly. Amen.

7

6 January

A PASSAGE TO PONDER

Thus says the LORD, who makes a way in the sea

And a path through mighty waters,

Who brings forth the chariot and horse,

The army and the power

(They shall lie down together, they shall not rise;

They are extinguished, they are quenched like a wick);

'Do not remember the former things,

Nor consider the things of old.

Behold, I will do a new thing,

Now it shall spring forth;

Shall you not know it?

I will even make a road in the wilderness

And rivers in the desert.'

Isaiah 43:16–19

Read the passage slowly and let the Author speak to your heart. Ask yourself these questions as you ponder this passage:

- What does it say?
- What does it mean?
- What is God saying to me?
- How will I respond?

7 January

The God of glory appeared to our father Abraham when he was in Mesopotamia, before he dwelt in Haran, and said to him, 'Get out of your country and from your relatives, and come to a land that I will show you.'

Acts 7:2–3

Reading: Hebrews 11:8–12

How did Abram feel walking through the gates of Ur for the last time? He went, it seems, without complaint, opting for the trade route north, which meandered through rugged, desert land.

It took a journey of 600 miles, involving months of travelling and living out of a tent, to reach the city of Haran. Months of hoping the next watering hole wouldn't be dry, and that there would be enough grass for their flocks. The city man was becoming a nomad. But when they got as far as Haran, Abram stopped there. In fact, he did more than stop: he settled there.

Had God told him to? No. Why did Abram not journey on when he had started so well? Was the man of faith going to settle for halfway? What about God's promise, if Abram obeyed?

Abram's problem was partial obedience. 'Get out of your country,' God had said. No problem. 'From your family.' *Ah, I'll just take my orphaned nephew, Lot, with me.* 'From your father's house.' *But my father is old; he needs me.* And Abram's lesson in obedience fell at the first hurdle. It seemed perfectly reasonable to him, but then Abram didn't know what God did – how Lot would be nothing but trouble, or that Abram's idol-worshipping father would delay God's blessing in his life.

To Abram's credit, he never looked back, or went back, to Ur. It was always his intention to follow God. He simply allowed his emotions and spiritual immaturity to get in the way of full obedience. Thankfully, God was developing a friendship with this brave man, and spoke to Abram again. And Abram left Haran and headed toward Canaan, where God met with him once more.

Lord, I can be easily sidetracked by what seems good, but is not necessarily Your will for me. Help me to listen carefully and obey wholeheartedly. Amen.

8 January

It was by faith that Isaac blessed his two sons,
Jacob and Esau. He had confidence in what God
was going to do in the future.

Hebrews 11:20, NLT

Reading: Genesis 22:1–8

The four men slowly trekked through wilderness terrain, their donkey laden with wood. Isaac thought his father quiet, but put it down to recent family tension over Ishmael. Perhaps once they'd made their sacrifice on Mount Moriah, his father would be in better spirits. So Isaac quietly followed the man whom he loved and respected; who had taught him about the covenant-keeping God. He couldn't have imagined what would happen next.

Later, when Abraham laid Isaac on that wooden altar, bound hand and foot, the young man didn't resist or fight back. He could easily have overpowered the old man and run for his life. But he didn't. Instead, he lay back on the wood and watched his beloved father raise the knife high above his head, ready to slay *him* – the son of God's promise!

And in that moment of horror, the result of Abraham's willingness to obey God's command by faith, Isaac heard God's voice for the first time. 'Abraham! Abraham! Lay down your knife ... for now I know that you truly fear God. You have not withheld even your beloved son from Me' (Genesis 22:11–12, NLT).

Is it any wonder, when the time came to commit his own sons to God's faithfulness, that Isaac did so without holding back? He had learnt from the master of faith, his own father, on that hill outside Jerusalem years earlier, that God can be trusted, even with what is most precious to us. Abraham believed that even if Isaac were to die, God would raise him to life again in order to fulfil His promise to make a great nation through his descendants.

Isaac had personally experienced the reward of costly faith, therefore, 'He had confidence in what God was going to do in the future' (Hebrews 11:20, NLT).

God of the everlasting covenant, I leave my future with You, confident that You can be trusted with whatever lies ahead. Amen.

9 January

By faith Moses, when he became of age, refused to be
called the son of Pharaoh's daughter, choosing rather
to suffer affliction with the people of God than to
enjoy the passing pleasures of sin.
Hebrews 11:24–25

Reading: Hebrews 11:23–29

For Moses, life was looking good. In spite of a shaky start he was now a member of an opulent family, living in one of the strongest kingdoms on earth. He had been given the finest education available, lived in luxury, and faced a future that most could only dream of.

But he wasn't happy. Moses knew deep down that he didn't belong in the palace of the kings. Childhood memories of a God not made by human hands, or covered in gold, woke the young prince from his sleep. In classes on the victories of Egypt his mind often wandered to stories of another community – the Hebrew citizens of Goshen: a nation of slaves who served the very people Moses had been taught to call his own.

They were poor. He was rich. They lived in hovels. He lived in a palace. They were nobodies. He was somebody. They had no future. He had everything to look forward to. Or had he? Moses couldn't get away from the fact of his birth, couldn't get away from the injustice and inhumanity he was party to every day. What could he do? He was only one man. But the day came when he could no longer straddle the fence. The man who was to become Israel's deliverer came to a place in the road of life where he had to choose, not necessarily what might seem best for him, but what was right. Yet amazingly, when that happened, neither side wanted him (Exodus 2:11–15)! Instead he found himself in a lonely place, but it was there God could finally shape him for the job that lay ahead.

And it all began with a choice.

Lord, life is filled with all kinds of choices. What seems best may not be right for me. Help me to leave the outcome with You. Amen.

11

10 January

Be still, and know that I am God.
Psalm 46:10

Reading: Psalm 46

It would be forty years before Moses would return to Egypt. And it took every one of those years for God to ready the man of His choice for the Exodus. Moses had to lose his Egyptian-ness, his need for position and power, his confused identity. He had to learn what it was like to eat more dust than fine food, to lie on rocks instead of silk sheets, to be another man's servant, to herd stubborn sheep through the wilderness, before leading an obstinate people across the desert.

But more important than all of this, Moses had to learn the art of stillness in order to hear God speak. In the mundane of life's ordinary tasks, away from the limelight, in the backwaters of Midian, this man was getting to know God. And God was in no hurry.

That fact always amazes me. God is never in a hurry. We fill our days with family, work, church and even ministry, believing that busyness equals godliness, that activity equals spirituality.

Yet, in reality, the times of greatest spiritual growth come when we are obedient to God's command to be still. For Moses, stillness came with life in a foreign and difficult place. Only then, and with the passage of time, did Moses hear God speak.

Recently this verse in Psalm 46, to 'Be still, and know that I am God', has been tugging at my heart. 'But how can I slow down, Lord? I'm so busy with life and ministry . . . and it's for You, Lord,' I've argued. Yet the consequence of my busyness is often that I end up serving from an empty cup.

'Be still, child,' the master cup-filler whispered, as family and health issues moved me to a different place. It hasn't been easy, but I'm listening for His voice again in the ordinary everyday, and learning that change is not to be feared. It is God's way of reminding us that knowing Him is more important than serving Him.

Lord, teach me to seek for stillness. Remind me that it is there I will find You. Amen.

11 January

'For with God nothing will be impossible.'
Luke 1:37

Reading: Exodus 14:13–16

The hospital lift doors closed slowly as the conversation with self began. *Why didn't you ask God to heal her?* Unwilling to admit my habit of praying safe prayers, I rehearsed the content of what I had actually prayed. I had asked for God's help, wisdom for the doctors, relief from pain, and peace for both patient and family. Surely that was all good?

But why do you never ask God to heal someone? Not just 'someone' – that person you were just with?

Because I didn't want to get their hopes up, I replied to self. *God doesn't always heal, or not in the way we want Him to.* But my logic couldn't lift my heart from my boots.

It can be so easy to quote Luke 1:37, can't it? But there are times when the outward expression of faith drags behind the words.

When Moses heard God say, 'But lift up your rod, and stretch out your hand over the sea and divide it. And the children of Israel shall go on dry ground through the midst of the sea' (Exodus 14:16), he did just that. The Egyptian army was almost upon them. The Red Sea blocked their escape. They were trapped! It was time to move beyond mere words – time to act, in faith, believing that the God who had said He would deliver them would actually do it. But it still required one thing from Moses. In faith, he had to lift up his rod and stretch out his hand over the sea, and then God would divide it.

That day, there was no safe option available for the man who had once run away. The door was opening for Moses to learn that 'with God nothing will be impossible'. And 'nothing' means not anything! That's a reality I also need to learn.

Lord, I want to move beyond the safe this year, and learn to pray and act in faith, believing that with You absolutely nothing is impossible. Amen.

13

12 January

'But My servant Caleb, because he has a different spirit in him and has followed Me fully, I will bring into the land where he went, and his descendants shall inherit it.'

Numbers 14:24

Reading: Numbers 13:26–33; 14:6–9

There was nothing safe about Caleb!

Under the leadership of Joshua, Caleb, along with ten other brave men, left the camp of Israel in the wilderness and went on a reconnaissance mission. They were to stake out the land God had promised to give them, and bring back a report to Moses. What was the land like? Would they be able to occupy it and live there as God had promised them? Straightforward enough, you might think. There was just one problem: the report would include the perspective of twelve different men! Ten of them chose to exclude God's word on the matter.

The majority report was catastrophic: 'the people living there are powerful, and their cities and towns are fortified and very large ... we even saw giants there' (Numbers 13:28, 33, NLT). It was accurate to a point, but they had left God out of the equation.

Caleb, on the other hand, had not! 'The land we explored is a wonderful land! And if the Lord is pleased with us, He will bring us safely into that land ... He will give it to us!' (Numbers 14:7–8, NLT).

Caleb and Joshua did not discount the difficulties, but rather included God in the reckoning. Theirs was a different perspective, and the outspoken Caleb wasn't afraid to add faith to the report.

Forty years passed before Caleb got to stand in the Promised Land, but God rewarded the faith of the man who remembered what he had seen the day the Red Sea parted in response to an act of faith and obedience.

Perspective is vital in every journey God is asking us to make.

God, who drew back the waters of the Red Sea, help me to look through the lens of faith and see Your plans from the perspective of heaven. Give me a 'different spirit', like that of Caleb. Amen.

14

13 January

A PASSAGE TO PONDER

If the clouds are full of rain,

They empty themselves upon the earth;

And if a tree falls to the south or the north,

In the place where the tree falls, there it shall lie.

He who observes the wind will not sow,

And he who regards the clouds will not reap.

As you do not know what is the way of the wind,

Or how the bones grow in the womb of her who is with child,

So you do not know the works of God who makes everything.

In the morning sow your seed,

And in the evening do not withhold your hand;

For you do not know which will prosper,

Either this or that,

Or whether both alike will be good.

Ecclesiastes 11:3–6

Read the passage slowly and let the Author speak to you. Ask yourself these questions as you ponder the passage:

- What does it say?
- What does it mean?
- What is God saying to me?
- How will I respond?

14 January

'O Lord God of our fathers, are You not God in heaven,
and do You not rule over all the kingdoms of the nations,
and in Your hand is there not power and might,
so that no one is able to withstand You?'
2 Chronicles 20:6

Reading: 2 Chronicles 20:5–15

King Jehoshaphat wasn't looking for an answer to this question.

Grammatically it's a rhetorical question, a confidence-booster for the person asking. For in the reply to the rhetoric, Jehoshaphat was reminding himself that the God whose help he so desperately needed was all of these things, and more. The King was sorting out any perspective issues he might have had.

Yes, the nation's enemies were camped on their borders. Yes, they could easily invade and destroy them. Yes, disaster was imminent. Yet in this question Jehoshaphat's focus was on the greatness of God – the ruler over all the nations, who had such power that none could stand against Him: 'For we have no power against this . . . but our eyes are upon You' (verse 12).

Some words slip easily off our tongues when all is well with the world. The difficulty arises when disaster arrives at our address. All of our big plans and self-reliance don't cut it at such times. I know. I've been there, had more than my share of difficulties and even disasters. During those times, glib recitation of Scripture did little to rescue me from pain, until I learned to recognize the One behind the words and promises.

You see, Jehoshaphat changed his focus. When an unbeatable enemy surrounded the nation, the King took time to recognize God's greatness. God's response? 'Do not be afraid . . . for the battle is not yours, but God's' (verse 15).

After years of sitting beside sickbeds and graves, I've discovered that focusing on the One who 'has measured the waters in the hollow of His hand' (Isaiah 40:12) helps me to realize that *He, Himself* is all I need.

Great Commander of heaven and earth, help me to look beyond the battle and remember that it's not mine to win, but Yours. Amen.

16

15 January

'You're going to wear yourself out – and the people, too.
This job is too heavy a burden for you to handle all
by yourself. Now let me give you a word of advice,
and may God be with you.'
Exodus 18:18–19b, NLT

Reading: Exodus 18:13–23

Are you a team player? Or do you prefer to work alone?

I have to confess a leaning towards the latter. Sometimes we'd rather just get on with it ourselves. We might even think that no-one can do a job quite like we can. But, as my husband would say, 'A one-man band is noisy, inefficient and looks ridiculous!'

By the time Jethro met up with his son-in-law in the wilderness, Moses was busily playing the one-man band, and wearing himself out in the process. Yes, God had called him to lead the people out of Egypt and into the Promised Land, but Moses had mistakenly thought he had to do it all by himself. A few wise words from Jethro encouraged Moses to appoint other able men to deal with less important situations where he was not needed. Moses could then spend his time more beneficially with both God and men. And sanity was restored.

Could it be that some of us need to take a leaf out of Moses' book and recognize that God does not intend us to do everything by ourselves? Are you exhausted with all the running, yet you never seem to get very far?

The apostle Paul tells us in 1 Corinthians 12 that the church is one body, but made up of different members. *Each part needs the others.* We cannot say to another part of the body, 'I have no need of you' (verse 21). We are not meant to be loners. We function better together, the apostle tells us. God made us to be team players.

Lord, forgive me for the times when I am hard-headed, refusing to accept the help I need. Help me to recognize that accepting help is not failure but rather a willingness to be part of the 'body'. Amen.

17

16 January

'Have I not commanded you? Be strong and of good courage; do not be afraid, nor be dismayed, for the LORD your God is with you wherever you go.'

Joshua 1:9

Reading: Joshua 1:1–9

Moses needed Aaron for Egypt, but it was Joshua he needed once they had crossed the Red Sea. Joshua was a leader, but one who also knew the value of teamwork. During forty difficult years, Joshua faithfully served alongside Moses. I wonder, did Joshua ever say, 'If only . . .'?

Sometimes the new beginnings we desire take more time to come around than we ever hoped or imagined. Is there something you long to see changed? When the clock struck 12 am on 1 January, did you ask God again for something new to happen this year? Think how many New Years Joshua had waited for Israel's promised new beginning.

Certainly, he had learned much from the mighty Moses. The young Joshua was able to glean wisdom even from Moses' mistakes. Now Moses was dead. God declared that Joshua would be His chosen leader to finally enter the land. It had been a long time coming, but the promise was about to be fulfilled. Change was on the agenda! But it wasn't going to be easy.

Significant change rarely is. It's easy to dream big and to fill our hearts with longings for what we believe is better. But there are times when God asks us to be the answer to our own prayers, or to step up to the mark ourselves.

How did Joshua accomplish what Moses didn't? He took God at His word. He believed His promises, and got on with it. Later, with death imminent, he was able to address the Children of Israel and declare that 'every promise of the LORD your God has come true. Not a single one has failed!' (Joshua 23:14, NLT).

Thank You, Lord, that the promise You gave to Joshua still stands today. Help me bravely move forward knowing You are with me, wherever I go. Amen.

17 January

'And remember the words of the Lord Jesus, that He said,
"It is more blessed to give than to receive."'

Acts 20:35

Reading: 1 John 4:12–16

Birthdays have never been the same since our grandchildren came along. Even the ones you'd really rather forget, like those sensitively marketed as 'milestone'!

On one particular 'milestone' birthday I lay in bed feeling sorry for myself. *How could I be this old?* Then my phone pinged and up popped a WhatsApp video of two little people with their dad, shouting at the top of their voices, 'Happy birthday, Granny! See you l-a-t-e-r!' The greeting was accompanied by excited blowing of kisses and giggles, and I was instantly rebuked by their celebration of joy. After all, I have so much to be thankful for!

So, you've guessed it. It's my birthday today. Considering today's verse, and since this book is entitled *Journey with Me*, I thought I'd give you a gift – the gift of my favourite Bible verse to mull over today. Those who are familiar with my earlier writings might be surprised at my choice. It's not Isaiah 43:2 or 40:31 as you might think, but rather 1 John 4:14, tucked in the middle of today's reading:

And we have seen and testify that the Father has sent the Son as Savior of the world.

For me, it is on this verse that everything else hangs. How do I know I am loved? Because the Father sent the Son – demonstrating His love for me. How can I trust God with my pain? Because the Father sent the Son, who knows all about suffering. How can I be certain that God has dealt with my sin? Because the Father sent the Son to be the Saviour of the world – including me. How can I be convinced of my eternal destiny? Because the Father sent the Son, who has gone to prepare a place for me (John 14:1–3).

Heavenly Father, I am blessed beyond measure by the gift of Your Son. Let this truth guide my steps and guard my heart today and always. Amen.

18 January

'For bodily exercise profits a little, but godliness
is profitable for all things, having promise of the life
that now is and of that which is to come.'

1 Timothy 4:8

Reading: 1 Timothy 4:6–11

I once joined a gym. I also once bought an exercise bicycle. I've tried on numerous occasions to learn to swim. As a teenager I once ran a cross-country race, and came last. For a short time I was LB (left back) for the school's under-14 B hockey team, before they eventually decided to leave me back in the changing room. I've tried badminton, tennis, round-the-table table tennis and even fencing. But you've guessed it – I'm not the sporty type!

So, two weeks into the New Year, how are you doing with those resolutions? Is the gym still pulling you in? Or what about the diet? Oops, shouldn't use that word – 'new eating habits' sounds better.

Well, this morning's weekly grocery shop took longer than usual as I checked out the fat and sugar content of my purchases. Low-sugar popcorn won over the big bar of chocolate – this time! Why is it that chocolate always looks more appetizing and value-for-money than a Granny Smith anyway?

I envy you 'fit' types, but usually not for long. Sorry, but the verse at the top of the page is a beautiful encouragement to people like me, especially at this time of the year when media advertising adds to my guilt. And yes, you are right, the apostle Paul is actually saying that exercise is good for you – so keep it up. However, the advice he gives here, writing to his young mentee Timothy, is all about priorities.

It is godly living, Paul tells us, that should be the focus of our lives. It's the one thing that will outlast these bodies, and even make a difference for eternity.

Lord, You made my body to be Your holy temple. Help me to look after it better than I do now, but may my focus always be on the ways You can purify my heart. Amen.

19 January

Elisha then returned to his oxen, killed them, and used
the wood from the plough to build a fire to roast their
flesh. He passed around the meat to the other ploughmen,
and they all ate. Then he went with Elijah as his assistant.

1 Kings 19:21, NLT

Reading: 1 Kings 19:19–21

The sun was up, and so was Elisha.

He may have been the son of a wealthy farmer, but he wasn't afraid to get his hands
dirty. Sweat trickled down his bare back, his calloused hands holding firmly on to
the plough. In front of him, eleven teams of oxen made their mark deep in the
earth. Elisha stood behind the twelfth team, controlling the strong piece of wood
to make a straight furrow.

But today was to be no ordinary day for the farmer's son.

Out of the corner of his eye Elisha saw the figure of a man walk towards him. The
visitor looked weary, his age and demeanour indicating he'd travelled a long road in
both distance and life. The oxen trundled along as the man sidled up beside Elisha.
He said nothing, took off his cloak and threw it over the bare shoulders of the
ploughman.

Suddenly Elisha recognized the old man of the desert. Elijah! The prophet of God!
As he took his hands off the plough, he felt the coarse cloth of the cloak rub on his
skin, yet it held an altogether other significance for Elisha. He understood what
this strange gesture meant: *he* was to take Elijah's place. The young farmer from
Abel Meholah would one day be God's mouthpiece for the nation!

Elisha didn't struggle, didn't question. He simply dismantled the plough, made a
fire from the wood and cooked the oxen that represented the life he was leaving
behind. He 'burned his bridges', we might say today – and then had a farewell
party! 'Then he arose and followed Elijah, and became his servant' (1 Kings 19:21).

*Lord, help me not to be afraid of what You are asking me to do today. If bridges need to
be burned, may I be willing! Amen.*

21

20 January

A PASSAGE TO PONDER

'But why do you call Me "Lord, Lord," and do not do the things
which I say?

Whoever comes to Me, and hears My sayings and does them,

I will show you whom he is like:

He is like a man building a house, who dug deep

and laid the foundation on the rock.

And when the flood arose, the stream beat vehemently against
that house,

And could not shake it, for it was founded on the rock.

But he who heard and did nothing is like a man who built a house
on the earth without foundation,

Against which the stream beat vehemently;

And immediately it fell.

And the ruin of that house was great.'

Luke 6:46–49

Read the passage slowly and let the Author speak to you. Ask yourself these
questions as you ponder:

- What does it say?
- What does it mean?
- What is God saying to me?
- How will I respond?

22

21 January

'And as soon as we heard these things, our hearts melted;
neither did there remain any more courage in anyone
because of you, for the LORD your God, He is God
in heaven above and on earth beneath.'

Joshua 2:11

Reading: Joshua 2:1–13

Have you ever checked out your genealogy? Are you familiar with your family roots?

I'm amazed at the fascination people have with their ancestors. A huge industry has emerged to help people discover more about their past. Televised celebrity searches explore where, or more accurately from whom, they originated. There's disappointment if they don't discover royalty, scandal or a murderer way back in their family history, while great delight is produced by the discovery of a hero. It seems everybody wants to be somebody.

And we all enjoy a good love story, don't we? And there is none more romantic than that of Ruth and Boaz. The latter was a man much respected for his dignity, honesty and leadership. But wait a minute. Surely Boaz' genealogy was pretty suspect? After all, he was the son of Rahab, the prostitute from Jericho (Matthew 1:5)!

How did Rahab ever get to be in the genealogy of Israel's great king, David, and consequently named in the very lineage of Jesus (Matthew 1), with a background like that? Simple. God didn't look at her background. He looked at her declaration of faith. This woman knew God by His covenant name, Yahweh, and she was prepared to die as a traitor, if need be, for daring to side with the people of God.

Rahab was a wise and courageous woman. When she looked back on Jericho lying in rubble on the day that she left, she was still a stranger to these people, but God had other plans for her. He is the God of change, after all (2 Corinthians 5:17).

Thank You, Lord, that I am a product not of my past, but of the change that You have brought into my heart because of Jesus. My future lies in Your hands. Amen.

23

22 January

'And she will bring forth a Son, and you shall call His name JESUS, for He will save His people from their sins.'

Matthew 1:21

Reading: Matthew 1:18–25

There's something about that name: *Jesus*.

Not a day goes by that I don't use it. I cannot praise or pray without the word tumbling from my lips. Neither can I imagine thoughts and dreams that do not include His name. It's frequently used in conversation with others, yet probably not as often as it should be.

It is gentle, soothing, peaceful and serene. At the same time it is powerful, disturbing, challenging and strong. What is it about that name?

I've heard it revered and worshipped, misused, abused and blasphemed. But one thing is certain: this name always evokes a response. Loved or hated, it cannot be ignored, no matter how hard you may try.

Jesus.

I love repeating it in the quiet place, singing it out with the crowd, listening to it preached on and prayed over. I've whispered it to my daughters when seizures racked their tiny frames, and shouted it out in anger when I couldn't work out what the Bearer of the name was doing with my life, or theirs. I've spoken it out, swallowed it down, and I've let it wash over my soul. Because I've discovered that there's power in that name: power to save, to heal, to calm, to guide and to give peace.

Jesus.

He is as close as the whisper of the word, convincing me of His presence, even in the storm. At times it was all I could say – all I needed to say, when there was nothing more to be said.

Who could have imagined, when the angel instructed the carpenter to call his wife's baby *Jesus*, how life-changing that name would be throughout the world, across the centuries, and in the lives of people like you and me?

Lord Jesus, one day every knee will bow at the mention of Your name (Philippians 2:10). Today I do it thankfully, in praise and worship. Amen.

23 January

But the angel said to him, 'Do not be afraid, Zacharias,
for your prayer is heard; and your wife Elizabeth will
bear you a son, and you shall call his name John.'
Luke 1:13

Reading: Luke 1:5–17

When our first child, a little girl, was born, her daddy announced that we would call her Cheryl. It means 'darling', and I couldn't argue with that. She stole our hearts from that very first day until she left us ten short years later, and, oh, how well she carried that name.

Today, children's names often follow trends rather than passing on family names. It was completely different in Bible times. Names always had significance then. Apart from the common practice of continuing family names, a child's name could express what was going on politically, socially or religiously around the time of their birth.

The English version of the name Zacharias was told to give his son is 'John'. In Hebrew it is 'Yochanan', meaning 'Yahweh is gracious'. The fact that Zacharias and Elizabeth would have a child in their old age was in itself proof of Yahweh's graciousness, but John's birth was about more than answering the prayers of a childless couple. God had plans for this boy, who was to grow into the man who would announce and prepare the nation for the coming Messiah.

And the boy John 'grew and became strong in spirit' (verse 80). He was 'great in the sight of the Lord' (verse 15), and one day the Messiah Himself said of him: 'I assure you, of all who have ever lived, there is none greater than John the Baptist' (Matthew 11:11, NLT). He carried the name well.

We too carry a name, given to us by God: 'Christian'. Conferring that name on us cost the Son of God His life, reminding us, and those we meet, that God is still gracious. I wonder how well we wear that name?

Yahweh, Lord of all, may Your name always be clearly evident in my life. May I wear it well, unashamed that I belong to Jesus. Amen.

25

24 January

'I am the bridegroom's friend, and I am filled with joy at His success. He must become greater and greater, and I must become less and less.'

John 3:29–30, NLT

Reading: John 3:22–31

When you read these words, it's no surprise that Jesus said 'there is none greater than John the Baptist' (Matthew 11:11, NLT). John's humility is staggering.

You see, John knew his place. And that was to prepare the people for the coming Messiah. His way of life was unusual: his dress unconventional, his eating habits repulsive. Yet people travelled from all over the country to hear this wild-looking desert man call them to repent and get ready for the coming Messiah.

Even the Jewish leaders were curious of the crowd-pulling baptizer. 'Who are you?' the spiritual elite asked. 'Elijah returned? The long-awaited Prophet perhaps?' (John 1:19–21).

John was turning heads and gathering crowds. The wilderness weirdo was quite an unlikely celebrity. He even had his own disciples – men who recognized the Baptizer as a spiritual man. A special man, sent by God to a nation who had known only heaven's silence for the four hundred years before he appeared on the scene.

And his disciples were affronted when they saw the crowds starting to follow Jesus and leave John behind. But John soon put them right. 'I told you that I am not the Messiah,' he reminded them.

The man thrust into the limelight by God to do a specific job was willing to step back into obscurity just as quickly. John even goes on to declare 'joy at his [Jesus'] success' (3:29), adding that it was essential for him to become less as Jesus became greater.

Evidently obedience was more important to John than recognition. Pride had no place in his heart. Personal rejection wasn't on his radar.

God in heaven, may I be just as willing to step back when You lead as I am to step forward. It's Your will that matters, not mine. Amen.

26

25 January

Examine yourselves to see if your faith is really genuine.
Test yourselves. If you cannot tell that Jesus Christ
is in you, it means you have failed the test.

2 Corinthians 13:5, NLT

Reading: Psalm 139:1–12, 23–24

January is a great month for stocktaking.

The kitchen cupboards are checked to see exactly what's in there, and what's out of date is dealt with. What's broken is disposed of, and what's new is called into service.

Stocktaking doesn't only make good practical sense; it's also a biblical principle for our spiritual life. Paul encourages us here to examine, test and assess ourselves for spiritual life and growth. But what's involved?

Honesty is the place to start. Is my Christian life based on Christ's forgiveness following repentance, or am I still trying to work for my salvation? How am I doing with following Jesus' agenda rather than my own?

We also need to discover what's broken, so that we can either dispose of it or seek to repair it. How is my prayer life? Do my relationships on Facebook get more attention than my Bible? What about my temper, timekeeping, relationships? We are not always good at owning up to what's wrong in our lives, or admitting to possessions that shouldn't be there. Bad habits? Wrong attitudes?

While no-one else knows us like we know ourselves, it is also true that there is a danger of self-examination being carried out either through rose-tinted spectacles or through the fog of negativism. Spiritual stocktaking is not twenty-first-century flagellation, but an honest assessment of our hearts and actions. For that we need God's help. In Romans 12:2 Paul explains that God can transform us and show us His will when we don't copy the behaviour of the world. How? By changing the way we think. Sounds like decluttering is on the agenda!

Lord, I want to know Your good, pleasing and perfect will for my life. Help me to examine my heart honestly and then do what's needed to make that happen. The transformation I gladly leave to You. Amen.

27

26 January

He heals the brokenhearted
And binds up their wounds.
Psalm 147:3

Reading: Psalm 147

As you were engaging in spiritual stocktaking, did you come across something in your inventory that is impacting your life? Is there an 'elephant in the room'? Something so big, so broken, that it has come between you and God? You have discovered a broken heart.

I know that 'elephant'. He lived in my life for quite some time.

When our first daughter was branded by a paediatrician as a child who 'would never be normal', I was full of hurt, anger, disappointment . . . mostly directed at God. I found it difficult to talk to Him, never mind listen to Him. I was broken-hearted. Nothing made sense any more. My confidence in the One who declared that He knew the plans He had for me (Jeremiah 29:11) was shattered. The 'elephant in the room' blocked my view of who He really is, and how He could bring about the healing my broken heart needed.

Little by little I had to learn to trust God with the things that I didn't understand. Perhaps that was the 'faith' that Paul was really alluding to in yesterday's reading. As a young mother I discovered that faith is all about the tough stuff, and in life's difficult classroom I began to feel the Master Physician bind up my wounds. With His touch, 'the elephant in the room' began to shrink in size and I was able once again to communicate with the only One who, as the psalmist says, 'heals the brokenhearted'.

God knows about the 'elephant' in your room. He wants to shrink it in order that you might once again catch a glimpse of Him, the One who is bigger than your broken heart. You'll find that the other broken things in your spiritual inventory will be repaired one by one as you choose to trust Him with the things that you don't understand.

God, I give You permission to deal with the 'elephant' in my room. Heal my broken heart, that I might catch a glimpse of You once more. Amen.

27 January

A PASSAGE TO PONDER

This is the message which we have heard from Him and declare to you,

that God is light and in Him is no darkness at all.

If we say that we have fellowship with Him, and walk in darkness,

we lie and do not practice the truth.

But if we walk in the light as He is in the light,

we have fellowship with one another,

and the blood of Jesus Christ His Son cleanses us from all sin.

If we say that we have no sin, we deceive ourselves,

and the truth is not in us.

If we confess our sins, He is faithful and just to forgive us our sins

and to cleanse us from all unrighteousness.

If we say that we have not sinned,

we make Him a liar, and His word is not in us.

1 John 1:5–10

Read the passage slowly and let the Author speak to you. Ask yourself these questions as you ponder:

- What does it say?
- What does it mean?
- What is God saying to me?
- How will I respond?

28 January

When the Lord saw her, He had compassion
on her and said to her, 'Do not weep.'

Luke 7:13

Reading: Luke 7:11–17

It's difficult to miss the fallout when two worlds collide, as they did on one particular day outside the city of Nain.

One large group of people was leaving, on their way to bury the only son of a widowed lady, now alone in this world.

The other equally large group was heading into the city. Still euphoric from the healings they'd witnessed the day before, the last thing they wanted was to be stopped by a funeral. Tradition dictated that they must now join the procession and head back down the dusty road. Perhaps if they'd arrived earlier, Jesus might have healed the young man and spared the woman's grief. Too late now!

How wrong that thought! For the One who declared Himself to be 'the resurrection and the life' (John 11:25), even death does not mean it is too late. He arrived in Nain at exactly the right time. And Jesus' heart was so deeply touched by the woman's grief and loss that he ignored ceremony, defiling Himself in the process, and raised the boy to life. What a different crowd returned through the city gate!

But that's typical of what Jesus does. He specializes in bringing dead things back to life. For some it will be relationships repaired, marriages mended, employment renewed, sins forgiven, bodies healed or joy restored. For others it will not be a return of what is lost, and that can be difficult, but instead it will be the addition of something new altogether. A closer walk with God. The tangible touch of God's love through others. A realization that now is not all there is, and that what is beyond is worth waiting for.

When our world collides with His, it is that He might give us 'a future and a hope' (Jeremiah 29:11).

God of compassion, thank You for caring about the losses in my life. Take them and breathe new life into them by the power of Your Holy Spirit. Amen.

29 January

And He said to him, 'Follow Me.' So [Levi] left all, rose up, and followed Him.

Luke 5:27–28

Reading: Luke 5:27–32

We think we have problems with the taxman today! In Jesus' day, the people had to pay taxes to the occupying Romans and to the local government authorities. They also had to pay temple tax. Tax collectors were, at best, unpopular, and those who lined their pockets with 'added extras' were despised. In addition, foreigners were taxed at the point of entry to the country, which contact rendered the tax collector ceremonially unclean. Levi, or Matthew as we know him better, was in a no-win situation as far as his reputation was concerned.

Was there any chance of a new start for him? A wealthy businessman, from a Levite background, Levi knew the Jewish Scriptures well. And he was probably one of those seeking change who had visited John the Baptist to ask what they should do about their unpopular jobs. Yet collecting 'no more than what is appointed' (Luke 3:13) wasn't bringing about the change that he longed for. Jesus passed by his tax booth near Capernaum one day, and with two words Levi's life was totally revolutionized.

'Follow Me,' was all that the Rabbi from Nazareth said. But the tax collector was finished with counting money for himself and others. The trappings of wealth no longer satisfied. By the time Jesus said, 'Follow Me,' Levi had already counted the cost. 'So he left all, rose up, and followed Him' (Luke 5:28).

Have you heard Jesus' call? Make no mistake: there's nothing glamorous about it. Whenever we experience His call, cost is always involved. Inevitably there will be a leaving of some kind, whether it's our sin, our ambitions or our comfort. But the best bit is that it also involves journeying with Jesus. 'Following' means Jesus is the One marking the trail, and He is always present, whatever terrain it crosses.

Lord, may my ears listen for Your call, my heart willingly respond, and my feet be quick to follow where You lead. Amen.

30 January

And when Jesus came to the place, He looked up and saw him, and said to him, 'Zacchaeus, make haste and come down, for today I must stay at your house.'

Luke 19:5

Reading: Luke 19:1–10

I meet a lot of people each year as I travel around. The extroverts are easy to spot, although there is often more going on behind all the talking and busyness than is seen on the surface. The introverts are more complicated to read. They prefer to make a dive for the safety of the kitchen afterwards, hiding with their elbows well submerged in soapsuds. I rarely get to hear their stories, but I often wonder what lies behind their shy smiles.

Are they simply life's quiet ones? Nothing wrong with that. Or have they been hurt, discouraged or, worse still, led to believe that they are somehow inferior to others?

The story of Zacchaeus has unfortunately been relegated to children's storybook material, not significant enough for us adults to pay much attention to. But this particular man fascinates me. He was obviously born with a height deficiency. I wonder, was he bullied as a child? Could that have been why he chose to make himself 'big' in other ways? Wealth, position and corruption certainly got him noticed, but for all the wrong reasons. As the town's most unpopular resident, it's doubtful that Zacchaeus hid in the tree for viewing purposes only. Remarkably, his encounter with Jesus had nothing to do with finger wagging.

To the Saviour, the little man was no different from anyone else. He needed to be changed from the inside out, but first he needed to know he was valued as an individual. Imagine what he must have thought when Jesus invited Himself to *his* house! Realizing he was loved, it didn't take long for Zacchaeus to become aware of his sin in the presence of the One who was treating him with undeserved kindness.

Extrovert, introvert, bullied or crook, may we hear You call us by name today, Lord, and experience Your life-changing love for us. Amen.

31 January

Seeing their faith, Jesus said to the paralyzed man,
'My child, your sins are forgiven.'

Mark 2:5, NLT

Reading: Mark 2:1–13

It's great to have friends, isn't it? Especially the kind who see what you need and then get on and do something about it. This story in Mark 2 is about friends like that: friends with initiative and ingenuity. In a nutshell, a paralyzed man is carried on a stretcher to Jesus, and Jesus heals him.

But wait, I've left a whole lot out, especially the bit about his friends not being able to get into the crowded house and digging a hole in the roof to lower their friend down through it! Mind you, they must have been both puzzled and disappointed with what they heard from their rooftop position. 'Your sins are forgiven,' the Rabbi said, rather than, 'You are healed.' All their effort for this?

The friends had made a common mistake. They thought the man's most important need was to walk again. It was something they could see, and something that was impacting his life in dreadful ways. They had heard that Jesus was a miracle worker, and believed without a shadow of a doubt that if they could get their friend to Him, he would be healed.

In fact, it was because of that very faith that Jesus spoke those words of forgiveness in the first place. The friends wanted their companion to have a life free from pain and suffering. A magnanimous gesture indeed, but incomplete – for Jesus could do so much more for the man than his friends ever dreamed. It's a reminder that the supreme task we have as friends is to introduce those we know and love to Jesus – to help them prioritize their greatest need as that of forgiveness. Not easy. There may be a few 'tiles to loosen' on the way, but Jesus will reward our faith.[1]

Thank You, Jesus, for the friend who brought me to the place where I first heard of Your great love for me. Amen.

33

February

1 February

Simon Peter said to them, 'I am going fishing.'
They said to him, 'We are going with you also.'
They went out and immediately got into the boat,
and that night they caught nothing.
John 21:3–4

Reading: John 21:1–14

Peter had started so well. On the day Jesus had told them He would 'make [them] fishers of men' (Matthew 4:19), it is recorded that Peter and his brother Andrew 'immediately left their nets and followed Him' (Matthew 4:20).

Peter had burned his bridges, just like Elisha. He had counted the cost of leaving all to follow Jesus, and had got up and gone. Impressive. In fact, the fisherman turned out to be the bravest, boldest and most loyal of all the disciples.

So if he was all this, what's with the verse at the top of the page? Fishing? Hadn't he left all that behind? We don't see Elisha return to farming. *What happened to all the promises you made, Peter?*

Life happened. Jesus had died. No, it was more than that – He had been crucified! The whirlwind three years was over. Jesus had left them. But wait. I thought Jesus had risen from the dead? He had been speaking to them not long before Peter stepped on to the boat! *What really went wrong, Peter?*

Life happened. Peter had messed up. He hadn't kept his promise to 'go with [Him], both to prison and to death' (Luke 22:33). Instead, Peter had kept his distance, denied Him and run away. Is it any wonder that he went back to fishing? I mean to say, Jesus wouldn't want him now, would He? Surely all that talk of sending them to take His message (John 20:21) was for the others, not for Peter? He was an utter failure! Best if he went back to fishing.

But Jesus hadn't finished with Peter. Neither is He finished with us.

Lord, I confess the 'Peter streak' that runs through my life. Put simply, I don't always get it right either. Help me not to run away, but to run to You. Amen.

2 February

'Friends, have you caught any fish?' . . .
'Simon, son of John, do you love me more than these?'

John 21:5, 15, NLT

Reading: John 21:15–22

I've stood on that beach. The one where Jesus cooked those fishermen breakfast.

It's small and stony, and, oh, so quiet. As I pushed the stones between my feet I felt I could see the risen Lord there, and pictured in my mind's eye where He might have lit the fire to feed the men who had toiled all night and caught nothing.

'Cast the net on the right side of the boat,' Jesus shouted across the still water, 'and you will find some [fish]' (John 21:6). Why didn't He say, 'What are you doing fishing for fish? I told you to fish for men!'

Only three hundred feet from the shore, signs of the 'old' Peter began to re-emerge when he jumped into the water and swam to shore to get to Jesus. And I walked the walk that Jesus took with Peter after breakfast, reciting the firm but loving words of a forgiving Saviour as the same stones crunched under my own feet centuries later.

'Simon, son of Jonah, do you love Me more than these?' (21:15).

Peter's head hung low, his heart heavy with regret. 'Yes, Lord; You know that I love You' (verse 15). Would he ever move beyond the test he'd failed the night of Jesus' arrest? Three times Peter had denied the Lord. Now Jesus was giving the broken disciple three more chances at the same question: 'Do you love Me?' And do you love Me more than fishing, Peter?

'Yes. Yes. Yes,' the big fisherman replied. 'Lord, You know all things; You know that I love You.' That was enough for the God of the second chance.

Walking back to the rest of the group, I thought of the many times I'd broken promises to the Lord. I'm so glad He knows that I love Him, glad that He still offers the second chance today.

Thank You, Lord, that, with You, failure isn't final. You know that I love You. Amen.

3 February

A PASSAGE TO PONDER

As you therefore have received Christ Jesus the Lord,

so walk in Him,

rooted and built up in Him and established in the faith,

as you have been taught, abounding in it with thanksgiving.

Beware lest anyone cheat you through philosophy and empty deceit,

according to the tradition of men,

according to the basic principles of the world,

and not according to Christ.

For in Him dwells all the fullness of the Godhead bodily;

and you are complete in Him,

who is the head of all principality and power.

Colossians 2:6–10

Read through the passage slowly and let the Author speak to you. Ask yourself these questions as you ponder:

- What does it say?
- What does it mean?
- What is God saying to me?
- How will I respond?

4 February

I have been crucified with Christ; it is no longer I who
live, but Christ lives in me; and the life which I now live
in the flesh I live by faith in the Son of God,
who loved me and gave Himself for me.

Galatians 2:20

Reading: Philemon

Onesimus was glad of the cooling sea breeze, but this was one stretch of ocean that
the young man had vowed he would never cross again. First time round it was
meant to be his route to freedom. Escape from a life of slavery was his plan, until
he met Paul. The apostle, himself a prisoner of Rome, was more free than any man
Onesimus had ever known. And it was because of Paul that the runaway was now
heading home.

Onesimus knew that his master had the legal right to end his life once he returned
to Colossae. Little wonder that his stomach churned. But Onesimus was returning
a changed man, and in his possession was a letter from Paul, a friend of Philemon,
his master. Would it make any difference?

'I appeal to you for my son Onesimus,' Paul had written, 'that you might receive
him forever, no longer as a slave but more than a slave – a beloved brother'
(Philemon 10, 15–16).

You see, the runaway had discovered in Rome that it wasn't a change in location
that brought freedom, but a change of heart. The new life he had dreamt of while
still a servant could only be found 'by faith in the Son of God, who loved me and
gave Himself for me' (Galatians 2:20). He had finally realized that running away
wasn't the answer. He had to deal with the past. And deep in his heart Onesimus
knew that, whatever happened at Colossae, he would always be a free man –
because of Jesus.

*Lord Jesus, thank You that forgiveness comes through Christ alone. But if there are
things in my past that I need to deal with, then please give me the courage of Onesimus
to stop running away, and to face them. Amen.*

5 February

'Have I been with you so long, and yet you have not known Me, Philip? He who has seen Me has seen the Father; so how can you say, "Show us the Father"?'

John 14:9

Reading: John 14:1–11

It's so embarrassing when someone chats to you but you haven't a clue who they are. So you nod and smile, hoping that the penny will drop. My worst faux pas was when a young woman approached me with great enthusiasm and hugs. I hadn't a clue who she was, but I couldn't fudge it this time. I had to admit that I didn't remember her, and asked her name!

Imagine the embarrassment when she told me that she was a missionary who had stayed in our home, and how she'd never forgotten our kindness to her. Yet, standing in front of her, I didn't feel that I knew her!

Philip had been with Jesus for three years. He'd been one of the inner circle of disciples who had heard more than the crowds who followed the Lord from place to place. He'd sat at table with Him, watched Jesus perform the miraculous, experienced His love personally and watched as He dealt compassionately with the lowest in society. Yet, even after all that, it appears that Philip hadn't fully understood who Jesus really was.

He didn't *really* know Jesus the way he thought he did.

No matter how long we've been on the road with Jesus – and for some of us that's been many years – I wonder how we'd reply if Jesus put the same question to us? If we were each to take out a blank piece of paper and write down what we've learnt about the Saviour over the past six months (okay then – the past year!), how much of the page could we fill? Can we determine to make the apostle Paul's lifetime ambition, that he states in Philippians 3:10, our prayer too? Because today's prayer is truly what knowing Christ is all about.

Lord, I want to know You and the power of Your resurrection, and the fellowship of Your sufferings, starting today. Amen.

6 February

'I will even make a road in the wilderness and
rivers in the desert.'

Isaiah 43:19

Reading: Isaiah 43:16–21

The sign on the motorway gantry flashed '40mph'. *That would be nice*, I thought, as I glanced at the speedometer displaying only 15mph!

The rain and wind relentlessly beat against the car. I was in a traffic jam going nowhere fast. Was the holdup purely down to the weather? I reached for the car radio just in time to catch the travel news: 'A lorry has overturned on the A1 causing traffic chaos. Drivers are advised to take another route, and avoid the area.'

I didn't know another route! I was in unfamiliar territory and all my directions to the meeting were from that road – which was now completely blocked! Frankly, I despaired of ever reaching my destination.

I eventually managed to get off the motorway and park in a shopping centre. The storm was now at its height, and I just wanted to turn and go home. There was no way I would make the meeting in time, and it was highly unlikely that anyone would venture out in such awful weather anyway. I felt ready to give up.

The only thing I could do was to phone the lady who had booked me, expecting her to say, 'No point in going on – head for home.' But she didn't. Instead she came to meet me, taking me along the back roads to reach the church. The roadblock was no problem to her; she knew the way around it, as did fifty other brave souls. And what a night of blessing we had together.

Life frequently throws all kinds of blockages our way, and we have no idea how to get through. We might even feel ready to give up. Make that call. Pray! Contact the One who knows the way around, or through, because God specializes in making a way where there is no way. Ask the Children of Israel.

God of heaven, I'm stuck here. I don't know how to move forward. Please show me the way. I'm listening for Your directions, Lord. Amen.

7 February

For you did not receive the spirit of bondage again to fear,
but you received the Spirit of adoption by whom
we cry out, 'Abba, Father.'
Romans 8:15

Reading: Romans 8:12–17

'I like living here,' the young boy said, his eyes constantly flitting for fear of making contact. 'They feed me.'

His throwaway remark declared an altogether different life previous to the one he was now experiencing with prospective adoptive parents. How sad to think that a full tummy was his only benchmark of a new beginning, the shrug of his shoulders an indication that perhaps, one day, he might belong. Might even be loved.

The desire to belong is universal. So much so that when family links are weak, and love absent, the human psyche searches for an identity of any kind that will give purpose and fulfilment of some sort. Clubs, associations and gangs, even terrorists, open welcoming arms, declaring, 'Join us. We'll be your friends, your family, whatever you need.'

The apostle understood that human need. While his letter to the Romans is a mammoth theological treatise on justification by faith, Paul adds a tender touch by shifting the attention of his readers firmly to the question of identity. His pastor's heart longs for them to understand the root of belonging, and how that changes the whole perspective into one of being rather than doing.

Having spent a considerable amount of time on how these new believers couldn't live the life required by God, the apostle goes on to explain their adoption into God's family. As children of God they belong. And so do we. Fear need no longer be our master. We have a Father, an Abba, and a completely new family too. We are the much-loved children of the God of heaven. Now that's what I call a benchmark upon which to build our identity.

Thank You, Lord, that alongside my new life in Christ, I get to call You, Abba, Father. Teach me more about what it means to be a child of the King. Amen.

8 February

How great love the Father has lavished on us,
that we should be called children of God!

1 John 3:1, NIV

Reading: 1 John 3:1–3

What comes to mind when you hear the word 'father'? Do you smile, get excited and feel thankful? Or are your palms sweaty, your mouth dry and your stomach churning?

Unfortunately, not everyone has good memories of their father. You may not even know who your father is. Biologically there must have been one, of course, but that's as far as it goes. He's been absent, missing in your life. For others, their father has been there in the worst of ways. Anger, abuse and violence are so often the three most prevalent words they associate with the male figure many of us couldn't imagine living without. And yet, with so many different examples of fatherhood in our world, God has chosen to reveal himself to His creation as 'Father'. How good to know that, just because there are counterfeits, it doesn't mean we can't trust the perfect original.

God is different from all the rest – even the good ones! There's no-one like Him. He is the very best of fathers, and available to every one of His children, whatever our earthly family history or experience.

The apostle John speaks of God's 'lavish' love in calling us His children. He describes Him as an extremely generous father. This Father is not one to be feared, or hated . . . or ignored. Rather, this is where our true spiritual identity starts. We belong. Truly belong. And John goes on to expand what it means to be children of God, for 'what we will be has not yet been made known (verse 2, NIV). There's more ahead! This is only the beginning.

As we get to know our Heavenly Father, we discover that He is not only generous with His love, but is also our protector, guide, teacher, provider, drier of tears . . . and never, ever absent!

Heavenly Father, I am so glad to be called Your child! Thank You for adopting me into Your family. I belong! Amen.

9 February

'So do not worry, saying, "What shall we eat?" or "What shall we drink?" or "What shall we wear?" For the pagans run after all these things, and your heavenly Father knows that you need them.'

Matthew 6:31–32, NIV

Reading: Matthew 6:25–34

My dad makes the best chips around! Add in sausages, eggs, tea, bread and butter, and you've got the Frasers' Saturday night special. De-licious!

One particular night we were reminiscing about food favourites when we were growing up, and I suddenly remembered something we hadn't eaten for years: 'Dad, do you remember when you used to make those jam butty pasties for a special treat? I loved them! You haven't made them in years!'

Mum and Dad suddenly gazed at their empty plates, uncomfortably silent. I was shocked as Dad revealed their secret. He explained that jam butty pasties were what they had resorted to making when they had literally no money with which to buy any food. Dad would spread jam on slices of bread, clap them together, dip them in flour-and-water batter, and drop them into hot fat to make them crispy. Then he'd call us for tea, announcing, 'Special treat night! Jam butty pasties!' And we'd cheer and tuck in, not realizing the tears that had been shed earlier.

I don't think I've ever been as proud of my parents as I was that day. I never realized the extent of the financial hardship they'd faced in the early years of their marriage. I only ever remember being loved, encouraged . . . and fed! As far as I am concerned, my dad was always a wonderful provider for his family.

Our Heavenly Father has no such problem with limited resources. He always has enough to meet His children's needs. Jesus tells us in this passage what we must not worry over, and then goes on to remind us that if we seek God's kingdom first, then all these other 'things' will be ours as well (Matthew 6:33).

Lord, I want to be a Kingdom seeker. Thank You, Father, for knowing my needs and providing for me when the time is right. Amen.

45

10 February

A PASSAGE TO PONDER

In that hour Jesus rejoiced in the Spirit and said,

'I thank You, Father, Lord of heaven and earth,

that You have hidden these things from the wise and prudent

and revealed them to babes.

Even so, Father, for so it seemed good in Your sight.

All things have been delivered to Me by My Father,

and no one knows who the Son is except the Father,

and who the Father is except the Son,

and the one to whom the Son wills to reveal Him.'

Then He turned to His disciples and said privately,

'Blessed are the eyes which have seen the things you see;

for I tell you that many prophets and kings have desired to see

what you see, and have not seen it, and to hear what you hear,

and have not heard it.'

Luke 10:21–24

Read the passage slowly and let the Author speak to you. Ask yourself these questions as you ponder:

- What does it say?
- What does it mean?
- What is God saying to me?
- How will I respond?

46

11 February

As a father has compassion on his children,
so the LORD has compassion on those who fear him.
Psalm 103:13, NIV

Reading: Psalm 103:13–18

I could see it coming, but was helpless to stop it! In a split second our little grandson fell from the top of the armchair, banging his head and shocking his system (and ours!) in the process. Before a scream had time to leave the two-year-old's lips, his dad sprang to his feet, scooping him up in his strong arms. For the next few minutes Daniel clung to him as if superglued, face buried in his daddy's neck, barely taking in enough air to squeal! In his pain, only Daddy would do.

There's nothing like pain to focus the mind.

Pain stops you in your tracks. It disorients, diverts your attention, unsettles your whole body and concentrates your attention on one thing – how to get rid of it! And while you are seeking for answers, it is compassion that brings comfort: the assurance that while you suffer, someone cares, someone is with you through the pain, someone offers a shoulder for you to cry on.

Pain is part of life's reality. Facing it alone needn't be.

Undoubtedly, God puts family and friends into our lives for that very reason, but there are some types of pain when only 'Daddy' will do. For those times when no-one else understands, or perhaps even knows, only our Heavenly Father is available, and able, to provide the compassion and love we need. It is possible to experience the reality of Deuteronomy 33:27, and to feel that 'underneath are the everlasting arms'. These Fatherly arms will never get tired holding us; neither is there a time limit to His caress because, as the psalmist reminds us, He 'has compassion on those who fear him'.

Abba, Father, thank You that You are always ready to scoop me up when only 'Daddy' will do. Thank You for those everlasting arms. Amen.

12 February

The Lord is faithful to all his promises
and loving towards all he has made.

Psalm 145:13, NIV

Reading: Hebrews 6:13–20

How good are you at keeping promises?

With the best will in the world, we try. Yet there are times when the promised visit or phone call isn't made, the children don't get to the park, the homemade curry becomes a takeaway. Much more serious promises also fall by the wayside, with devastating consequences. Those made at the front of a church on a wedding day, or to a child who, craving approval, constantly misses a parent's face at their special event. Unfulfilled promises leave disappointed children, friends, work colleagues, husbands and wives in their wake. People who trusted us; people we failed.

Excuses are easily found. Life invariably gets in the way sometimes. An unexpected illness. A day filled with too many other things. The clock that wouldn't wait for me to do what I'd said I would. Some things can be made right; others aren't that easy, especially the heartbreakers: the trust destroyers.

Conversely, our Heavenly Father is the great promise-keeping God. He never breaks His word. He always delivers what He says He will. At the end of his life, Joshua declared to the gathered multitude that not one promise of God had failed (Joshua 23:14). What a statement! Throughout the difficult journey into the Promised Land, Israel's great general had proved that what God promised He always did. No exceptions!

Fast-forward to the days of the early church who were reminded how, 'after he had patiently endured, [Abraham] obtained the promise' (Hebrews 6:15). God came through for Abraham. He can do it for you too, the writer to the Hebrews declared.

I've seen too many images of troubled children waiting for the absent dad to turn up on time, talked to too many women damaged by promises never kept by the man who has their heart.

That will never happen with our Father God, for He cannot lie!

Father, thank You that I can have absolute confidence in Your promises. I can leave my heart safely in Your hands. Amen.

13 February

God is our refuge and strength,
A very present help in trouble.
Therefore we will not fear,
Even though the earth be removed,
And though the mountains be carried
into the midst of the sea.
Psalm 46:1–2

Reading: Psalm 46

The Psalms are a remarkable collection of poetry and songs written by a number of different people. David was responsible for writing some seventy-three of them. Down through the ages, multitudes have found them a source of comfort and encouragement in times of trouble. They also reveal a lot about God's character and His relationship with His people, Israel.

Psalm 46, for example, was probably written following God's miraculous deliverance of Jerusalem during Hezekiah's reign. Sennacherib, King of Assyria, had laid siege to the city after decimating many other towns and villages in Judah. Around 185,000 soldiers had surrounded Jerusalem's walls. It was only a matter of time before the city was counted in Sennacherib's victory roll. Or so the Assyrian king thought. But he hadn't reckoned on the power of the God of Israel to protect what was His. On one night, in response to Hezekiah's prayer, God sent His angel through the enemy camp. The following morning Sennacherib found the corpses of thousands of his fighting men. He never troubled Israel again (2 Kings 18 – 19).

Our God is a protecting God, and He knows those who are His (2 Timothy 2:19). He is our Father. We are His children. And if we learn anything from Psalm 46 it is that whatever we are facing – however difficult or even impossible the situation might seem – God has promised His presence (verse 1), His help (verse 5), His stability (verse 2), His deliverance (verse 8–9) and His protection (verse 7).

Our part?

'Be still, and know that I am God,' the Father tells us (verse 10). We can rest in Him.

God of the nations, I rejoice that You are my Father. Nothing is too big for You. I don't need to be afraid, for You are my refuge and my strength. Amen.

14 February

He brought me to the banqueting house,
And His banner over me was love.

Song of Solomon 2:4

Reading: Song of Solomon 2:8–14

It was Valentine's Day. I was fourteen years old. The postman hadn't left any mail with my name on it. Well, it was Sunday – a Valentine card might still come on Monday. Unbeknown to me, I was in for a surprise that Valentine's Day – and love was the key!

As I made my way down the road that evening I half hoped that the girl who had invited me to the youth meeting wouldn't turn up. But there she was, waiting at the gate. By this stage I wasn't brave enough to turn back, so we made our way into a hall packed with teenagers. I hid in the crowd, feeling slightly out of place and wondering why on earth so many teenagers would want to be here on St Valentine's night?

The atmosphere was electric! *Surely this can't be church?* I was slightly embarrassed that I didn't know the songs they sang, but wow, they sang about Jesus in ways I'd never heard before. *They're actually excited about God!* Someone read from the Bible as if they were reading from the best book in the library. *It doesn't sound like your normal lectionary reading to me.* Then this guy stood up and told us how he had come to know Jesus as his Saviour. And he was so happy about it – he said that Jesus had changed his life! Looking around the room I could see that everyone was truly happy. Instantly I knew that I wanted what they had.

Later, in my own room, I recognized that being a Christian wasn't about going to church, but about a Man who loved me so much that He had died on a cross for me. That night I welcomed Him into my heart as my Saviour.

Lord, thank You for the day I fell in love with Jesus! No-one else will ever love me in the way You do. Calvary proves it! Amen.

50

15 February

'And he arose and came to his father. But when
he was still a great way off, his father saw him and had
compassion, and ran and fell on his neck and kissed him.'
Luke 15:20

Reading: Luke 15:11–32

Some stories are worth returning to.

Each of our grandchildren has a favourite book that they drop on my lap again and again. They know every word, yet with every retelling they listen as if for the first time. They are enthralled. And that's just how I feel about this story that Jesus told. But what is it that keeps drawing me back?

Is it the every-family nature of the story that crosses both centuries and cultures? The airing of family squabbles more akin to TV soaps? The picture of a soft-natured father compared to a selfish younger son? The reminder that money only brings fair-weather friends? The martyr complex of the older brother? The bravery of the prodigal heading home to face the music after he had really messed up? Or the heart-warming image of the father patiently watching and waiting every single day for his child to return?

No. What enthrals me most in this story is the picture of the father *running* to meet his wayward boy. You see, back then it was unusual, nay, improper, for an Eastern father to run. But this father didn't care what others thought of him. His son, who 'was lost' was now found, who 'was 'dead' was now alive again (verse 32). Forget protocol. This father ran!

It's easy to look at this parable as the story of a son who's lost his way, or even as a tale of two sons. (The older brother hardly shines here!) But this story is about a father who has his children on his heart. A father who runs! This is the Father Jesus wants us to know.

Heavenly Father, thank You that You are the Father who runs! How wonderful to know that You have me on Your heart even when I don't behave as a child of God should. Amen.

51

16 February

'Can you search out the deep things of God?
Can you find out the limits of the Almighty?'
Job 11:7

Reading: Ephesians 3:14–21

How is it that we read of the incomprehensible nature of an all-powerful God, whose ways are 'past finding out' (Job 9:10; Romans 11:33), and yet the very same God says 'I will be a Father to you' (2 Corinthians 6:18)? Can we know what we don't understand? Isn't that a contradiction?

Absolutely not! But it does stretch the mind.

The fact that a holy God has chosen to reveal Himself at all to those of finite minds and sinful hearts is the very demonstration of the love He has for His creation, and in particular His children. The method He chose to show Himself in times past was 'by the prophets', but He 'has in these last days spoken to us by His Son' (Hebrews 1:1–2). We may never be able to understand everything about God. And that's okay. Some mysteries we need to leave with Him, but many of them are revealed in His Son. And that is precisely how we get to know the Father. Jesus clearly tells His disciples in John 14:9, 'He who has seen Me has seen the Father.'

How do we know that our Heavenly Father is compassionate, just, loving, gracious, present, all-seeing, all-powerful and working out His plan in our lives? We look at Jesus. How can I be sure that I am His child, and that the inexplicable God of whom Job speaks is my Father? We trust in the One who says, 'I am the way, the truth, and the life. No one comes to the Father except through Me' (John 14:6).

Incomprehensible? Certainly. Knowable? Absolutely! He is God, after all, and with Him 'nothing will be impossible' (Luke 1:37).

Lord of Heaven and Earth, I stand in awe at Your greatness. Thank you for revealing Your glory, and doing it through Your Son. Unworthy I stand, amazed to be called Your child. Overwhelmed that You are my Father, I am eternally grateful. Amen.

17 February

A PASSAGE TO PONDER

'And as Moses lifted up the serpent in the wilderness,

even so must the Son of Man be lifted up,

that whoever believes in Him should not perish but have eternal life.

For God so loved the world that He gave His only begotten Son,

that whoever believes in Him should not perish

but have everlasting life.

For God did not send His Son into the world to condemn the world,

but that the world through Him might be saved.

He who believes in Him is not condemned;

but he who does not believe is condemned already,

because he has not believed in the name of the only begotten Son of God.'

John 3:14–18

Read the passage slowly and let the Author speak to you. Ask yourself these questions as you ponder:

- What does it say?
- What does it mean?
- What is God saying to me?
- How will I respond?

18 February

In the beginning God created the heavens and the earth.
Genesis 1:1

Then God said, 'Let Us make man in Our image, according to Our likeness.'
Genesis 1:26

Reading: Genesis 1

For me, afternoon TV is useful for only one thing – making time spent at the ironing board move more quickly! But during mindless viewing I have learned some important things. Within the plethora of programmes about antiques I discovered that the true value of an item is not necessarily in how it looks, or even whether or not it is flawed. Rather, its worth is determined by the name etched on the base, or scrawled in the corner of a painting.

A designer label turns a mediocre pot into a desirable piece of chinaware, an oil-on-canvas into a masterpiece.

When the Designer of the universe created the heavens and the earth, and everything in between, He finished His creative process by making man different from all the rest. The One who placed the stars in space saw His work as incomplete until He made man.

What made us different? Why did God hand over control of 'every living thing that moves on the earth' to mankind (verse 28)?

Because He chose to make us unique out of all that He had made. Unlike all the rest, man alone was created in His image (verse 26) – 'patterned after Himself' (NLT). Uniquely designed. Created for relationship, not merely with those around us but with God Himself.

In fact, we display the most important designer label on earth. Even on our very worst days we carry His mark. This mark determines our true value in a world that attempts to send out a message that we came from nothing, are here for no purpose and are headed nowhere when we die. Oh how wrong that message is.

Our worth before God is incalculable – flaws and all!

Creator of the universe, help me to see just how precious I am. I'm designer made! I carry the mark of God on my life. Amen.

19 February

You saw me before I was born.
Every day of my life was recorded in your book.
Every moment was laid out before a single day had passed.
Psalm 139:16, NLT

Reading: Ephesians 2:4–10

I am particularly proud of a small painting of a tiger's head which hangs in our home. It is the work of a young woman from our church who is currently at art college. Artists are creators. They either create something for us to observe – to beautify or challenge; or something with purpose, for us to use. Many, of course, manage to achieve both.

When God created us, He put purpose into our lives. We aren't just here; we are here for a reason. Ignoring that truth causes all kinds of problems in our society. The soaring suicide rates tell a very sad story. After all, when things get tough, what's the point in living when we've been told that we've come from nowhere, are here for no purpose, and when we die that's it?

How different from what the psalmist says. Imagine. God saw us before we were born. He knew every day we would live on this earth. And more importantly, the One who created us had already planned every moment before we took our first breath! As a mother of two profoundly disabled children, that brings me great comfort. Some dared to say their lives were pointless, but God knew our daughters before they took a breath. He also knew the impact they would have, not only on our lives, but also on the lives of many others. Cheryl and Joy may not have been able to walk or talk, sing or see, but they taught us how to love without expecting anything in return, how to bear one another's burdens, and how to trust in God when all the usual props have been removed. Their lives had purpose. And so do ours.

Thank You, God, that You created me with purpose. Help me to live it out, that others might see Your workmanship in me. Amen.

20 February

Long ago the Lord said to Israel: 'I have loved you, my people, with an everlasting love. With unfailing love I have drawn you to myself.'

Jeremiah 31:3, NLT

Reading: Jeremiah 31:1–9

I realize that I am a very fortunate woman. I have never known a time in my life when I was not loved. Even on the days I haven't particularly felt loved, I have known that I am.

Sadly, that is not the case for everyone. Too often love and affection are used as bargaining chips in a relationship. Love is seen as something to be earned, not given freely. The journey home from work, or, perish the thought, school, is filled with an agonizing dread: *What will their form be like today? Will hugs or horror follow the turning of the key in the door?*

How wonderful to know that our Heavenly Father is altogether different. These words, 'I have loved you . . . with an everlasting love', were written long ago to a people in exile, who had suffered much. Yet they carry down through the centuries to us as His children today. And the love the Father is expressing is of a kind that cannot be replicated, even in the best of human relationships.

Think with me what being loved 'with an everlasting love' means.

God's love has no beginning and no end. He didn't decide one day to start loving you, and He won't wake up one day and declare that He doesn't love you any more. His love is constant, not flighty; unchanging, always the same; incomparable, there is absolutely nothing else like it!

And we are assured that God gives His love to us without reserve. He never holds back to see how we are going to behave. There is no price tag to fool us into thinking His love can be bought, bargained for or earned. So there is no use trying!

He quite simply loves you and me. No strings attached.

Thank you, Father, that You love me unconditionally. Help me to bask in the warmth of it today . . . and every day. Amen.

56

21 February

But God showed His great love for us by sending
Christ to die for us while we were still sinners.

Romans 5:8, NLT

Reading: Romans 5:1–11

It's one thing to say that we are precious because God has made us, or that the same God loves us with an everlasting love, but how can we really know that those words are true? Why should we believe them?

Words are cheap! Words aren't worth the paper they're written on! What she says and what she does are two different things!

Perhaps you've used those phrases yourself. They are all forms of everyday parlance because experience tells us that words on their own are merely puffs of air. Too often, words are spoken and promises are made, but nothing happens. Except perhaps, that disappointment results and trust is lost: relationships may even be damaged. So why should we believe what we've been considering these past few days?

Nice words. But can they be trusted?

There's another phrase that helps us with this one: actions speak louder than words!

Yesterday we looked, briefly, at the quality of God's everlasting love. Today, the words from Romans 5:8 throw light on a completely different dimension of that love. They tell us how God backed up His words with action! This kind of action is alien to our human thinking. Let's face it, there are some people we find difficult to like, never mind to love. And even within our closest relationships we sometimes have to work at loving the other person. Muttering the right words isn't always enough.

God did more than talk. He demonstrated to us that He meant it when He said He loved us. How did He do it? He sent His own Son, Jesus, to die for us in order that we might understand His great love for us. And He did it, not while we were His friends but 'while we were still sinners' (verse 8).

Proof enough? Absolutely! We are loved completely!

Thank You for the cross, Lord. I need no other proof that You love me. Amen.

57

22 February

This is real love. It is not that we loved God,
but that He loved us and sent His Son as a sacrifice
to take away our sins.

1 John 4:10, NLT

Reading: 1 John 4:7–11

Cheryl brought us much love simply by her presence. Her smile lit up our lives.

Paul's arrival, however, brought with it the treasure of watching a child do everything that parents without a disabled child take for granted. In one of the games we played when he was still very small, Paul would ask, 'How much do you love me, Mummy?' And he would add, 'This much?' as he held his chubby fingers inches apart.

'Oh no!' I would reply. 'I love you much more than that.'

'Do you love me this much?' he'd continue, stretching his hands further apart with each enquiry. Eventually he'd balance precariously on tiptoe, arms stretched to the limit, face contorted, and squeak, 'Do you love me this much, Mummy?'

By this stage I'd be on my knees in front of him, and with one sweep I'd stretch my arms way beyond his fingertips, exclaiming, 'No, Paul! I love you this much!' Much hilarity and hugs would follow.

However, boys will be boys, and following some naughtiness on his part I banished him to the sofa to think on his misdemeanour. A few short minutes later I heard his footsteps behind me. I turned from the sink to witness a saddened expression on his wee face and his fingers held slightly apart. 'Do you love me this much, Mummy?'

'No, Paul,' I replied, much to his surprise and upset. 'I love you this much,' I continued, kneeling in front of him and stretching my arms further than ever before. 'What you do doesn't change my love for you. I'm your mummy!'

'I'm sorry, Mummy,' he replied, with the tightest of squeezes.

True love doesn't dissipate when we get it wrong. God loves us when we mess up. His arms will always stretch beyond ours. He is our Father!

Thank You, Lord, that Your arms always stretch beyond mine, even when I mess up. Amen.

23 February

You will show me the path of life;
In Your presence is fullness of joy;
At Your right hand are pleasures forevermore.
Psalm 16:11

Reading: Psalm 16

The phone in our hotel room rang twice. She was on her way! That thought was enough to shoot a smile across our faces. The door rapped, and I stood to attention like an excited schoolchild on prize-giving day. Responding immediately to the knock, Granda Philip opened the door wide. And there she was – a miniature delight of beauty and excitement, blond bunches bouncing as she ran into my arms.

'Morning, Granny and Granda!' she exclaimed, stretching out to include Granda in the three-way cuddle. 'It's time for breakfast!'

Three days of our family holiday in Malta had already passed, and sharing that fun time with our three-year-old granddaughter and her parents was surpassing what the beautiful island had to offer.

'And do you know what, Granny?' Bethany continued, her little hands firmly holding my cheeks to make sure I was paying attention. 'The sun is shining – again!'

My husband's fondest memory of that holiday is watching his little grandchild skip down the corridor in front of us, stopping every short distance to turn, smile and make sure we were still on her tail. Sometimes it's the little things that bring the greatest delights.

The psalmist reminds us today that, in spite of the tough stuff that life throws our way, joy and pleasure are to be found in the Father's presence. Are you finding smiles hard to come by at the moment? Perhaps it displays a need to spend more time with Him?

Rekindle the joy. Remember: behind the clouds the sun is always shining. Or should that be – the Son!

Lord Jesus, help me to remember that You are the One at the Father's right hand. And it is in You that I find life's greatest pleasure. Amen.

59

24 February

A PASSAGE TO PONDER

Who shall separate us from the love of Christ?

Shall tribulation, or distress, or persecution, or famine,

or nakedness, or peril, or sword?

As it is written:

'For Your sake we are killed all day long;

We are counted as sheep for the slaughter.'

Yet in all these things we are more than conquerors

through Him who loved us.

For I am persuaded that neither death nor life,

nor angels nor principalities nor powers,

nor things present nor things to come,

nor height nor depth, nor any other created thing,

shall be able to separate us from the love of God

which is in Christ Jesus our Lord.

Romans 8:35–39

Read the passage through slowly and let the Author speak to you. Ask yourself these questions as you ponder:

- What does it say?
- What does it mean?
- What is God saying to me?
- How will I respond?

25 February

And not only that, but we also glory in tribulations,
knowing that tribulation produces perseverance.

Romans 5:3

Reading: Romans 5:1–5

ONLY TWO ICEBERG LETTUCE PER CUSTOMER.

The hastily scrawled notice drew my attention, not least because I couldn't imagine anyone requiring more than two iceberg lettuces in the month of February! The smaller scribble underneath provided some explanation: 'due to the unforeseen weather conditions in Europe'. That made me smile. Not only did television images of snow on the beaches of southern Spain come to mind, but a rather perverse humour towards those poor individuals who'd paid for winter sun only to find themselves throwing snowballs along the shore.

So the poor iceberg lettuce couldn't hack a bit of bad weather! The salad plates of Britain were apparently going to suffer.

Pushing my supermarket trolley further on, I couldn't help but consider another scene I had witnessed only the day before. It was also a piece of vegetation, but this one gallantly pushes through the hard soil of winter year after year to produce such fragile beauty that it always makes me gasp with admiration. The snowdrop. Tiny. Delicate. Stunning. It looks like it shouldn't be there, that it couldn't possibly have survived the difficult journey of pushing through hard, frozen earth only to arrive where the sun won't give it any warmth. Yet it does, and more than that: the cold wind will shake its fine frame, and snow might even reduce its height, but it will stand its ground, declaring to all who dare to look that it's a survivor! And a beautiful one at that!

God of the seasons, I am only too aware that life isn't always summer. When the blasts of winter blow heartache my way, give me the strength to persevere, and to push through the tough stuff. And may I emerge displaying a delicate beauty that onlookers will witness as the strength that only comes from You. Amen.

61

26 February

But when the fullness of time had come,
God sent forth His Son, born of woman, born under
the law, to redeem those who were under the law,
that we might receive the adoption as sons.

Galatians 4:4–5

Reading: Galatians 4:1–7

I know little of the intricacies of adoption law, but I do know the emotional trauma it can cause couples waiting for the court's final decision. My husband and I have twice acted as sponsors for a couple waiting to hear whether the children they had already grown to love would be allowed to become members of their family once and for all.

The adoption route is a harrowing experience; the length of time involved nothing short of brutal. The couple can never quite be sure how the decision will finally fall until they receive confirmation of the court date. On that day they, along with their precious child, will stand before a judge who will stamp the adoption papers declaring the child a member of their family. Fostering has ended. The child now belongs – permanently. And to prove it, they are given a new name – the family name. The old has gone; the new has come!

When I look at the adopted children I know, I am deeply touched. These kids had such a difficult start in life, but then someone *chose* to love them and make them part of their family.

It's also like that for we who have become God's children. Sin had orphaned us. But God chose to love us, to make us part of His family. The adoption route was not easy, and cost the death of His Son to draw us to Himself. But then one day our adoption papers were signed, and stamped by the Spirit, making us God's children once and for all (Romans 8:16). We belong.

And as part of God's family we too have been given a new name – Christian – Christ's ones . . . for all time. The old has gone; the new has come (2 Corinthians 5:17)!

What an amazing feeling, Lord, to know that because of Jesus I am part of Your family! Forgiven. Loved. Adopted. Thank You! Amen.

27 February

Let us therefore come boldly to the throne of grace,
that we may obtain mercy and find grace to help
in time of need.

Hebrews 4:16

Reading: Hebrews 4:14–16

Imagine: as part of the family of God we are loved, forgiven, adopted and given a new name. And that is only the beginning. One of the most precious privileges we enjoy as children of God is open and free access to the Father at any time.

The writer to the Hebrews reminds us that we can approach God's throne with a confidence that almost verges on impudence. 'Come boldly,' we are told. We are His children. God will have an audience with us at any time. But wait, it's more than the formality of a royal audience we can expect. It's an intimacy with our 'Abba, Father', as Paul reminds us (Romans 8:15). The word 'Abba' in Aramaic is the same word we use for 'Daddy' today. While reverence is essential when we pray, it's good to remember the 'Abba' nature of God's character towards us.

Remarkably, the King of kings, our Father, welcomes us into His presence. He doesn't have a complex appointment system in operation, or a list of options to search through in order to reach Him. The hours we can access Him are 24/7. He is never unavailable. In fact, when we speak with Him, He:

- never puts us on hold;
- won't say, 'We'll talk about it later';
- doesn't limit the time we can spend with Him.

There isn't any topic we can't discuss with Him. And He doesn't enjoy the company of one of His children more than another. God has no favourites (Acts 10:34).

The only quantifying factor in our access to our Heavenly Father is *how much we choose to use it*. Sometimes I wonder if my absence might make Him say, 'Where have you been? I've missed you.'

Forgive me, Lord, for the times when I haven't shown up, when I feel too busy to speak with You. Thank You that it's never too late to reconnect. Amen.

63

28 February

Eye has not seen, nor ear heard,
Nor has it entered into the heart of man
The things which God has prepared
for those who love Him.

1 Corinthians 2:9

Reading: 1 Peter 1:3–9

Go on . . . read today's verse again! Check your pulse if these words don't make your heart beat faster. Yet, the privileges we enjoy now from God's hand are as nothing compared to the future inheritance He has laid up for those who love him. It's beyond our imagination. New heaven. New earth. New bodies. New life. New air. New Jerusalem. No pain. No sickness. No sorrow. No hate. No hunger. No death. And that's only the beginning!

When our son was in London at music college, I would count the days each term until he returned home. The house was cleaned; his bedroom made ready. All his favourite foods filled the fridge, including extra treats, of course. A suitcase of dirty clothes was worth the work just to welcome him home!

Obviously, we'd keep in touch by phone while he was away, but it didn't compare with being in the same room and speaking face to face. It was his presence we loved. The warmth of his smile. The excitement he generated when rehearsing all that had happened since he'd last been home. For me, I loved to hear him say, 'So Mum, what are you reading?' That's what family reunions are all about – sharing, loving and being together.

The words of Jesus in John 14 give me that sense of longing for a 'family' reunion, of looking forward to what lies ahead. Imagine: He's preparing a place for me – in His Father's house! I get to meet face to face the One I've been speaking with at a distance for years. To sit with Him, walk with Him, enjoy His presence and feel the warmth of His smile. And all because I am His child.

I can't wait, Lord, for that day when I shall see You face to face. Thank you for the privilege that is mine as a child of the King. Amen.

March

1 March

But you received the Spirit of adoption by whom we cry out, 'Abba Father.'
Romans 8:15

Reading: John 1:10–14

I love how Jesus used stories to teach profound truths (Matthew 13:34). He explained what people needed to hear in the simplest way possible. Let's have a go!

The young woman's hand shook as she slipped the invitation out of its envelope. She couldn't believe her eyes:

You are invited to a Royal banquet to be held in the Palace.

But how would she get there? What would she wear? She read on:

A carriage will collect you and dress will be provided.

She was overwhelmed. How come she had been invited?

The doorman welcomed her inside. They were playing a new song, and the music captivated her. Surrounded by incredible beauty, the young woman tiptoed into the great hall, a tiny bead of sweat forming on her brow. The room was filled with such joy. Laughter floated through the air. Everyone else looked like they – she searched for the word – belonged. And her heart beat faster. She watched as the King tenderly embraced a child, while the Prince spoke with another guest.

Panic set in. 'What am I doing here?' her heart screamed. 'I don't deserve to be here!' But she couldn't find the exit. So she slid down against the wall when the dinner bell rang, hiding in a corner as the others went to the feast.

That's when she heard a voice above her. 'My child, what are you doing here? The Father is looking for you. He wants you to sit at the table with Him.'

'But I don't belong here,' she replied. 'I'm not good enough.'

'Of course, dear. No-one is good enough. But you're family now. I know. I signed your adoption papers.'

As He reached forward, she took the Spirit's hand, and rose to her feet to take her place at the table.

Thank You, Father, that I am adopted. I am Your child. Forgive me for sitting in the corner of the Palace, when I should be dining at Your table. Amen.

2 March

But as many as received Him, to them He gave the right
to become children of God, to those who believe in
His name: who were born, not of blood, nor of the
will of the flesh, nor of the will of man, but of God.

John 1:12–13

Reading: John 1:11–14

God has no grandchildren! However, we have discovered that He does have children whom He has adopted into His family.

But how can I be sure I am a member of God's family? Can I truly know that He is *my* Father, and that I am His child?

The answer to these questions lies in today's Scripture. You see, becoming a child of God has nothing to do with heredity: having Christian parents or grandparents won't make us Christians. Neither can someone else drag us into God's family, or plan for us to be included, no matter how deeply they wish it for us.

Our rebirth, or adoption, comes through God alone. Our part is clearly explained at the start of John 1:12: 'as many as received Him, to them He gave the right to become children of God'. Receive whom? Jesus, God's Son. How?

- *Recognize* our sinful nature, and our inability to do anything about it (Romans 3:23).
- *Repent* of our sin, and *believe* the good news that Christ died for us (Romans 5:6–8).
- *Confess* that we cannot save ourselves, and *call* on the name of the Lord to save us from our sin (Romans 10:13).
- *Tell others*: 'For with the heart one believes unto righteousness, and with the mouth confession is made unto salvation' (Romans 10:10).

If it helps, feel free to use the prayer below, and trust God, by the Holy Spirit, to do the rest! Oh, and . . . welcome to the family!

Dear God, I know I am a sinner, and that only Christ's sacrificial death on the cross can make me right with You. Please forgive me, and make me Your child. Thank You for hearing and answering my prayer. Amen.

68

3 March

A PASSAGE TO PONDER

There was a man of the Pharisees named Nicodemus,

a ruler of the Jews.

This man came to Jesus by night and said to Him,

'Rabbi, we know that You are a teacher come from God;

for no one can do these signs that You do unless God is with Him.'

Jesus answered and said to him,

'Most assuredly, I say to you, unless one is born again,

he cannot see the kingdom of God.'

Nicodemus said to Him, 'How can a man be born when he is old?

Can he enter a second time into his mother's womb and be born?'

Jesus answered, 'Most assuredly, I say to you,

unless one is born of water and the Spirit, he cannot

enter the kingdom of God.

That which is born of the flesh is flesh,

and that which is born of the Spirit is spirit.

Do not marvel that I said to you, "You must be born again."'

John 3:1–7

Read the passage slowly and let the Author speak to you. Ask yourself these questions as you ponder.

- What does it say?
- What does it mean?
- What is God saying to me?
- How will I respond?

4 March

Therefore with joy you will draw water
From the wells of salvation.

Isaiah 12:3

Reading: Isaiah 12

I had been tasked with picking some flowers to grace my mum's hallway. She had made her wishes clear: 'Get something nice and colourful.'

So I browsed the excellent display, trying to choose something special but which wouldn't cost a fortune. There are two varieties of flowers that she often chooses for herself but I wanted to surprise her with something different. That particular day, the display buckets were brimming with too much choice! Having walked round and round a few times I suddenly noticed a pile of cardboard boxes sitting at the end of the stall. Lying on their side, completely dry, piled on top of each other and held together with two elastic bands were what looked like bunches of green sticks! *Yes!* Search complete: Mum will love these.

Dry, stick-like, green things – not a flower to be seen? How come?

They were daffodils. The first of the season. All they needed was twenty-four hours in water and, hey presto . . . they would bloom in brightest yellow! A visual delight so close to winter's end.

It's amazing how many everyday items come with the instructions: 'Just add water.' Its transformative power can change the dullest and driest into something beautiful.

Jesus told the woman at the well in John 4:14 that whoever drinks of the 'water' that He gives will never thirst again. He went even further to explain to her that it would produce everlasting life for those who drink it. Of course, Jesus was speaking of the life to be found only in Him. Transforming, life-giving, drought-chasing Water of Life! And it will never be in short supply!

If you are feeling dry and stick-like today, why not drink from the well that never runs dry, and watch . . . for your soul will blossom!

Lord, I rejoice that the water from the wells of salvation will never run dry. Thank You that You can deal with my soul's dryness, and produce something beautiful as I drink from You. Amen.

5 March

This is the day the LORD has made;
We will rejoice and be glad in it.
Psalm 118:24

Reading: Psalm 118:19–29

Perhaps that's not what you wanted to read this morning.

Maybe there's not much to rejoice or be glad about in the next twenty-four hours. Same old, same old. Work, home, housework, TV. The daily grind. Nothing much to get excited about. Or maybe this is the day you go to the hospital for test results, and you doubt you'll be rejoicing afterwards. Then there's that grave to visit, and coming back to an empty house delivers no smiles.

Surely the psalmist is thinking of one specific day in his life? He couldn't possibly mean today – here and now – could he? Maybe he's speaking about the Sabbath. We always try to think of something to rejoice about on a Sunday. It seems right somehow.

Not so. The psalmist hasn't had one of those 'everything in the garden is rosy' days that makes him want to praise the Lord. Quite the opposite, in fact. Life for him personally, and for the nation, has been very tough. He uses such words in the psalm as distress, violence and destruction. Hardly much to sing about. Why, then, does he decide to rejoice and be glad? Because the day he is speaking about is none other than the day of salvation! He not only recognizes what God has done in their past, but he even prophesies in verse 22 about the coming Saviour. That's what 'is marvelous in [his)] eyes' (verse 23).

Whatever is going to happen, the psalmist makes a deliberate choice: 'We *will* rejoice and be glad in it' (verse 24, emphasis mine). They are going to live, and not die (verse 17)! The day of salvation is a reality to him – something to shout about!

How much more should it be for we who have Jesus. Praise is a choice. Let's choose well today.

Loving Saviour, thank You that we still live in the day of salvation – this day the Lord has made. I choose today to rejoice and be glad in it. Amen.

71

6 March

'Is this not the fast that I have chosen:
To loose the bonds of wickedness,
To undo the heavy burdens,
To let the oppressed go free,
And that you break every yoke?'
Isaiah 58:6

Reading: Isaiah 58:1–8

The Children of Israel loved to make a public display of misery when they were observing fast days. They liked to make a big deal of any short period of personal sacrifice. A gaunt, melancholy face was a sure sign of fasting, which they hoped would draw compliments for their perceived state of holiness.

Not much has changed! Many of us will commiserate with others when Lent begins. Six weeks without chocolate, pizza or Facebook might even result in mutual backslapping, while we secretly wonder how long we'll manage to hold out this time round. And what will it do for our personal holiness? Isaiah reminded the people that God isn't interested in flagellation for personal brownie points. What He wanted was sacrifice that changed lives, and not merely our own.

So when we're making our pancake stack today, it's unlikely to clear the house of restricted foods for the Lenten fast. But it could be the opportunity to thank God for all His goodness and to ask Him to encourage reflection and repentance in our lives. Reflection on all that God's Son sacrificed so that we might be freed from our wickedness and released from everything that oppresses. Repentance for all that holds us back from following Him the way we ought.

For some, it might involve fasting to help focus the mind. For others, it might involve giving sacrificially to remind our hearts what that feels like. However we choose to prepare to commemorate Easter, let's do it with worshipping hearts.

God of Heaven, thank You for the selfless plan of salvation. As I contemplate Lent, may I be willing to put self aside and take time to remember all that Jesus laid aside for me. Amen.

7 March

Blessed are those who are generous,
because they feed the poor.
Proverbs 22:9, NLT

Reading: 1 Timothy 6:17–19

For some communities of the Christian church, Lent is a more important part of the church calendar than for others. Yet I for one am glad that the Lenten profile has been raised within the ranks of those of us who are less comfortable with formal forms of worship and liturgy. After all, who among us should not give more careful consideration to all that Christ has done for us? Too often the cross of Christ is brushed over with unbefitting familiarity, while the fact of the resurrection is not celebrated as it should be, for fear of looking foolish.

Lent can focus our minds and hearts on allowing the Easter truths to captivate our hearts once more. After all, the message we have is exciting, life-changing stuff!

Some people find that engaging in some form of personal sacrifice is the aid they like to use for reflection. They give something up as a reminder of all that was given up for them. The loss of something they enjoy for a period of time frees them to contemplate more fully on the cross, and the great sacrifice made by the Saviour for our redemption.

Others focus on giving during Lent to remind them of the generosity of God in the giving of His Son, and of Christ in willingly offering Himself. Organizations have even sprung up to help people give creatively, not only of money, but also of time and acts of kindness. They encourage us to think of others rather than ourselves for the forty days leading up to Easter. Ultimately, both the self-denial approach and the acts of kindness approach are intended to hone our thoughts more keenly on both the horror and the freedom brought about that first Easter. Any other result would render us hypocrites!

God of Heaven, as I contemplate all Your Son has given for me, may I be stirred to generosity of heart, that others may seek You. Amen.

73

8 March

Live no longer as the ungodly do, for they are hopelessly confused . . . You must display a new nature because you are a new person, created in God's likeness – righteous, holy and true.

Ephesians 4:17, 24, NLT

Reading: Ephesians 4:17–24

It doesn't take a genius to recognize that a coin has two sides. Nor does it take much thought to work out that privilege always has a companion tagging along, her 'sterner sister' – responsibility!

Oh dear. It's one of those words that invariably evokes a groan. The dictionary doesn't soften it any with its definition of *accountability*, *duty*, *obligation*, and wait for it . . . *taking the blame*! Undoubtedly, our delight is to enjoy the privileges associated with being children of God, but what of the sterner sister? Is responsibility the other side of God's 'adoption' coin?

Paul, writing to the new Christians in Ephesus, certainly seems to confirm that. Reminding them of their new position in Christ, he tells them not to live like the ungodly, but rather to make their new nature clearly evident. Seems pretty straightforward: the children in God's family have a responsibility to live differently from those around us.

Thankfully, and before the panic sets in, Paul explains the 'how to' very quickly when in Ephesians 5:1 he says, 'Therefore be imitators of God as dear children.' God doesn't ask the impossible of us without giving the wherewithal to achieve it. He recognizes that we cannot live differently and display a new nature in our own strength. But it *is* possible when we discover that we have a mentor unlike any other. Jesus said, 'Let Me teach you, because I am humble and gentle, and you will find rest for your souls' (Matthew 11:29, NLT).

Perhaps 'responsibility' isn't stern but rather just another privilege. After all, look who is our teacher! And it won't be front-of-the-class instruction. We get to walk beside Jesus, learning as we go.

Heavenly Father, I can only live this life You have called me to with Jesus walking by my side. Thank You that I can learn from You, Jesus. Amen.

9 March

'I am the vine, you are the branches. He who abides in Me, and I in him, bears much fruit; for without Me you can do nothing.'

John 15:5

Reading: John 15:1–8

We become like the people we live with. It's an old saying that constantly proves itself true. Observe one of the younger members of your family and it won't be long before you identify facial expressions or walking gait that remind you of parents or grandparents. At times the likeness is uncanny.

It's no different in God's family. The more time we spend in God's presence, the more like Him we become. Imitate your Father, Paul exhorts us in Ephesians 5:1, in order that we might live differently. 'He who has seen Me has seen the Father,' Jesus tells Philip in John 14:9. If we are to become like the Father, as Paul says, then it will only happen as we spend time with Jesus.

John 15 teaches us about the vine life. While the fruit of the plant hangs from the branches, it can't exist without the life-giving properties of the main vine. For from within the roots and through the trunk flow the nutrients and liquid the plant needs, not only to live, but also to produce fruit. Branches are pretty useless on their own. Jesus makes that very clear when He identifies Himself as the true vine, and believers as the branches. We can't do anything without Him! Our spiritual life and effectiveness only happen because of what we receive from Him. We cannot live differently from those around us if we are not attached to Him, the true vine.

There's something exhilarating, yet restful at the same time, in knowing that my responsibility is merely to remain in Him. It's Jesus Who is charged with my spiritual growth as long as I abide, remain, stay attached. That's beautiful.

Lord Jesus, thank you for making it possible for me to abide in You. Without You I can do nothing. With You all things are possible. Teach me what it means to abide. Amen.

10 March

A PASSAGE TO PONDER

'Moreover when you fast, do not be like the hypocrites,

with a sad countenance.

For they disfigure their faces that they may appear to men

to be fasting.

Assuredly, I say to you, they have their reward.

But you, when you fast,

anoint your head and wash your face,

so that you do not appear to men to be fasting,

but to your Father who is in the secret place;

and your Father who sees in secret will reward you openly.'

Matthew 6:16–18

Read the passage slowly and allow the Author to speak to you. As you ponder, ask yourself these questions:

- What does it say?
- What does it mean?
- What is God saying to me?
- How will I respond?

76

11 March

Then Jesus spoke to them again, saying, 'I am the light
of the world. He who follows Me shall not walk
in darkness, but have the light of life.'
John 8:12

Reading: Isaiah 55:8–13

There are times when the delights of Christmas stretch right through to spring. Especially when you discover that restaurant gift voucher tucked away in the study drawer – an overdue Christmas treat to be enjoyed beside the sea.

Portballintrae nestles on Northern Ireland's beautiful north coast. It boasts only one shop, but hundreds of holiday homes. The permanent residents enjoy the peace and quiet of strolling along the empty sands all winter, avoiding jostling with large numbers of visiting city-dwellers on weekends and in the summer months. On this particular March day we dined overlooking a peaceful bay, and the view was stunning.

It's strange how a few hours away from the grind can be so relaxing in such surroundings. What surprised us even more was that it was still daylight at 6.20 in the evening. All the more time to gaze at the lapping waves. We were both very tired. Lately life had been too busy; weeks chasing each other faster than ever. So the extra daylight added to the enjoyment, and also confirmed that spring was on the way. Soon the long dark days of winter will come to an end, and daylight will last until as late as 10.30 pm!

Darkness had fallen by the time we turned the car towards home, and I couldn't help but laugh at the sight of one patch of the sky clinging stubbornly to the very last piece of light against the encroaching darkness.

How comforting to know that darkness is not our permanent state, that one day the sun will shine again, and there will be more 'light' to enjoy as each day passes. If it's still winter in your heart, take courage, spring is on its way!

Father of the seasons, You who know the importance of winter in my life, give me patience to wait for spring, for it shall surely come. Amen.

12 March

'And the sheep hear his voice; and he calls his own
sheep by name and leads them out.'

John 10:3

Reading: John 10:1–6

In our generation, farming sheep in the West is very different from the shepherding
of sheep we read about in Bible times: a tradition that is still used by many Eastern
shepherds today.

Considering the reputation sheep have as being rather dumb animals, I've always
wondered somewhat how an individual sheep would, or could, respond cleverly
when the shepherd called its name? That is, until we visited Israel.

In the Nazareth Village (designed as it would have been when Jesus lived), we
gathered around a rickety sheep pen, which housed some sheep and goats. The
animals weren't paying any attention to us as they munched on a pile of hay at
the far end of the pen. The shepherd told us to call them. So some members of
our group called and whistled in an attempt to coax the animals to head in our
direction. All without success. They were too busy eating.

Then the shepherd spoke, raising his voice ever so slightly. One brief sentence was
all it took, and then it happened. The sheep and goats instantly turned and ran
across the pen to the one whose voice they recognized above all others. There was
no mistaking it. The sheep knew their master.

The sight of the new lambs in the fields near our home at the moment remind me
of how Jesus described Himself as the Good Shepherd. Remarkably, He knows
every one of His sheep by name and calls us to follow Him. I'm so thankful for the
times I've clearly heard Him speak my name, calling me to Himself when I've been
in desperate need of His care. However, in today's noisy world, we need to ensure
that other voices are not drowning out the One that really matters.

*Great Shepherd of the sheep, help me listen carefully for Your voice above the many that
seek my attention. May my response be instant, for only You know exactly what I need.
Amen.*

13 March

Then Jesus said to them again: 'Most assuredly,
I say to you, I am the door of the sheep . . .
If anyone enters by Me, he will be saved,
and will go in and out and find pasture.'

John 10:7, 9

Reading: John 10:7–10

Shepherding in Bible times was normally done far from home. The arable land was tilled and planted near to the villages and towns. But looking after sheep had to be done away from where they might destroy other human food sources. And finding pasture for the flock was not always easy in Israel's arid landscape. Often shepherds were away from home for long periods of time. They had plenty of time to get to know their woolly companions, while the sheep learnt quickly to become utterly dependent on the shepherd for everything.

Yet the land was far from hospitable. Perilous terrain, wild animals and thieving men were only some of the dangers from which the shepherd had to protect his flock. So every night the shepherd would construct a temporary pen of rocks and wood to keep his sheep safe. He'd stand in the pen and call each one by name and the sheep would follow the shepherd in. Then he would lie across the opening they'd entered by to ensure that none would go looking for a midnight snack. The shepherd himself became the door, keeping his flock safe from themselves and from the possible attacks of beasts and man. When morning came, he would move aside and allow the sheep to graze once more.

Aren't you glad that Jesus is our door? The One who calls us by name is the One who brings us into pastures that will sustain us. He is also the One who protects us from anything or anyone seeking to harm us. He keeps us safe. He is utterly dependable, completely trustworthy. We are totally safe in the Shepherd's care.

Thank You, Lord, that You provide my sustenance and my safety. You are the Shepherd whom I can trust completely. You are the door through which I find life and security. Amen.

14 March

'I am the good shepherd . . . As the Father knows Me,
even so I know the Father; and I lay down My life
for the sheep.'

John 10:14–15

Reading: John 10:11–18

If King David had been standing in the crowd listening to Jesus that day he would have understood exactly what Jesus was saying. Shepherding was a dangerous job. Hadn't David boldly declared the killing of a lion and a bear as worthy credentials to fight against the giant Goliath (1 Samuel 17:36)?

But if we look at the tense Jesus uses here in John 10:16, we see He isn't declaring His willingness to lay down His life for His sheep; He is confirming a fact: 'I lay down My life for the sheep.'

It would take the slaying of Shepherd Jesus to make the sheep truly His own, and His death to provide the ultimate protection of those who were His. Through the resurrection He would take up His life again, making eternal provision also possible. Jesus isn't merely Shepherd for the here and now. One day He will call us heavenward.

Unfortunately, the religious leaders had little time for shepherds, who were often despised for their lack of education. The study of the Torah was simply not possible if you spent most of the year distant from the synagogue. Ironic, really, as without shepherds there would be no lambs available for the sacrifice required by the same law the Pharisees held to so tenaciously. And yet Jesus identified Himself with the role of the shepherd rather than with the religious. Hardly surprising when we recall that Isaiah prophesied of the Messiah, 'He is despised and rejected by men' (Isaiah 53:3).

So what is our response to this great Shepherd of the sheep? Reject Him? Follow Him? One thing is sure: He continues patiently to call us by name.

Thank You, Lord, for laying down Your life for me. I look forward to the day when I shall hear You call me heavenward. Until then I choose to follow You, great Shepherd of the sheep. Amen.

15 March

'And other sheep I have that are not of this fold;
them also must I bring, and they will hear My voice;
and there will be one flock and one shepherd.'

John 10:16

Reading: John 10:15–21

To be compared with a sheep is not hugely flattering!

Rightly or wrongly, they don't exactly get good press in the wisdom stakes, do they? The one thing they are good at, though, is on the community front: they love being together in groups. Experts say that a lone sheep is either lost or ill. According to sheep research (yes, there is such a thing), sheep have inbuilt grouping mechanisms primarily for safety against predators. They need to be in sight of at least five other members of the flock or they become stressed.

Middle Eastern shepherds were only too aware of this, and those with small flocks often joined with others to search for pasture. But they were still shepherds of their own flock. Even within travelling groups there would have been disagreements. Abraham and Lot were a case in point (Genesis 13:7). Shepherds liked to have their flock close by or there could be ownership and other problems. In fact, separation went beyond sheep business. In spite of the Old Testament teaching about welcoming strangers (Leviticus 19:33–34), the Jews were suspicious of outsiders.

What Jesus said here in John 10:16 was revolutionary. He declared that He had sheep 'which are not of this fold' – not Jews! He would be Shepherd to *all* who responded to His call. And there would be one flock . . . and only One Shepherd. I for one am glad that the Shepherd's call can be heard by Gentile sheep from every tribe, race, colour and creed.

And remember, He calls us by name!

Thank You, Lord Jesus, that there is room in Your flock for everyone who responds to Your call – including me! Help me make it easy for others to hear You call their name. Amen.

81

16 March

For the message of the cross is foolishness to those
who are perishing, but to us who are being saved
it is the power of God.

1 Corinthians 1:18

Reading: Romans 3:19–26

Green garments of all kinds will be brought out from the closets of millions tomorrow. Politicians and heads of state will don an emerald tie or pin on a little clump of shamrock. Rivers and beers will be dyed green, while famous buildings will reflect the colour most closely associated with a small country situated on Europe's westernmost edge.

Yes, tomorrow is St Patrick's Day. It is a day more celebrated across the world than any other national festival on earth. Everyone loves the Irish, it seems. An excuse for a party if ever there was one.

Patrick would turn in his grave if he could see what happens in his name.

As a sixteen-year-old boy he was kidnapped from Roman Britain and enslaved for six years in Ireland before escaping to his homeland. Those difficult years brought him to God. But the image of pagan Ireland would not leave his soul, and saw him return here to preach the gospel, winning thousands to the Saviour and establishing the Christian church. His writings are filled with quotes from the book of Romans, hence today's reading. The real Patrick knew nothing of snakes, leprechauns or charms, but he knew plenty of Christ. Hymn-writer Cecil Frances Alexander translated St Patrick's Breastplate, showing us Patrick's heart. This is the man we should celebrate: his Saviour, the One we ought to follow.

> Christ beside me, Christ before me,
> Christ to comfort and restore me,
> Christ beneath me, Christ above me,
> Christ in quiet, Christ in danger,
> Christ in hearts of all that love me,
> Christ in mouth of friend and stranger.[2]

Lord God, I celebrate today those who, at great personal cost, brought the gospel to my homeland. Give Your children a heart like Patrick, to spread this wonderful message to those who still need to hear it. Amen.

17 March

A PASSAGE TO PONDER

Good and upright is the LORD;

Therefore He teaches sinners in the way.

The humble He guides in justice,

And the humble He teaches His way.

All the paths of the LORD are mercy and truth,

To such as keep His covenant and His testimonies.

For Your name's sake, O LORD,

Pardon my iniquity, for it is great.

Psalm 25:8–11

Read the passage slowly and let the Author speak to you. Ask yourself these questions as you ponder:

- What does it say?
- What does it mean?
- What is God saying to me?
- How will I respond?

18 March

And Adam called his wife's name Eve,
because she was the mother of all living.
Genesis 3:20

Reading: Genesis 3

Eve had it all! The perfect man, the perfect home, the perfect body, and the profound delight of walking with God in the garden every day.

Yet by the time she gave birth to her first child she had lost it all! Ejected from her beautiful home, the relationship she had with her husband was forever damaged. Her beautiful body now experienced pain; wrinkles would one day furrow her brow and stiffness gnarl those supple joints. How did it all go so terribly wrong? And worse still, what example had she left for those yet unborn?

The agony of childbirth at least delivered a beautiful son to caress in the night hours when, I suspect, guilt tore at Eve's heart. But never could she have dreamt, when she kissed Cain's sweet head, that she held in her arms the one who would rob her of her second-born in the years to come. For Abel would be murdered by the very child who brought her joy when she likely thought there was no more for her – the one who 'cheapened Paradise', in John White Chadwick's words.[3]

Yet we cannot point a finger at this failing woman without recognizing that we too make mistakes, for we are all children of Eve.

Eve's error, which set the dominoes falling with such catastrophic consequences, was to listen to the wrong voice. The serpent's first words (Genesis 3:1) caused Eve to doubt those spoken by her Creator, and to pander to what she wanted over what God had planned. Unfortunately she didn't only listen; she also acted on Satan's lies. The result was life changing for all of us!

Today, many conflicting voices vie for our attention and response. Whom we listen to is important not only for us, but also for the children who receive our legacy.

Lord, help me not to listen merely to what 'seems' right, but instead to listen carefully for Your voice, and to filter all the rest through Your Word. Amen.

19 March

He restores my soul;
He leads me in the paths of righteousness
For His name's sake.
Psalm 23:3

Reading: 1 John 1:5–10

Eve was by no means the only one in the Bible to make a mess of things.

I think one of the reasons why I love the Bible so much is that it doesn't only tell the stories of the great and the good. Nothing is hidden, and I'm glad, because the Bible isn't about great individuals, it's about a great God. And this great God specializes in:

- making the sad glad again;
- turning our disappointments into joy;
- taking our disasters and doing something miraculous with them;
- transforming the sinner into a saint.

How does He do all this?

'He restores my soul,' the psalmist reminds us. And David, the writer of Psalm 23, knew only too well what it was like to listen to the wrong voices, especially the ones in his own heart that urged him to fulfil his own desires first.

Eve suffered for her sin in so many ways, but God is in the restoration business. When her heart was broken by Abel's murder, and Cain's banishment because of it, she had another son. Eve named the little boy Seth, saying, 'God has granted me another child in place of Abel, since Cain killed him' (Genesis 4:25, NIV). In these words we see Eve acknowledging God's kindness and merciful provision for her. Perhaps even a sense that God still loved her reached into her brokenness.

All was not lost for Eve. God's restoration had begun in her soul.

God of Heaven – the great Change-maker – thank You that You are able and willing to restore my soul. Lead me in those 'paths of righteousness' that David speaks of, and divert my feet from walking where my soul would be harmed and Your name disgraced. Amen.

20 March

Then Jesus said to His disciples, 'If anyone desires
to come after Me, let him deny himself,
and take up his cross, and follow Me.'
Matthew 16:24

Reading: Ruth 1:1–17

Eve and Ruth were poles apart in more than life experience. Eve started with perfection and ended in loss and pain. Ruth's life was catapulted into loss and pain early on, and ended in what we might call fairy-tale fashion. Except her life was no work of fiction!

We could approach the retelling of Ruth's story from different angles: how she coped with personal disaster, her exemplary character, her amazing faith, moving from pagan foreigner to a follower of the God of Israel. But it's her sacrifice that captures my heart.

Ruth was faced with the challenge of sacrifice after her world fell apart, and she stepped up to the plate and took it on. When her mother-in-law, Naomi, urged both of her daughters-in-law to go home after all three women had lost their husbands, Ruth refused to go. Instead she told Naomi that she would return to Israel with her: 'Entreat me not to leave you,' Ruth said, 'or to turn back from following after you; for wherever you go, I will go; and wherever you lodge, I will lodge; your people shall be my people, and your God, my God' (Ruth 1:16).

She made a deliberate choice to leave behind the security and comfort of home to accompany her mother-in-law back to her home, with the likelihood of never seeing Moab again. The journey would be long and difficult, and Ruth knew, as a foreigner, that a welcome might not await her. Naomi could make no promises; there was no offer of a bright future. Instead, Ruth chose sacrifice, because her journey was more than geographical. She had set her heart on knowing Naomi's God. And she believed the price was worth it.

Heavenly Father, the best things in life require sacrifice. Help me to be willing to take on the challenge of sacrifice with the same willingness that Ruth displayed. Amen.

86

21 March

God is not unjust; he will not forget your work and
the love you have shown him as you have helped
his people and continue to help them.

Hebrews 6:10, NIV

Reading: Ruth 4:13–21

Sacrifice is an old-fashioned concept these days. Surely the 'deny himself, and take up his cross' concept that Jesus spoke about in Matthew 16:24 doesn't really apply to me, does it? Wasn't it for a different time? True, it's not easy theology. But it's what Jesus said needs to happen if we desire to follow Him.

Centuries earlier, Ruth had faced head on the challenge of sacrifice. What she came to discover is that sacrifice has unexpected rewards. God is no man's debtor. He does not need our sacrifice. Nor does He need to pay us back, for He owes us nothing. We, on the other hand, owe Him everything, while He continues to give, and give again.

Ruth gave up her family . . . God gave her a new one.

She left behind the possibility of marriage, culturally speaking . . . God gave her a godly husband.

She thought she would never be a mother . . . God gave her a son.

Added to all this, Ruth's prayers were answered, for Naomi's people became her people and, better still, Naomi's God became her God.

On the darkest of days, I wonder whether Ruth ever felt like giving up? In the depths of her sacrifice, could she ever have imagined how God would reward her? I certainly doubt she ever dreamt that her name would be mentioned in the lineage of the Christ, but it was (Matthew 1:5).

You see, there is no way that we can outgive God. We might think we are making the most profound sacrifice, but the writer to the Hebrews reminds us that He will not forget our work and our love. He sees it all. It does not go unnoticed by Him.

Father, thank You that no matter how hard we try, we cannot outgive You. Sacrifice is a lifestyle choice exampled by Your son, Jesus. I choose today to follow Him. Amen.

87

22 March

Looking unto Jesus . . . who for the joy that was set before Him endured the cross, despising the shame, and has sat down at the right hand of the throne of God.

Hebrews 12:2

Reading: Matthew 21:1–11

Six thousand years had passed since God had promised a 'Seed' that would bruise Satan's head (Genesis 3:15). The waiting ended with the birth of a baby boy to a virgin mother in a stable in Bethlehem. Thirty-three years later, Jesus faced His destiny as He gazed across the Mount of Olives to the city of Jerusalem.

All that waiting in eternity, all those years restricted in human form, for this very moment. I wonder what the human Jesus thought and felt? He knew all about the betrayal and the lies that lay ahead. The arrest, beatings, rejection, abandonment and crucifixion would come as no surprise. But for the first time in all of eternity He would be separated from His Father. Alone, He would die, because our sin would be placed on Him. That was His destiny.

Why did He ever get on that donkey? Why did He set His face to go to Jerusalem? The writer to the Hebrews tells us that it was 'for the joy that was set before Him' (12:2). Joy? What joy could Jerusalem possibly hold for Him?

The eternal joy:

- of obedience to the Father's will;
- of defeating sin, death and hell;
- of providing an inheritance for us that can never fade (1 Peter 1:4);
- of leaving the constraints of time to sit once more at the Father's side.

Beyond the horror of the cross Jesus saw the wonder of the resurrection: *There was joy ahead!* That's why He got on that donkey!

And because He made that Palm Sunday journey, we too can face our 'Jerusalem', whatever it might hold for us. 'Consider Him,' we are told, 'lest you become weary and discouraged in your souls' (Hebrews 12:3). There is joy ahead!

Thank You, Jesus, for getting on that donkey! Thank You for reminding me that there is joy ahead. Amen.

88

23 March

And the eye cannot say to the hand,
'I have no need of you.'
1 Corinthians 12:21

Reading: 1 Corinthians 12:12–26

My total knee replacement surgery was carried out in a centre of orthopaedic excellence. The surgeon was at the top of his field. The physiotherapists knew exactly how to get joints and muscles moving again. The nursing staff were skilled at concocting pain medication regimes. Each one had an endgame in mind: eventual pain-free joint movement for the patient. So they constantly focused on the bigger picture.

Two days after surgery I watched a staff member working outside. I was fascinated by how meticulously he worked. No shortcuts were taken as he got on with his job, totally on his own: none of his bosses could see what he was doing. He took real pride in his work! Not once did he slack or slow down. I think he was in on the bigger picture too. He knew how important his job was in ensuring patients reached their goal of returning to a more normal life after surgery.

The focus of my admiration? The bin-washer!

Yes, this amazing man spent ages power-hosing bins at the back of the clinic. Every square inch was meticulously cleaned. My guess is that he had been told that it only takes one little bit of dirt or one tiny organism to undo the work of the surgical team. Infection is the most feared word in orthopaedic surgery. In the big scheme of things, the bin-washer is needed as much as the surgeon.

As children of God, we are members of Christ's church, each one precious, important and needed exactly where God has placed us. There is no hierarchy. Our Big Picture is God's glory. Directing our focus on that transforms how we perform any task He asks of us!

Lord, keep my focus on Your glory, that I might recognize the importance of anything You ask me to do. I am proud to work for such a Master. Amen.

24 March

A PASSAGE TO PONDER

Sacrifice and offering You did not desire;

My ears You have opened.

Burnt offering and sin offering You did not require.

Then I said, 'Behold, I come;

In the scroll of the book it is written of me.

I delight to do Your will, O my God,

And your law is within my heart.'

Psalm 40:6–8

Read the passage slowly and let the Author speak to you. As you ponder, ask yourself these questions:

- What does it say?
- What does it mean?
- What is God saying to me?
- How will I respond?

25 March

'For My thoughts are not your thoughts,
Nor are your ways My ways,' says the LORD.
Isaiah 55:8

Reading: 1 Kings 17:8–16

In today's high-tech age, information can be beamed into our living rooms from across the world and instantly displayed via TV news. Much of it is disturbing, none more so than pictures of mothers holding dying children in their arms. I know something of that pain, having lost two of our three children to complex medical disorders. But I cannot imagine the horror of losing an otherwise healthy child simply because I cannot feed him or her. That's an altogether different kind of pain.

Unfortunately, this is not new to our world.

In today's reading we encounter a widowed mother leaving her little boy at home in order to gather a few sticks so that she can cook one final meal with what she has left. Soon they would die from the ravages of famine. All hope had gone. No husband meant no-one to provide for them. Even her sacrificial offerings to Baal, the god of the harvest, had gone unnoticed. She had done all she could.

Never could she have imagined that deliverance would come from a stranger who looked as hungry as she did. A stranger who asked the impossible from her: bread from the mouth of her starving child. But this stranger would introduce her to a God who did things differently. A God who keeps His promises; a God who would surprise her by simply turning up!

What do we do when we run out of options? How is it that sometimes we're beaten whichever direction we take? Why does it appear that our calls for help seem destined for disappointment? Is there no way out?

It might feel like that, but don't give up! Remember, God doesn't always use recognized channels to come to our aid. Listen carefully for His voice, because He is listening for ours. All is not lost.

Lord, You are often unpredictable, but always trustworthy. When everything else fails, I know You will find a way. Help me to rest in that truth. Amen.

26 March

Then the word of the LORD came to him, saying,
'Arise and go to Zarephath . . . I have commanded
a widow there to provide for you.'
1 Kings 17:8–9

Reading: 1 Kings 17:13–16

Elijah was no stranger to obedience. Whatever God asked of him, Elijah got on with it. No questions asked. Even when God told his prophet to leave Israel and go into what some would describe as alien and dangerous territory, it didn't faze Elijah. We simply read, 'So he arose and went to Zarephath' (1 Kings 17:10).

However, obedience to the God of Israel was a completely new experience for the starving, widowed mother Elijah met at the gate of the city. Yet somehow she instantly recognized the bedraggled man asking bread from her as a follower of another God. Otherwise why would she reply, 'As the LORD your God lives'? And for the first time in her life this nameless woman was asked to put feet to faith in the One she already recognized as 'living'.

'Do not fear,' the man of God said to her, explaining that if she were obedient, the Lord God of Israel would see to it that she and her son would not die, but live. 'The bin of flour shall not be used up, nor shall the jar of oil run dry, until the day the LORD sends rain on the earth' (1 Kings 17:14).

Make the last morsel of bread for a stranger and not her son? How could she agree? Yet how could she not? For the request was laced with promise. Promise not from a beggar, but from the very God of Israel! As she ran home I believe her steps were quickened by a hope that had eluded her for a very long time. In the days to come, shaking the bin of flour would remind her that it's not faith that matters, but in whom we place our faith that makes all the difference.

Lord, may my feet follow You in faith, even when my head would want me to doubt. Amen.

27 March

'For you have found grace in my sight,
and I know you by name.'
Exodus 33:17

Reading: 1 Kings 17:13–16

Who was this woman to whom God showed such love and compassion?

We don't even know her name. In her day, a woman's name was only of importance when related to her husband. Once he died she became a nonentity, with no-one to provide for her . . . until, that is, her son became a man. For this woman to lose her son as well as her husband would be disastrous. He was her only hope of a future.

Was she destined to become another nameless statistic of the enveloping famine? Nothing could be further from the truth as far as God was concerned, for when God set His plan of protection and provision in motion for His servant Elijah, He had someone else on His mind. God could have sent Elijah to a wealthy family just as easily as to this starving, poverty-stricken woman, but that's not God's way. Yes, He wanted His servant to realize that He could care for him beyond Israel's borders, but He also wanted a broken woman to know that she mattered just as much.

Each morning, when she shook that bin of flour and lifted the flask of oil, the widow of Zarephath not only re-encountered the miraculous, but also had daily confirmation that the God of heaven loved her. Her identity was no longer determined by her husband's name but by the grace of God. He was the One who knew her name. Much lay ahead for this precious lady, but for now she was experiencing a new life, one that was about more than being able to bake bread each morning. The God who knew her name wanted her to know His. And little by little she would come to know much more than that.

Lord, there are days when I feel invisible and unloved. But feelings are often wrong. Thank You that You know my name, and have me on Your heart. Amen.

28 March

'But no one says, "Where is God my Maker,
who gives songs in the night?"'
Job 35:10

Reading: Job 35:9–11

Music is surely one of the greatest gifts our Creator has given to the human race!

Is there anything more exhilarating than standing with a few thousand others, singing words of praise at the top of your voice? Such glorious sound causes your heart to pound and your toes to tingle. Or can there be anything more touching than the quiet lyrics of an old chorus offered to the Audience of One while you are alone with Him? The sense of awe and privilege suddenly transforms an ordinary place into a sanctuary of worship.

Yet there are times in all of our lives when the song seems to have been silenced by the rigours of life, the tiredness of our human frame, the sadness in our souls. It is at those times that I find the music of others is the channel God frequently uses to encourage and remind me that I am still loved ... and that He continues to be in control. Such words are soothing to the soul.

> I heard the voice of Jesus say,
> 'Come unto Me and rest;
> lay down, thou weary one, lay down
> thy head upon My breast.'
> I came to Jesus as I was,
> weary, and worn, and sad;
> I found in Him a resting place
> and He has made me glad.
> (Horatius Bonar, 1846)[4]

Thank you, Lord, for the 'songs in the night'. Rekindle the flame of praise in my heart, for its blessing will surely return to touch my life. Amen.

29 March

But Mary kept all these things and pondered them in her heart.
Luke 2:19

Reading: Luke 1:26–33

March may seem a strange time to be reading part of the Christmas story, but with Mother's Day approaching in the UK my thoughts can't help but turn to Mary.

She was the teenager addressed by an angel as 'highly favoured', 'blessed among women', while announcing, 'the Lord is with you' (Luke 1:28). She was the woman whom God chose to carry His Son, the long-awaited Messiah. The privilege all Jewish woman longed to have was to be given to Mary of Nazareth. Hers was no high-class family. Her father no military general. There was nothing of note about her, in fact. Apart from one thing: Mary was God's choice to bring up His Son. A revelation she didn't shy away from. A calling she didn't reject.

Motherhood would not be easy. Her pregnancy was classified as shameful because it came before the completion of her marriage to Joseph, the man to whom she was betrothed. Did she tell those who berated her of the angel's visit? Doubtful. Who would believe that the child she carried was conceived by the Holy Spirit? Even the child's birth happened in an inauspicious stable far from home.

It's no wonder that on that night promised by the angel Mary had plenty to ponder over. A crowd of visiting shepherds speaking of angel choirs and messages from God. And what of Simeon's words a short time later, that one day a sword would pierce her soul because of this child (Luke 2:35)? How could that be when Jesus was destined to be King? For now, Mary would do what any mother would: bring up her son as best she could. The rest she would leave in God's hands, for hadn't the angel told her that 'with God nothing will be impossible' (Luke 1:37)?

Lord, thank You for the example of Mary, who was prepared to follow You in obedience. May I be close enough to hear You speak, and bold enough to walk in faith, believing that nothing is too hard for You. Amen.

30 March

Her children rise up and call her blessed.
Proverbs 31:28

Reading: Psalm 95:1–7

The famous motto of the internationally renowned florist, Interflora, rolls off the tongue easily: 'Say it with flowers!'

Whether forecourt-purchased bunches or intricately designed floral masterpieces, flowers have been used, by most of us to say many things. 'Sorry!' 'Congratulations!' 'Happy birthday!' 'I love you!' 'Thank you!' 'Happy anniversary!' 'With sympathy.' But at this time of the year the greeting most often attached will be, 'Happy Mother's Day!'

In the United Kingdom we celebrate Mother's Day on the fourth Sunday in Lent, falling between mid-March and mid-April. The rest of the world celebrates it on the second Sunday in May. This is one day that should be celebrated, not least because being a mum can feel like the most difficult job in the world at times, especially in a society that looks for women to be all things to all people. Too many young women feel pressured into fulfilling career roles alongside being 'super-mums'. Bookshelves are laden with 'How to' titles about raising perfect kids, while parents at school gates discuss with pride the age *their* child walked or got his or her first tooth – as if somehow that was down to parenting success!

Measuring up against the 'in crowd' can be soul-destroying for young mums. Let's make sure we encourage and compliment those who might be finding the responsibility daunting. Mothers don't need unsolicited advice, but a 'you're doing a great job' could make their day.

And for those of us fortunate enough to still have our mums, saying 'thank you' with flowers is great, but using actual words will mean even more! The psalmist encourages us to praise the Lord – to develop an attitude of gratitude. And we do have so much to be grateful for! The New Testament writers take it one step further by telling us to encourage one another (1 Thessalonians 4:9). No-one deserves that encouragement more than Mum! Do it today!

Lord, thank You for my mother. Bless her life today. Please encourage those mums who are finding the responsibility tough today. Amen.

31 March

A PASSAGE TO PONDER

Strength and honor are her clothing;

She shall rejoice in time to come.

She opens her mouth with wisdom,

And on her tongue is the law of kindness.

She watches over the ways of her household,

And does not eat the bread of idleness,

Her children rise up and call her blessed;

Her husband also, and he praises her:

'Many daughters have done well,

But you excel them all.'

Charm is deceitful and beauty is passing,

But a woman who fears the LORD, she shall be praised.

Proverbs 31:25–30

Read the passage slowly and allow the Author to speak to you. As you ponder, ask yourself these questions:

- What does it say?
- What does it mean?
- What is God saying to me?
- How will I respond?

April

1 April

'This is My commandment, that you love one another
as I have loved you.'

John 15:12

Reading: 1 Corinthians 13:1–8

It's said that you can choose your friends but you can't choose your family!

While each of us displays family traits, it's amazing how different from each other members of one family can be, in spite of coming from the same gene pool. And I'm not speaking only of hair colour and height. In particular, differences in temperament can make for an explosive mix in siblings, especially in some of the more difficult growing-up periods. Thankfully, things usually change with maturity. Family is family, after all. A loving family should have each other's backs, laugh together, cry together, and display a commitment for each other that goes beyond friendship.

It's just the same when we become children of God. We have another, new family. A family joined by blood, Christ's blood, to whom we should also be committed. Siblings, whom we wouldn't necessarily choose as friends, but whom Christ has commanded us to love. And He goes on to tell us that we are to love them as He has loved us. That's a big ask, especially as we read in 1 John 3:16 that 'By this we know love, because He laid down His life for us'.

This love we are to have for other members of God's family is to be of the same sacrificial kind Christ had for us. And it's non-negotiable! Jesus commands us to love one another.

Why is it so important? Because, as Jesus tells us, we are being watched, watched by those who are looking for truth in what we do as well as what we say. 'By this all will know that you are My disciples, *if* you have love for one another' (John 13:35, emphasis mine). But remember, loving one another is a two-way street ... an absolute delight!

Lord Jesus, thank You that Your love knows no limits. Help me to love my brothers and sisters in Christ as You do. Thank You for those who have loved me because of You. Amen.

101

2 April

Though he was God . . . he gave up his divine privileges;
he took the humble position of a slave and
was born as a human being.

Philippians 2:6–7, NLT

Reading: Philippians 2:1–11

We have a saying in our house that goes like this: 'Don't do a Henman!'

For a number of years we watched the British Tennis Number One, Tim Henman, compete for the Wimbledon trophy. We would start by cheering with excitement but, invariably, we'd be reaching for a cushion to hide behind as it all started to fall apart. Soon a dejected Henman would head for the changing rooms once more. For us armchair critics, Henman's battle was lost in his head. He could play well enough to win. But did he believe it?

The battle for almost anything we find difficult is won first of all in our mind. A local gym poster is quite telling: *If you think you can do it and if you think you can't, you're right!*

There is much about living as part of God's family that seems utterly impossible. How can we possibly love one another as Christ loved us, as we read yesterday? How can we 'no longer live as the Gentiles do' (Ephesians 4:17)? Surely these are battles already lost. We don't have the ability to do these things by ourselves. Are we going to be forever heading dejectedly for the lockers?

Nothing has helped me more with these enormous challenges than Romans 12:2: 'Let God transform you into a new person by changing the way you think. Then you will know what God wants you to do, and you will know how good and pleasing and perfect his will really is' (NLT). As we allow Him to transform our lives, attitudes and behaviour by changing the way we think, it won't be long be before we start to think like Jesus, who 'gave up His divine privileges' and 'took the humble position of a slave' (Philippians 2:7, NLT).

Lord, I give You permission to change the way I think, in spite of the pressure of this world to squeeze me into its mould. Amen.

102

3 April

So accept each other just as Christ has accepted you; then God will be glorified.

Romans 15:7, NLT

Reading: Titus 3:5–7

Recently we've had a beautiful but most unexpected visitor to our garden. I haven't been quick enough to photograph him yet, which makes proper identification elusive. With the help of 'Professor Google' I think he, or she, might be a kestrel. But, whatever this small bird of prey is, he is stunning to see at such close quarters! What he is doing perched on our garden fence is a real mystery. He looks totally out of place in suburbia.

Have you ever felt out of place? Do you wonder if you really fit in God's family? Might you even have gone so far as to doubt you are God's child? Does it seem a bit surreal? You've prayed the prayer but still wonder if it was ever answered.

The apostle Paul was forever reminding members of the early church, and us today, of the fact of our salvation when we trust in Christ. While encouraging those in Rome to accept each other as believers, he also reminded them that 'Christ has accepted you' (Romans 15:7). No ifs, buts or maybes. Fact!

Then, when he wrote to Titus, who was pastoring the church on the island of Crete, he reminded those listening to the letter that Christ 'washed away our sins and gave us a new life through the Holy Spirit' (Titus 3:5, NLT). Fact! Our sins are forgiven. We now have new life through the Holy Spirit. We are indeed part of the family of God, whether we are new members or whether we have been on the journey for a long time.

Isn't it interesting that Paul told the believers in Rome that God is glorified when we accept each other as Christ has accepted us? No-one who has trusted in Christ should ever feel out of place in the family of God.

Heavenly Father, thank You that, because of Jesus, I am part of Your family. Help me to welcome others into this wonderful family who might otherwise feel out of place. Amen.

4 April

'For I have come down from heaven, not to do My own will, but the will of Him who sent Me.'

John 6:38

Reading: Luke 22:41–44

At time of writing, our Queen, Elizabeth II, has been the longest-reigning monarch ever to sit on the British throne. Sixty-five years all told. While she undoubtedly enjoys the privilege of position, wealth and fame, that is only part of the story, for duty and responsibility have been her daily companions ever since her father died while she was still a young woman. Her life is not her own – not even at the grand age of ninety-one.

Queen Elizabeth epitomizes duty: her country comes first. She has spent her very long life fulfilling a multitude of engagements annually on behalf of her beloved nation. In the past she has been judged harshly for appearing to put commitment to the crown before her own family. Yet she has never retaliated when she has been wronged. Her life is ordered by responsibility. She is to be admired.

That word 'responsibility' conjures up feelings of needs must, expectation and stoicism. Yet as far as Jesus was concerned, nothing could be further from the truth. For the Son of God, life was about more than duty and service; it was about devotion. Devotion was what motivated the Saviour to leave the glory of heaven in the first place. A devotion to His Father, whose heart Jesus knew only too well, was in turn motivated by love for each one of us.

Therefore, when Jesus spoke of coming to earth not to do His own will, but the will of His Father, He knew exactly what that would mean. Rejection, pain, death on a cross. Yet He persevered and carried out the Father's will, even through the agony of Gethsemane. 'Nevertheless not My will, but Yours, be done,' Jesus said (Luke 22:42).

Mere duty? Or heartfelt devotion? How will I respond to the Father today?

Thank You, Jesus, that Your response to the Father was one of utter devotion. Help me to follow Your example. Amen.

104

5 April

Beloved, do not think it strange concerning the fiery
trial which is to try you, as though some strange
thing happened to you.

1 Peter 4:12

Reading: John 16:25–33

Years ago our minister was preaching on how God speaks through His Word, and he commented, 'There are times when God repeats Himself to make sure we get the importance of what He is saying.'

Recently we have experienced a catalogue of family, and extended family, illnesses, which have at times been overwhelming.

Each day I've reached for my Bible, looking for little nuggets of encouragement. I also finish each day with two short readings from a couple of rather old devotionals, benefiting from filling my mind with something wholesome before sleep. You can imagine how surprised I was that both devotionals had the very same verse at the head of each reading! God was repeating Himself. However, the words shocked me, causing me to groan rather than bringing comfort: 'Beloved, do not think it strange concerning the fiery trial which is to try you, as though some strange thing happened to you' (1 Peter 4:12).

It was the sense of a future tense that made me groan a responsive, 'No Lord, not more!' Yet in an almost instantaneous response I heard these words from John 16:33 rise above the others: 'In the world you will have tribulation; but be of good cheer, I have overcome the world.'

How often I've spoken on those words from 1 Peter 4:12, where Peter reminds us that difficulty is not unusual in this life. While Jesus confirms that fact in John 16, He also reminds us that the victory against all that troubles our hearts and lives has already been won. He has 'overcome the world'. Our part is to trust Him while we wait for the final victory parade!

Lord, there are days when I just don't understand what You are doing, when pain is my daily companion. Rather than fight it, Lord, help me to rest in You, knowing You have it covered. Amen.

105

6 April

He has shown you, O man, what is good;
And what does the LORD require of you
But to do justly,
To love mercy,
And to walk humbly with your God?
Micah 6:8

Reading: Psalm 63:1–5

Have you ever sat in a meeting, perhaps a large convention or crusade, and sensed God speaking to you? The praise was wonderful, the atmosphere electric, and the preacher seemed to know just what you needed to hear. In fact, you'd go so far as to say you heard God speak clearly to your heart that day. Perhaps you even stood in response to the altar call to follow God's call on your life. The only problem is, you're not quite sure what that call actually is. So you've been seeking guidance, longing for revelation.

'I'd do whatever God asks me, if only I knew what that was,' you might say.

Too often we struggle with the issue of discovering God's will, when He simply wants us to get on with doing what He has already asked us to do.

- *Act justly*, God tells His people through the prophet Micah. Live each day with a determination to do what is right. Don't wrong individuals. Help those who are in need.
- *Love mercy*, God commands in this selfish world. Let loving kindness be the benchmark of our lives, for God has given us what we don't deserve, pouring His love and forgiveness on us.
- *Walk humbly with your God*, recognizing God's lordship over us. Develop an attitude of heart that seeks not our own way, but His. And get on with daily walking with Him.

Obedience to what's already revealed often leads to further and greater responsibility, if that's what God chooses to give us. But it's His prerogative; we are His children, after all . . . hopefully obedient ones, at that.

Heavenly Father, sometimes in our exuberance to discover Your will I forget that You have already shown me what You want me to do. Help me to be faithful and obedient in what You have asked of me. Amen.

106

7 April

A PASSAGE TO PONDER

And so dear brothers and sisters,

I plead with you to give your bodies to God.

Let them be a living and holy sacrifice –

The kind He will accept.

When you think of what He has done for you,

is this too much to ask?

Don't copy the behavior and customs of this world,

But let God transform you into a new person

by changing the way that you think.

Then you will know what God wants you to do,

and you will know how good and pleasing

and perfect His will really is.

Romans 12:1–2, NLT

Read the passage slowly and let the Author speak to you. As you ponder, ask yourself these questions:

- What does it say?
- What does it mean?
- What is God saying to me?
- How will I respond?

8 April

Take courage, all you people still left in the land,
says the Lord, take courage and work,
for I am with you, says the Lord Almighty.
Haggai 2:4, NLT

Reading: Haggai 2:5–9

I wonder, do you ever feel discouraged?

Perhaps I should qualify that question. Do you ever feel discouraged about the church? Or more specifically, your church? That part of God's family where you worship and that you call your spiritual home. Perhaps the enemy of our souls whispers in your ear, as he sometimes does in mine, 'What's the point? Nothing ever changes, people are still not saved, the prayer meetings are small, attendance numbers are dwindling.'

Sometimes those of us who worship in a small church fellowship can feel overwhelmed by what we witness in the mega-church world. But big isn't always beautiful. Didn't God choose a *small* nation to be His covenant people? Didn't He choose a *small* stable for Mary to give birth? Didn't He choose a *small* town to be home to His Son? Didn't He choose an unknown family to bring up the Messiah?

Long before Jesus' birth, when the Children of Israel were disappointed that the new temple wasn't as grand as Solomon's, the Lord said, 'For who has despised the day of small things?' (Zechariah 4:10). In fact, He declared that this temple would be the cause of great rejoicing: '"The glory of this latter temple will be greater than the former," says the Lord of hosts. "And in this place I will give peace"' (Haggai 2:9).

Through Haggai, the Lord encourages us to remain faithful. Keep at it, work for the Master, because He has promised, 'I am with you' (Haggai 2:4). Small or great, it matters not to God. And if it is His glory alone we seek, then size doesn't matter.

Lord, thank You for placing us within the community of a church family. Wherever that is, help us to be committed to it and work for Your glory alone. Amen.

9 April

Fix your thoughts on what is true and honourable and right.
Philippians 4:8, NLT

Reading: Philippians 4:6–9

At the time of writing, Donald Trump is President of the USA. He frequently rocks the world by what he says, often by tweeting. While he managed to become the most powerful political leader on the planet, I doubt he would have passed an entrance test for the diplomatic service! One of his more memorable accusations has been about 'fake news', which, it appears, simply describes anything he doesn't like.

Undoubtedly, there are times when it is difficult to know exactly what is true and what is not. The apostle Paul here encourages us to 'fix [our] thoughts on what is true'. Too often we allow our minds to linger on words that were spoken in haste, criticism or negativity. But what is it that we are to think on? What is true? Perhaps that should be: who is true?

Jesus described Himself in John 14:6 as 'the way, the truth, and the life', explaining further in John 8:32 that in knowing Him, the Truth, we shall be set free. Jesus is the One on whom we ought to fix our minds.

In Ephesians 6:11 Paul also tells us to 'Put on the whole armour of God', that we might stand against all the devil throws at us. That armour includes the belt of truth (verse 14). A Roman soldier's belt held everything together: his tunic to help him fight unhindered, and his sword, the essential battle weapon. Jesus is our belt of truth. He holds us together. He makes it possible for us to live our lives unhindered by the things that seek to hold us back, while Himself being the Word that is 'sharper than any two-edged sword' (Hebrews 4:12).

Fixing our eyes on Jesus allows our minds to be filled with the truth that He is, and the truth that He gives. There's no fake news with Him!

Lord Jesus, in this world of confusion and blurred lines, I choose today to fix my eyes on You, and to tune my ears to listening to what You say. For You are truth. Amen.

109

10 April

'He reveals deep and secret things;
He knows what is in the darkness,
And light dwells with Him.'
Daniel 2:22

Reading: Daniel 2:16–23

Much is written today about dreams and interpretations. It is a subject that can become an unhealthy obsession. For Daniel, the interpretation of Nebuchadnezzar's dream was a matter of life and death: he was asked not only the interpretation but also what the dream was in the first place! Daniel knew that such knowledge could only come by divine revelation, and that God is willing to reveal the deep and secret things. However, many of the mysteries of life will remain just that.

Centuries later, Jesus took a small group of men as His disciples and taught them for three short years. These men were nothing like Daniel. They were neither intellectual greats nor living in privilege but, as with Daniel, God was revealing deep and secret things to them. Only this time, they got to walk physically with the Truth every day. What must it have been like to be one of their number? To be privy to the revealing of mysteries as Jesus explained the deep things of God? To witness the miraculous on a daily basis? To hear words of prophecy, even though they didn't recognize it at the time? To live side by side with the One who fulfilled the very prophecy mankind had been waiting for from the days of Adam?

We live in days of even greater privilege, for God is still the Revealer of mysteries. He not only speaks through His written word; He is also present in us by the indwelling Holy Spirit. All we need to know in life is there for us to discover. How much we discover depends on our willingness to seek it out and on our prayerfulness for the Spirit to reveal it to us. Remember, 'He knows what is in the darkness, and light dwells with Him' (Daniel 2:22).

God of majesty and might, thank You that You know all things. May You be the deepest longing in my life, and Your Spirit my teacher. Amen.

110

11 April

Then our mouth was filled with laughter,
And our tongue with singing.
Then they said among the nations,
'The LORD has done great things for them.'
Psalm 126:2

Reading: Psalm 126

Our grandchildren's favourite piece of equipment at the local play-park is a boat-shaped swing with a normal seat at one end, perfect for the six-year-old, while the nursery seat at the other end suits the two-year-old. They love facing each other as the swing is pushed higher, playing off on each other's excitement and the thrill of the ride! Soon their laughter is so intense that it's impossible not to join in. Children's lives should be full of laughter. Unfortunately, that's not always the case.

Our first visit to a small refugee camp on the Thai–Burma border introduced me to the reality of children devastated by mankind's brutality. Their expressionless faces were an indicator of lives that had been robbed. We gave out food parcels to families hiding in the forest, with a promise to return the next day to play with the children. At first, the playtime was subdued, quieter than I'd ever witnessed. But it didn't take long before the smiles appeared, and then the sound of laughter filled that normally sad place so far from home. I wept. Tears of deep sadness for what these children had to endure, mixed with those of joy at the resilience of the human spirit. On that day they were children again.

Psalm 126 speaks of the unfettered joy the Children of Israel felt when they remembered how God had delivered them from captivity. They laughed and sang with sheer delight in their God, while those watching witnessed their praise to the God who had 'done great things for them'.

Happiness, sadness, freedom, captivity. Whatever our situation, the Lord has done great things for us. Through Jesus we have been freed from the captivity of sin. Do laughter, singing and praise feature in our response?

Father God, You undoubtedly delight in Your children's joy. May praise ring from my heart, for You have indeed done great things for me. Amen.

111

12 April

'I will not present burnt offerings to the Lord my God
that have cost me nothing.'
2 Samuel 24:24, NLT

Reading: John 12:1–7

Jesus was on His way to Jerusalem. No, more than that: Jesus was on His way to the cross. Sacrifice was on His mind.

It was a mere six days until the feast of Passover. Sacrifice was also on the mind of the multitudes making their way to the city, where the annual commemoration of Israel's exodus from Egypt would culminate in the sacrifice of the Passover lamb, the symbol of God's deliverance. Sacrifice of a different kind was on the mind of the zealots, who fought to rid their land of the Roman occupiers.

At the same time, two miles outside Jerusalem, sacrifice was enacted in a home in Bethany. There, Mary, a devoted follower of Jesus who often listened at His feet, seemed to sense the Lord's approaching death. As supper ended, Mary took an alabaster flask of expensive perfumed oil, broke it and poured the contents over the feet of Jesus. Then, in demonstration of her devotion, she unbraided her hair, using it to massage the oil into the Master's feet.

Judas berated her for wasting money. Jesus commended her sacrificial commitment to Him. Sacrifice? What sacrifice? The jar of spikenard held Mary's future. It could have provided a marriage dowry should she marry, or a means to live on should she not. Judas was right about one thing, though: what Mary poured over Jesus' feet was worth a lot of money, but it cost Mary more than money to give it to Jesus. It likely cost her future. Mary's sacrifice was an act of worship and devotion: total commitment. Price didn't come into it.

The prophet Samuel reminds us that King David refused to offer anything to the Lord that cost him nothing. Cheap faith is simply that – cheap!

Thank You, Lord, for willingly giving up Your life for me. May my offerings to You be marked by total commitment, whatever the cost. Amen.

13 April

'Hosanna!
Blessed is He who comes in the name of the Lord!'
Mark 11:9

Reading: Ephesians 4:11–16

How easily men's hearts change!

When Jesus arrived in Jerusalem, on what we now know as Palm Sunday, He was greeted by jubilant crowds. They were religious people, many even followers of Jesus, who were ecstatic that the Man who had raised Lazarus from the dead a few days earlier was now in their midst. They welcomed Jesus like a conquering hero! The spreading of palm leaves was a symbol of victory. The word 'Hosanna' means 'save now'. This crowd was celebrating in advance the victory of the One they believed would save them. The problem was that they only wanted saving from the Romans!

It wasn't long before the feelings of the crowd would be roused in a different way, not with acclamations of Messiah, but accusations of blasphemer. The crowd mentality is so fickle. One minute praising, the next minute condemning. Before long they were shouting, 'Crucify Him!' (Luke 23:21).

Yet a crowd is made up of individuals, each of whom chooses whether to remain and be swayed by those around, or to stand alone and remain loyalty to whom, or what, he or she knows is right.

It's easy to be critical of this swaying bunch, but what of us? Does my mind sway with every wind of doctrine (Ephesians 4:14)? Have I made promises to God that disappeared with the dawn of a new day? Has my zeal dulled, my commitment lost its edge? Do I prefer to follow what's trendy rather than search the Scriptures for myself?

And what of my loyalty to Jesus? Has it been dethroned by loyalty to self? Or have I decided to walk away from the crowd, once and for all?

Lord Jesus, forgive me for the times when I have followed the crowd instead of standing up for You. May my life display in words and actions that I belong to You, unashamedly. Amen.

113

14 April

A PASSAGE TO PONDER

The next day a great multitude that had come to the feast,

when they heard that Jesus was coming to Jerusalem,

took branches of palm trees and went out to meet Him, and cried out:

'Hosanna!

Blessed is He who comes in the name of the LORD!

The King of Israel!'

Then Jesus, when He had found a young donkey, sat on it; as it is written:

'Fear not, daughter of Zion;

Behold, your King is coming,

Sitting on a donkey's colt.'

His disciples did not understand these things at first;

but when Jesus was glorified, then they remembered

that these things were written about Him

and that they had done these things to Him.

John 12:12–16

Read the passage slowly and let the Author speak to you. As you ponder, ask yourself these questions:

- What does it say?
- What does it mean?
- What is God saying to me?
- How will I respond?

114

15 April

And He said to them, 'It is written, "My house shall
be called a house of prayer," but you have made it
a "den of thieves".'
Matthew 21:13

Reading: Matthew 21:12–17

No-one likes a hypocrite!

In Greek, the word 'hypocrite' is translated as 'actor'. It literally means 'playing a part'. In essence, you are not the real thing; you are just pretending. Our English dictionary defines a hypocrite as a fraud!

Yet in Jesus' day, the temple, of all places, was full of them. Under the guise of ensuring pilgrims had everything they needed to offer the required sacrifices, temple traders and moneychangers were cheating the faithful. Pilgrims and worshippers arrived with burdened hearts, ready to do business with God. Many of them had travelled long distances, making it impossible to bring with them the animals or birds required for sacrifice. Others had experienced the embarrassment of having their own animals rejected as 'unsuitable', resulting in the additional expense of buying from the overpriced traders in the temple forecourt. And to make matters worse, they couldn't use their own currency in the temple grounds. They had to use temple currency, and the exchange rate was exorbitant. The term 'daylight robbery' comes to mind.

Is it any wonder that Jesus was enraged on entering the temple? These people were pretending to care about the requirements of the Law but instead were using that same law to line their own pockets. Honouring God was the furthest thing from their minds.

Yet, in our distaste for the actions of these and countless others whose hypocrisy has been made public, we had better beware of those fingers pointing back at us. Am I sure that God's glory is the single motivating factor in all I do and say? Or could there be tables Jesus needs to overturn in my life?

Lord Jesus, as You examine my heart, make me willing for hypocrisy to be exposed, and give me a desire for Your glory to take its place. Amen.

16 April

'And whatever things you ask in prayer,
believing, you will receive.'
Matthew 21:22

Reading: Matthew 21:18–22

I wonder how you would spend your time if you knew you had only a few days left to live?

In spite of what lay ahead, Jesus continued with what He did every time He was in Jerusalem. He headed for the temple, ready for another day of teaching those who would listen, and challenging those who disbelieved. But the teaching started long before He entered the city. The disciples witnessed the Master curse the fig tree and explain to them the possibility of partaking in mountain-moving prayer ... through faith (Matthew 21:21–22). If only they'd believe!

Then, after the previous day's business of wreaking havoc with the table-turning incident, Jesus walked straight back into the temple colonnades and took a seat in the shade, the crowds heaving around Him.

You can imagine the conversation, can't you? *What will Jesus do today? Will He heal someone? Or make the Pharisees look foolish yet again?* Traders anxiously eyeing the Galilean, tempering their sales talk in the hope of keeping their supplies safe after yesterday's ructions. Temple guards gather, waiting to pounce should any trouble break out. Pharisees and Sadducees stiffen in arrogant resentment. The air is tense. But even the questioning of the chief priests and elders does not stop Jesus from doing what He'd planned. Time is now short, and Jesus made every word count. Only this time, instead of talking about the religious leaders, He addresses them directly. And what a message He gives. There is nowhere to hide.

Repentance is key. Judgment is coming. God is to be honoured with all your heart, soul and mind. Hypocrisy will fail. Israel will fall. And the message of salvation will be given to the Gentiles (Matthew 21:43).

Lord Jesus, help me to live this week as if it were my last. May my life count for eternity, and my words speak grace to those who need to know the way. Amen.

116

17 April

'I pray for them. I do not pray for the world but for those whom You have given Me, for they are Yours.'

John 17:9

Reading: John 17:9–26

It's so humbling when we hear the words, 'I've been praying for you.'

One of the silver linings to almost twenty years of caring for our disabled daughters was to experience this encouragement regularly. It was particularly true when one or other of them was in hospital. Much of the little time we had at home was spent answering the phone as friends or church folk asked for prayer updates. Often during the long days and nights, when I hardly had the strength to pray for myself, I knew that others held us and our precious children before the throne. Even today, long after the girls' deaths, I occasionally meet strangers who tell me how they prayed for us during those difficult years. We are blessed indeed.

Yet, in spite of all this, nothing touches my heart more than to know that when Jesus was on His way to the cross, He prayed for us. In fact, the Saviour also mentioned those of us believers living today in this prayer recorded in John 17: 'I am not only praying for these disciples but also for all who will believe in me through their message' (verse 20, NLT). His prayer has reached through the centuries to touch our lives today. So what did Jesus pray to His Father for us?

- 'Now protect them by the power of your name so that they will be united just as we are' (verse 11, NLT).
- 'To keep them safe from the evil one' (verse 15, NLT).
- 'Make them holy by your truth; teach them your word, which is truth' (verse 17, NLT).
- 'May they experience such perfect unity that the world will know that you sent me and that you love them as much as you love me' (verse 23, NLT).
- 'I want these whom you have given me to be where I am' (verse 24, NLT).

Lord Jesus, when I hear You pray, I feel Your heart for me. Thank You. Amen.

117

18 April

After that, he poured water into a basin and began
to wash his disciples' feet, drying them with the towel
that was wrapped round him.

John 13:5, NIV

Reading: John 13:1–17

The basin, jug and towel stood by the door: a common sight in every Eastern home. If you wanted to keep your house clean from what was carried in off the dusty roads, you made sure your feet were washed on entry, and certainly before you sat down to eat. Hospitality was an important part of Jewish culture, where welcoming guests into your home was recognized by washing their feet for them. The task would usually be carried out by a servant.

This particular room had been set up earlier for the Passover feast. Everything was ready for the expected guests – including the basin, jug and towel. The house-servant had already left when Jesus and His disciples arrived, and it seems that the men continued with all they'd been discussing on their way to the upper room. All that was left for them to do was eat. Or was it?

The basin, jug and towel stood silently by the door. But only Jesus heard their silent call.

Some of the twelve didn't even notice the Master rise from the table as they discussed the Pharisees' displeasure over Jesus' teaching from the prophet Isaiah. It was the water sloshing into the basin from the jug that first caught their attention, and the sight of Jesus' tunic on the floor that halted their conversation. *What is He doing?* Only Peter dared speak as the Servant King took off their sandals, one by one, and washed their dirty feet. And Peter's protestations held no sway with Jesus.

The basin, jug and towel had never been used by someone so great until that day, neither had those whose feet were washed ever received a finer example of servant leadership. Jesus on His knees . . . for them . . . for us.

Servant King, may I daily give my life to You as an offering of worship. No job too small. No place, or people, beneath me. Amen.

19 April

But He was wounded for our transgressions, He was bruised for our iniquities.
Isaiah 53:5

Reading: Mark 15:21–39

People were everywhere! The old shepherd much preferred the bleating of sheep to the Passover crowds! Yet what choice had they? Men kept sinning, so sacrifice had to be made continually . . . year after weary year.

There was a time, many years ago, when Hoshea really thought things would change. It was the night he heard the choir sing. But the crowd jostling him interrupted his thoughts. 'Where are they all going?' He could hear taunting cries: 'If you're the Messiah, save yourself!' Ahead, he saw the silhouette of crosses against the sunlit sky. Crucifixions! Hoshea tried to turn around on the stony road, but something stopped him in his tracks. A voice, calling out a name . . . one he used to whisper in the dark nights by the sheepfold. The One of whom the angel spoke . . . on the night Hoshea heard the choir.

'Jesus!' 'If You are the Son of God, save Yourself!'

The words pierced the old man's heart. It couldn't be Him – could it? He had waited so long since that night. Now he had to get to Jesus – it was all that mattered. He remembered the first time he had rushed to meet Him . . . on the night he had heard the choir.

'Jesus!' Hoshea called, the sight before him so shocking it took his breath away. The Man nailed to the centre cross was unrecognizable – His face beaten, a cruel crown of thorns pushed into His brow, a taunting sign pinned above His head: THIS IS THE KING OF THE JEWS! Falling on his knees in the dirt, the old shepherd was broken. Despite the passage of thirty-three years, and the unforgivable cruelty of man, Hoshea recognized the Man. He had been introduced to Him by an angel . . . on the night he had heard the choir.

'How could it be', Hoshea wailed, 'that the Christ could die on a Roman cross?'

With all my heart, Lord, thank You for the cross. Amen.

119

20 April

According to the law almost all things are purified
with blood, and without shedding of blood
there is no remission.
Hebrews 9:22

Reading: Isaiah 53:5–12

Punching the air with his fists, the simple shepherd who had been given the privilege of visiting the 'Saviour' at His birth shouted, 'You said it was "good news", that it would bring "great joy"! You said He was the Saviour – Christ the Lord! How can this be?'

Hoshea's distress was interrupted by one final cry from the Man on the centre cross: 'It is finished!' The old man gasped.

Jesus was dead! That much Hoshea did understand. Exhausted, he sat, for how long he didn't know, until the noise of an approaching soldier stirred him from his grief. Rising to go, Hoshea stared as the soldier pierced the side of Jesus with his spear ... the blood of the Crucified One now running down the rough wood to form a thick, mucky, red puddle on the dirty hill of Golgotha.

How often had he watched the priest kill the lambs he had brought from Bethlehem? How often had the old man given thanks for the sacrifice of those innocent beasts in order that his sins could be forgiven? How often had he watched their blood run down the altar, knowing it was for him? And suddenly he saw it! Suddenly he understood the words of the prophet Isaiah that he had learnt as a boy:

> He was wounded for our transgressions ...
> All we like sheep have gone astray ...
> And the LORD has laid on Him the iniquity of us all.
> Isaiah 53:5–6

And as Hoshea finally turned to go, he knew that somehow he hadn't seen the last of Jesus. This couldn't be the end! For in his head he heard the choir sing. 'Glory to God in the highest!' 'There is born to you ... a Savior, who is Christ the Lord' (Luke 2:14, 11).

Nothing happens by chance, Lord. You were born to die, and in Your death I have life. Your blood has cleansed me from sin. Thank You, Lord! Amen.

21 April

A PASSAGE TO PONDER

Now after the Sabbath, as the first day of the week began to dawn,

Mary Magdalene and the other Mary came to see the tomb.

And behold, there was a great earthquake;

for an angel of the Lord descended from heaven,

and came and rolled back the stone from the door, and sat on it.

His countenance was like lightning, and his clothing as white as snow.

And the guards shook for fear of him,

and became like dead men.

But the angel answered and said to the women,

'Do not be afraid, for I know you seek Jesus who was crucified.

He is not here; for He is risen, as He said.

Come, see the place where the Lord lay.

And go quickly and tell His disciples that He is risen from the dead,

and indeed He is going before you into Galilee;

there you will see Him.

Behold, I have told you.'

So they went out quickly from the tomb with fear and great joy,

and ran to bring His disciples word.

And as they went to tell His disciples, behold, Jesus met them,

Saying, 'Rejoice!'

So they came and held Him by the feet and worshiped Him.

Matthew 28:1–9

Read the passage slowly and let the Author speak to you. As you ponder, ask yourself these questions:

- What does it say?
- What does it means?
- What is God saying to me?
- How will I respond?

22 April

'Because I live, you will live also.'
John 14:19

Reading: 1 Corinthians 15:12–20

Most nurses and doctors will remember the first death of a patient they cared for. I certainly do. It was my first week working as a student nurse, and the patient was an elderly man. I don't know which was worse – watching him die, or tying an identity tag to his big toe after preparing him for the morgue!

Once qualified, I worked in cardiology, where part of my job was responding to emergency cardiac calls outside of the hospital with the Cardiac Ambulance team, or when patients suffered a cardiac arrest in other wards and departments. Resuscitation was a frequent task in my working life. Death was an unfortunate fact of life that we tried to hold back medically, but sometimes it beat us. That was never easy, especially as the deaths occurred suddenly, causing a huge shock to the families.

Nowadays, in pastoral life, my husband and I are still near the top of the list of first responders when death visits a family. It's a privilege to come alongside them during a time of deep pain, but it can ever be taken lightly. Death is never simple, never pretty. Every one of us will one day meet it head on.

Now there's a sobering thought to start your day! Well, it would be if Christ were not raised. Death is not the end, neither is it the final frontier, nor the great unknown, or the many other descriptions used by writers and filmmakers. Rather, death is transition time. Yes, our earthly bodies do cease to function, but only because 'these perishable bodies of ours are not able to live forever' (1 Corinthians 15:50, NLT). Instead they 'must be transformed into heavenly bodies that will never die'. Then we can declare, 'Death is swallowed up in victory. O death, where is your victory? O death, where is your sting?' (1 Corinthians 15:53–55, NLT).

This changes everything!

Thank You, Lord, that death has been defeated, and one day I too will be resurrected! What an amazing thought. Amen.

23 April

'Only fear the LORD, and serve Him in truth
with all your heart; for consider what great things
He has done for you.'
1 Samuel 12:24

Reading: Luke 23:55 – 24:10

Mary Magdalene has received bad press down the centuries, none of which you'll find biblical evidence for. It is unlikely she was a prostitute, and she was certainly not the wife of Jesus, no matter what the filmmakers say. Rather, God did great things for her through His Son.

Magdala was a small town within walking distance from Capernaum, where Jesus based His Galilean ministry. Mary's had been a difficult life, tortured by demonic possession, but totally transformed when she experienced Jesus' healing power (Luke 8:2). And her response to the One who had healed her and set her free was to devote her life, and means, to serving Him.

- Mary, along with Joanna and Susanna, travelled with Jesus and His disciples. They heard Jesus' teaching for themselves – an unusual opportunity for women. They undoubtedly helped with the men's practical needs, and helped fund the ministry of Jesus from their own resources (Luke 8:1–3).
- These women stayed by the cross. They watched the agony of Jesus' crucifixion to the very end, refusing to leave Him even when He died, choosing to stay until Joseph of Arimathea took down His body from the cross (Luke 23:50–53).
- Then they followed Joseph to the tomb. Their service for Jesus wasn't over (Luke 23:55).
- After the Sabbath, Mary and the others returned to anoint Jesus' body with the spices and oils they had hand-prepared (Luke 24:1).

Such devotion. Such loving service. And what was Mary Magdalene's reward? She got to see the risen Lord before anyone else!

Lord, I can never outgive You! May I be willing to follow this amazing example of devoted service and selfless giving, for You are worthy. Amen.

123

24 April

'Unless I see in His hands the print of the nails, and put
my finger into the print of the nails, and put my hand
into His side, I will not believe.'

John 20:25

Reading: John 20:24–29

Everyone likes to be a critic, especially where Thomas is concerned. In his defence, there's far more to Thomas' life than this well-known faux pas.

Thomas wasn't one of the big three so we don't read much about him in the Gospels, yet he faithfully followed Jesus. Then when Jesus wanted to head back to Judea after Lazarus had died, the disciples tried to dissuade Him (John 11). All except Thomas, who encouraged the others to accompany Jesus on this dangerous journey, even declaring a willingness to die with Him (verse 16)! His devotion to the Saviour was never in doubt.

Jesus' declaration in John 14:6 that He was 'the way, the truth, and the life' was in fact in direct response to Thomas' question. Jesus was explaining that He was going to prepare an eternal place for them to join Him after death. Only Thomas was brave enough to ask the question, 'How can we know the way?' His willingness to understand Jesus' words was not in doubt either. He wanted to know God and the way to His perfect heaven.

Okay, it doesn't take away from the fact that Thomas messed up big time when he flatly refused to believe that Jesus was alive. Unfortunately, the text does not show the heart behind the doubt. Was it grief? Anxiety? Disappointment? We don't know, except for one thing: when Jesus returned and said to Thomas, 'Do not be unbelieving, but believing' (John 21:27), Thomas didn't hesitate to respond in devotion and worship: 'My Lord and My God!' (verse 28).

In a world that ridicules those who believe in the resurrection, how do we respond? Do people hear us declare the living Christ as 'my Lord and my God'?

Lord Jesus, thank You that You are willing to forgive even my doubts. I declare You the Living Son of God, alive in me through Your Spirit. Amen.

25 April

Jesus said to her, 'Mary!'
She turned and said to Him, 'Rabboni!'
(which is to say, Teacher).
John 20:16

Reading: John 20:11–18

The English language sometimes does a disservice to the words translated from Hebrew that we find in the Bible. Hebrew words have layers of meanings. You peel back one meaning only to find another. That's certainly what we find here in Mary Magdalene's beautiful response to meeting Jesus on that resurrection morning.

People often addressed Jesus as 'Rabbi'. It simply meant 'Teacher' or 'Master', but, according to the Talmud, was only used correctly of those who had disciples. Disciples were a group of men who devotedly followed the teachings of one particular rabbi to such an extent that they were prepared to make new disciples themselves according to the same teaching. For example, the apostle Paul had declared himself to have been a disciple of Gamaliel (Acts 22:3) before his conversion. It was always Jesus' plan for His disciples to go and make new disciples one day (Matthew 28:19).

But the word used by Mary that morning, 'Rabboni', was on a completely different level. The word 'Rabbon' means 'Great Master' or 'Great Teacher'. There was no other teacher like Jesus, as far as Mary was concerned. No-one greater. And by adding the letter 'i' to the name she personalized it further, calling the risen Lord, 'MY Great Master!' Even as a woman, Mary made it clear that she was a disciple of the Great Master and Teacher, the risen Jesus.

On only one other occasion do we read of anyone calling Jesus 'Rabboni'. When blind Bartimaeus replied to Jesus that he wanted to have his sight restored, he called Jesus 'Rabboni'. My Great Master! (Mark 10:51). Could it be that this was why Jesus commended his faith as the reason for Bartimaeus' healing? The blind man saw something more than by physical sight.

How do we approach this Jesus? What name demonstrates how my heart worships the One who gave His all for me?

Saviour! Master! Friend! I worship You today with my whole heart. Amen.

125

26 April

'We had hoped he was the Messiah who had come to rescue Israel.'
Luke 24:21, NLT

Reading: Luke 24:13–31

There was no spring to the step of Cleopas and his companion as the seven-mile journey stretched before them. This was one Passover they'd never forget, but it was memorable for all the wrong reasons. The mutual farewell greetings between pilgrims – 'See you next year in Jerusalem' – were low key on the busy road. They were too deeply engrossed in all that had happened, too disappointed with unfulfilled expectations even to notice the man who had joined them on the journey. But the incredulity of his question soon grabbed their attention: 'What are you discussing so intently?' he asked them.

The conversation that ensued was typical of many that their unknown companion had engaged in during the previous three years. In fact, 'He expounded to them in all the Scriptures the things concerning Himself' (Luke 24:27). Yet for some reason they didn't recognize the risen Jesus as the One who was explaining to them the necessity for the cross – the very cause of their sadness and confusion. They only knew that, as He spoke, their hearts were changing from despair to expectation (verse 32). Could what the women had told them earlier that day, when they had returned from the empty tomb, actually be true?

'Suddenly their eyes were opened, and they recognized Him!' (Luke 24:31, NLT). The man they had hoped was the Messiah actually was, after all! Jesus hadn't let them down; they had simply allowed circumstances to cloud the truth already before them. Thankfully, Jesus was prepared to remind them, willing to take time with His discouraged disciples.

When we can't see the Saviour walking beside us on the road of discouragement, it doesn't mean He's absent. All we need is a little reminder of His presence, and if we open the Book we'll discover He's been there all the time.

Lord, sometimes I can't see You through the fog of circumstances, but You have promised always to be with me. Help me rest in that truth. Amen.

27 April

Then Jesus said to them, 'Do not be afraid.
Go and tell My brethren to go to Galilee,
and there they will see Me.'
Matthew 28:10

Reading: Matthew 28:5–10

After His resurrection, why did Jesus instruct His disciples to go to Galilee? He knew He would make an appearance in Jerusalem, the spiritual home of the nation. Why take them to the backwaters again?

For us, Easter Sunday is exciting and joyful, but back then the idea that Jesus had risen from the dead filled the disciples with all kinds of emotions – not least fear. They had no idea what to expect or what to believe, even though Jesus had told them this would happen (Luke 9:22). Neither the Romans nor the Jewish leaders would be happy. The disciples' lives would now be on the line. Is it any wonder they were afraid?

That's what I love about Jesus' words. The Saviour knew only too well how the disciples would react when they heard about the empty tomb. So, in His love, and with great tenderness, He sent them a message: 'I'll meet you in Galilee. Go home. You'll see Me there' (my paraphrase).

Galilee was home for these weary, confused and fearful men and women. It was the place they'd first met with Jesus, the place they'd experienced the miraculous, the place they'd first responded to His call on their lives. When they didn't know what to do or how to think, Jesus sent them home, with the promise that He would meet them there.

Home. The place we feel safest, where danger is usually kept outside the door. Home. Where we can kick off our shoes and be ourselves; where the stress of life is replaced by the comfort of the familiar. Home. Where we are known and loved. Home. Jesus promises to meet us there. In the routine of ordinary everyday life is the very place we should wait for Him. He'll turn up for sure.

Too often, Lord, I seek You at the 'big' spiritual events, when You are waiting to meet me at home every day. Amen.

28 April

A PASSAGE TO PONDER

In the same way, 'Abraham believed God,

so God declared him righteous because of his faith.'

The real children of Abraham, then, are those who put their faith in God.

What's more, the Scriptures looked forward to this time

when God would accept the Gentiles, too, on the basis of their faith.

God promised this good news to Abraham long ago when he said,

'All nations will be blessed through you.'

And so it is:

All who put their faith in Christ

share the same blessing Abraham received because of his faith.

Galatians 3:6–9, NLT

Read the passage slowly and let the Author speak to you. As you ponder, ask yourself these questions:

- What does it say?
- What does it mean?
- What is God saying to me?
- How will I respond?

29 April

I can do all things through Christ who strengthens me.
Philippians 4:13

Reading: Hebrews 4:14–16

White-van-man stopped abruptly in front of me on a busy approach road. I was perturbed by his unexpected action, especially as the car behind hooted furiously at the sudden stop. I had no idea what had happened to cause our delay, until I caught sight of something appearing by the front left wheel of the white van.

There she was, a mummy duck feverishly leading her little brood across the busy road: eight fluffy little ducklings racing behind her in a ruler-straight line. What a beautiful sight! I'm so glad Mr White-van-man had stopped in time.

As we drove on I couldn't help but think she was either a very brave mummy or a very foolish one, to attempt to cross that main road with such precious cargo. But then, there are times when we just have to do what we know is right! This is especially true when it's God who is asking.

The letter to the Philippians hadn't been written when that bunch of scared disciples realized precisely what it was that the risen Lord was asking them to do. They needed to be brave in the days ahead, while they waited for the coming of the Holy Spirit after returning to Jerusalem. The search was still on for Jesus' body, but Jesus had promised them power, Holy Spirit power, if they would step up to the mark and wait for His coming.

Billy Graham said, 'Courage is contagious. When a brave man takes a stand, the spines of others are often stiffened.'

After the encounter with Jesus on the beach, Peter once again became that brave man. As others followed his example, their spines were stiffened as they waited, and they soon discovered that the promise of Jesus was enough to strengthen them for those days in God's waiting room.

God, I'm not a very brave person, but the strength I need to obey is found in Christ. You only ask for that first brave step. Help me to take it. Amen.

129

30 April

What is Faith? It is the confident assurance that what we hope for is going to happen. It is the evidence of things we cannot yet see.

Hebrews 11:1, NLT

Reading: Hebrews 10:35–39

Too often the word 'faith' is prefaced by the word 'blind'. But taking a leap in the dark is not bravery; it's stupidity. There's nothing 'blind' about faith. There's no wishful thinking, no maybe, no perhaps. Rather, faith is a measured, rational response to something or someone based on what we already know about that thing or person.

When I take my little grandson to the park, he loves to walk along the wall leading up to the gate. Soon he'll happily jump off the end of it because it really isn't high. But for now, he waits until I hold out my arms and then he leaps confidently into my grasp. What is it that makes him jump? Bravery? Perhaps that was true the first time he did it. But now it's faith . . . he knows I'm going to catch him. And every time I do, his confidence grows. He has 'confident assurance' that I'll catch him. And I delight in knowing that he trusts me.

Faith plays a huge part in our relationship with God, and is something He delights in (Hebrews 11:6). But faith has nothing to do with walking blindfolded over the edge of a cliff, hoping God will catch us. Instead it has everything to do with what we already know about the One who has proved Himself again and again in our lives: the One who loves, protects, guards and guides us. Undoubtedly, there are times when He asks of us what seems impossible, but as that is His speciality, we can trust Him even with that.

Remember: 'For He Himself has said, "I will never leave you nor forsake you." So we may boldly say: "The Lord is my helper; I will not fear. What can man do to me?"' (Hebrews 13:5–6).

Heavenly Father, may I jump willingly when You tell me to, confidently assured that You will always catch me. Amen.

May

1 May

'God is Spirit, and those who worship Him
must worship in spirit and truth.'

John 4:24

Reading: John 4:19–26

It never ceases to amaze me the lengths to which Jesus went to meet particular individuals. The woman in this story was a most unlikely case in point, and to say that Jesus 'needed to go through Samaria' (John 4:4) was more about His heart for lost souls than good travel planning.

In the middle of this Samaritan woman's encounter with Jesus, a strange conversation develops – a conversation about worship. Remarkably, this immoral woman, ostracized even by her own community, tries to engage Jesus in spiritual debate! Declaring the visitor to be a prophet (verse 19), she tries to move the subject away from herself to the old divisive Jewish/Samaritan controversy – where should they worship? Mount Gerazim or Jerusalem? She makes the same mistake we make today: showing more interest in the 'Where', 'How' and 'When' of worship than to 'Whom' our worship should be directed.

Jesus sets her straight, explaining that worship is not about mountains or temples, but rather that the Father is seeking true worshippers (verse 23): those who 'worship in spirit and truth' (verse 24).

It's easy to make the mistake of confusing turning up for church as worship, although that's an important part of it. Or that worship is only about what we sing, say or pray, although that is important too. Rather, worship is an attitude of heart that doesn't end with the music, or dissipate when the alarm goes off on Monday morning. It is a daily response to who God is, which develops into a lifestyle. It is who we are. It marks us out from everyone else around us.

Heavenly Father, You continue to seek true worshippers today. With the help of Your Spirit, may I develop an attitude of heart that becomes a lifestyle of worship. You are worthy of no less. Amen.

2 May

Oh come, let us worship and bow down;
Let us kneel before the LORD our Maker.

Psalm 95:6

Reading: Psalm 95

While the dictionary defines the word 'worship' as 'to show profound religious devotion', it doesn't explain that every person on the planet is actually a worshipper. First encounters with tribal people groups, whether by anthropologists or missionaries, reveal that they are worshipping people groups. Their focus of worship may be evil spirits or ancestors, but they are worshippers – showing profound devotion.

Walk the cities or villages of the Far East and you'll see a statue of the Buddha along every road. There, people will feed the Buddha ahead of their own children. They are worshippers – showing profound devotion. Visit any mosque and you will see row upon row of kneeling, chanting men, called to prayer five times every day. They are worshippers – showing profound devotion. Venerating the thousands of Hindu gods consumes the life of millions, but they do it with profound devotion – they are worshippers.

Atheists may think they don't worship, but their profound devotion to what they think disproves the need to worship God makes them worshippers. In the West, thousands cram into sporting events, chanting their profound devotion to their sporting heroes, while temples to fashion are jam-packed, taking from us what we do not have in order that we might look good. We are all worshippers!

Why this compulsion to worship? Simple: we are hardwired that way. We were created with a spiritual dimension (Genesis 1:27). Augustine said, 'Thou has made us for Thyself and our hearts are restless 'til they find their rest in Thee.'[5] Psalm 95:3 declares, 'For the LORD is the great God, and the great King above *all gods*' (emphasis mine). While the sad fact is that millions across our world can't escape the pull to worship, we who know Christ are privileged to approach the One True God, and we have the opportunity to express our profound devotion to Him. But do we?

Lord of all creation, I worship You today above all others. Amen.

134

3 May

'Do not worship any other gods besides me.
Do not make idols of any kind.'

Exodus 20:3–4, NLT

Reading: Matthew 4:8–11

It was A. W. Tozer who said, 'An idol of the mind is as offensive to God as an idol of the hand.'6

We know about the many idols of gold and silver that kept the Children of Israel out of the Promised Land for forty long years. It seems as if every time Moses had his back turned they were collecting jewellery for yet another great 'meltdown'! It's difficult to understand how they couldn't recognize an idol as something no more powerful than the one who made it, especially when their need for gods they could see and touch was a constant stumbling block to the true worship that Jehovah demanded.

Yet, are things really all that different today? Are we prepared to identify the idols in our own lives? Is there an 'idol of the mind' that is interfering with worshipping God 'in Spirit and truth', which Jesus said was required of us in John 4:24?

- Whom, or what, is foremost in my thoughts? Have I created an idol?
- Whom, or what, do I love more than anything else? Have I created an idol?
- Whom, or what, will I give my time to, spend my money on? Have I created an idol?
- Who, or what, will ultimately have my profound devotion? Have I created an idol?

Shocking, isn't it? It is all too easy to create idols of mind, heart and activity without being aware that we are doing it. Yet they will block our relationship with the One who should be first in our hearts. And that is idolatry!

'Search me, O God, and know my heart; test me and know my thoughts. Point out anything in me that offends You, and lead me along the path of everlasting life' (Psalm 139:23–24, NLT). Amen.

4 May

'Holy, holy, holy is the LORD of hosts;
The whole earth is full of His glory.'

Isaiah 6:3

Reading: Isaiah 6:1–8

If asked to describe whom the focus of our worship actually is, I wonder how we'd reply? The picture we form in our minds is often reminiscent of a child's collage. We stick together little pieces of what we know, and like, about God, to produce an image that we can understand. Often that image is inadequate, incomplete and lacking in the one thing the seraphim wanted Isaiah to be absolutely clear about. Above everything else, God is holy. He is other than anything we can imagine, which is why 'the whole earth is full of His glory' (verse 3).

So aware are these angelic beings of this truth that they cover their faces in reverence and their feet in humility when they are in God's presence (verse 2). In this moment of glimpsing God's glory, Isaiah is overwhelmed with a sense of personal sin and unworthiness. 'My destruction is sealed,' he laments. 'For I am a sinful man and a member of a sinful race. Yet I have seen the King, the Lord Almighty' (verse 5, NLT).

Even in today's Christian culture we are in danger of becoming overfamiliar with the God of heaven. Yes, we are the privileged children of God. Yes, because of Jesus we have automatic access to the throne room of heaven. Yes, our sins are forgiven, and we are clothed in Christ's righteousness. But God is not our buddy. He is still the One who is holy: 'unique, set apart, unlike all others' as is the sense of the Hebrew word.

Have we lost the wonder? Do we even recognize who He is? If we dare to ask for a glimpse of His glory, could we stand in His presence? Because the One we worship *is* the One who is Holy, Holy, Holy!

I bow before You, Lord, God of heaven and earth. I dare to ask for a glimpse of Your glory, that my worship may always be fitting in Your Holy presence. Amen.

5 May

A PASSAGE TO PONDER

For the Lord is great and greatly to be praised;

He is also to be feared above all gods.

For all the gods of the peoples are idols,

But the Lord made the heavens.

Honor and majesty are before Him;

Strength and gladness are in His place.

Give to the Lord, O families of the peoples,

Give to the Lord glory and strength.

Give to the Lord the glory due His name;

Bring an offering, and come before Him.

Oh, worship the Lord in the beauty of holiness!

1 Chronicles 16:25–29

Read the passage slowly and let the Author speak to you. As you ponder, ask yourself these questions:

- What does it say?
- What does it mean?
- What is God saying to me?
- How should I respond?

6 May

'Who is like You, O LORD, among the gods?
Who is like You, glorious in holiness,
Fearful in praises, doing wonders?'
Exodus 15:11

Reading: Exodus 3:1–6

At first Moses didn't realize what was going on. This runaway Prince of Egypt hadn't expected to meet with God face to face in the wilderness. Surely temples and places of worship are more appropriate for such encounters? He was soon to discover that God often chooses to meet with us where there's nothing to distract.

The sad thing is, it took a while for Moses to see God in what was happening right in front of him – burning bush and all. Only when God told Moses, 'Take your sandals off your feet, for the place where you stand is holy ground' (Exodus 3:5), did he respond by hiding his face in worship.

In spite of that shaky start, Moses began his long journey with God: a journey of discovering the holiness of God and what it means to walk with Him. By the time Moses stood on the banks of the Red Sea looking back at Egypt, we hear him unflinchingly declare who God is: 'Who is like You, glorious in holiness, fearful in praises, doing wonders?' (Exodus 15:11). He'd got it in one! First and foremost God is holy, and worthy of our praise. Moses speaks of God 'doing wonders', for He is the One who flung the stars into space (Genesis 1:16), who measured the waters in the hollow of His hand (Isaiah 40:12), who stretches out the heavens like a curtain (Isaiah 40:22). Little wonder then that He was able to deliver His people from the Egyptians in Moses' day (Exodus 15:13), and us from our sin today (Colossians 1:13–14).

Praise finally came easily from the stammering lips of the man God had found in the wilderness years earlier, for Moses had now seen the glory of God. When that happens, worship is the only response.

Lord, forgive me for being slow to respond to who You really are. May my worship reflect something of the reverence due to Your holy name. Amen.

7 May

For Christ also suffered once for sins, the just for the unjust, that He might bring us to God.
1 Peter 3:18

Reading: Isaiah 53

Journey with me from Moses' vantage point above the Red Sea, past Isaiah's vision of God's glory in the temple, and across the centuries to a rocky outcrop outside Jerusalem. Here, in this most unlikely of places, we get to see for ourselves who God is.

In appearance He is a young man, Jesus by name, but there is nothing beautiful to attract us to Him. Unbelievably, He is hanging on a Roman cross, clearly despised and rejected by His own people, forsaken by those who called themselves His friends. His face is more disfigured than any man's, making Him barely recognizable to the few women bravely standing nearby. The humiliating nakedness of His tortured body is an affront to decent Jews, so they turn away as they pass by. His tunic is now a mere gambling object for the soldiers playing at His feet. The scene is about as far away from Isaiah's vision of God in the temple as you could get. And no-one is worshipping the prisoner on the cross.

And the young man cries, 'My God, My God, why have You forsaken Me?' (Matthew 27:46), His Father's abandonment piercing His heart more painfully than the crown of thorns tearing at His flesh. Feel the earth shake and watch the skies blacken, as their Creator bows His head. And the blood of the Son of God runs down that cross-shaped altar, declaring our deliverance – we are redeemed! The price for our sin has now been paid with all the revulsion we ought to feel for it . . . but instead it is laid on Him – Jesus!

And, finally, one man worships, for, in the darkness, the Roman centurion has seen God face to face: 'Truly this was the Son of God!' (Matthew 27:54).

Lord Jesus, I bow in adoration at Your feet, for You alone make it possible for this sinner to approach a holy God. Thank You. Amen.

8 May

Because it is written, 'Be holy, for I am holy.'
1 Peter 1:16

Reading: 1 Peter 1:13–21

'There is a great market for religious experience in our world,' says Eugene Peterson in his book *A Long Obedience*. 'There is little enthusiasm,' he continues, 'for the patient acquisition of virtue, little inclination to sign up for a long apprenticeship in what earlier generations of Christians called holiness.'[7]

Holiness. It's one of those words that makes us feel uncomfortable. It has the feeling of a bygone age: a Puritanical list of dos and don'ts intended to help us gain favour with God. Is holiness a disguised call back to legalism?

When Paul wrote to the new Christians in Ephesus, telling them, 'Be imitators of God as dear children' (Ephesians 5:1), he wasn't laying a burden on them; he was reminding them that they were made in the image of God (Genesis 1:27). God is holy, therefore they were made to be holy. *Impossible!* we might very well cry, if it were not for the invitation of Jesus in Matthew 11:29: 'Take My yoke upon you and learn from Me.'

The call to holiness was never meant to be a test to pass or fail, but rather a commitment to a life yoked up with the Holy One. As we harness up with Christ, He teaches us how to think, live and worship as the set-apart children of a holy God. It's the presence of Jesus alongside us in this 'long apprenticeship' that Peterson speaks about, which makes us holy.

St John of the Cross, a sixteenth-century friar, put it like this: 'I no longer want just to hear about you, beloved Lord, through messengers, I no longer want to hear doctrines about you, nor to have my emotions stirred by people speaking of you. I yearn for your presence.'

Yearnings like this are only fulfilled when we yoke up for the long haul with the Holy One.

Thank You, Jesus, that holy living is possible when I make a deliberate choice to yoke up with You. Teach me Your ways, Lord. Amen.

140

9 May

Therefore, if anyone is in Christ, he is a new creation;
old things have passed away; behold,
all things have become new.

2 Corinthians 5:17

Reading: Acts 16:11–15

We are fortunate to live in a country with four distinct seasons, demonstrating how God's creation is constantly changing. In fact, God is a God who changes things. It's His speciality. The apostle Paul speaks in today's verse of how God makes all things new. When God touches our lives, He doesn't leave us the same: we are changed because of Christ.

In Acts 16 we are introduced to a number of people, including a wealthy businesswoman called Lydia, who lived in Philippi. There was no synagogue in the city, so devoted Jews prayed at a riverside location. Lydia was religious to some degree; in fact, the passage tells us she 'worshiped God' (Acts 16:14). But Paul discovered that this lady, and the others gathered, had only a limited knowledge of God in spite of their desire to worship Him.

How beautiful to read that when Lydia heard Paul speak of Jesus, 'the Lord opened her heart to heed the things spoken by Paul' (Acts 16:14). On that day this precious lady discovered that religion wasn't enough, and God changed her heart. It didn't take her long to make her commitment public by being baptized. And, of course, she was hungry to hear more, so an invitation to Paul and his companions to stay at her home seemed the ideal solution. God not only changed Lydia's heart, He also changed her home.

It's easy to identify with the Christian church by turning up on Sunday with everyone else, but that won't change our hearts, or our homes for that matter. Only God can do that. The question is, are we prepared to heed what we're told about the Saviour, like Lydia did, and then allow Him to change us?

Lord, You know exactly what needs to change in my life, and in my home. Open my heart, I pray. Amen.

141

10 May

Yes, and all who desire to live godly
in Christ Jesus will suffer persecution.

2 Timothy 3:12

Reading: Acts 16:16–24

I wonder whether Lydia realized when she decided to follow Jesus that her community might not see it as acceptable. Probably an understatement. Her life changed dramatically, which wouldn't have been easy for someone who had built a reputation for herself as a distinguished businesswoman in a world dominated by men.

Yet it wasn't too long after Paul and Silas had moved into Lydia's home that trouble visited. It was only a matter of time before the businesswoman would be a regular visitor to the city jail where the two visiting preachers were being held, accused of teaching 'customs which are not lawful for us' (Acts 16:21). While Caesar-worship was the religion of the Romans and their annexed provinces, this particular charge spawned from greedy slave-masters. But it was enough for Lydia to see clearly what her local community thought of Christian teaching. They had rioted because of it!

Did she ever ask herself what the town gossips said about her at the market-place? Did she fear for her business, or her reputation with the authorities? I doubt it, or at least, if they did, she dealt with it, because when the prisoners were released from prison they went straight back to Lydia's house, where the first church in Europe was now meeting (Acts 16:40).

Lydia had counted the cost of following Jesus. God had met with her at the river on that particular Sabbath, and He had changed her – both heart and home. She had no intention of denying Him now, even if persecution were to come knocking on her door again.

Writing to Timothy, Paul tells him, and us, that persecution is not only to be expected, but it is normal if we are followers of Christ. What if persecution were to come knocking on our door? Have we a heart like Lydia's?

Lord, persecution is not what I seek, but when it comes, help me to be brave like Lydia. Amen.

11 May

'For you will be His witness to all men
of what you have seen and heard.'
Acts 22:15

Reading: Acts 16:25–34

What would you do if you had been unfairly imprisoned and then a miraculous earthquake shook open the doors of your cell in the middle of the night? I would hightail it out of there! Surely this was God's provision for Paul and Silas? But Paul didn't run. In fact, according to our reading, none of the prisoners took the opportunity to escape. They stayed put.

Escaped prisoners invariably cost a Roman jailer his life. A full jailhouse must have seemed miraculous to the jailer that night, especially as the earthquake should have led to a breakout. Then to receive kindness from a man he'd cruelly treated and fastened in chains was almost too much for him.

Why did Paul not run when he had the chance? Why stay in a place of danger when it seemed that God was providing a way out of persecution? His actions provide the answer, along with the clear memory of his call by God following his conversion in Damascus. Paul, the one-time persecutor himself, was now God's witness, and he took his call very seriously indeed. His own safety didn't come into it. There was a man in that prison who needed to hear what Paul had 'seen and heard': a man who would have died if Paul had thought only about himself. That man was the jailer!

The same jailer collapsed to his knees in disbelief, and relief, when he discovered that the prisoners were still there. Undoubtedly, he'd already heard the talkative preacher's message when he'd locked him in chains earlier. There in the darkness he knew exactly what to ask: 'Sirs, what must I do to be saved?'

Philippi had yet another convert, all thanks to the grace of God and a man obedient to God's call.

Lord, You choose to use people like me to tell others of Your great love. May I be Your faithful witness, whatever else is going on around me. Amen.

143

12 May

A PASSAGE TO PONDER

And Hannah prayed and said:

'My heart rejoices in the LORD;

My horn is exalted in the LORD.

I smile at my enemies,

Because I rejoice in Your salvation.

No one is holy like the LORD,

For there is none besides You,

Nor is there any rock like our God.

Talk no more so very proudly;

Let no arrogance come from your mouth,

For the LORD is the God of knowledge;

And by Him actions are weighed.

The bows of the mighty men are broken,

And those who stumbled are girded with strength.'

1 Samuel 2:1–4

Read the passage slowly and let the Author speak to you. As you ponder, ask yourself these questions:

- What does it say?
- What does it mean?
- What is God saying to me?
- How should I respond?

13 May

'For the Lord does not see as man sees;
for man looks at the outward appearance,
but the LORD looks at the heart.'
1 Samuel 16:7

Reading: 1 Samuel 16:6–13

We used to have such fun hearing about the celebrities our son, and his now wife, met when they were studying music in London. One such phone call went something like this: 'Hey, Mum, I've had such a surreal day. I was sitting at Sting's grand piano giving Pierce Brosnan's son a piano lesson.' Beat that for name-dropping!

Truth is, we live in a society besotted with celebrity. Fans will stand outside a building for hours if they believe a certain someone to be inside, while parents often choose to name their children after the rich and famous. Part of the package of growing up invariably includes a desire to 'make a name' for yourself. I well remember early rejections by publishers that included the comment that 'nobody knows your name'. And 'names' sell books.

Have you ever struggled with invisibility syndrome? I'm nobody special – nobody knows my name. I've never done anything exciting – nobody knows my name. I'll never achieve anything great – nobody knows my name.

The Bible is full of people whose lives have a deep impact on our own. Some we know well, while for many others we don't even know their names. But God does, and He has revealed their stories in His Word to teach us many things, for example:

- Social standing doesn't impress Him.
- Intellect doesn't make us better than others.
- Wealth won't influence the One who owns it all.
- Beauty doesn't make the man, or woman.
- Fame curries no favour with God.

No matter how many people are totally unaware of my existence, God knows that I am right here, and He knows my name. And He never forgets it. We are never invisible to the One who really matters.

Thank You, God, that I am not invisible to You. You see me, You know me and You love me. Amen.

145

14 May

Elkanah . . . had two wives: the name of one was Hannah,
and the name of the other Peninnah. Peninnah had
children, but Hannah had no children.

1 Samuel 1:1–2

Reading: 1 Samuel 1:1–3

'I know you,' said the lady as she cornered me in the supermarket aisle. 'You're the woman who lost two children, aren't you?' she continued, loudly. 'I've read your book.'

My heart sank. I wanted to tell her that I am more than the sum of past circumstances, but she kept on talking about 'how sad it was', and that 'the book made me cry'. A cynical inner voice scolded, 'Well, you *did* write the book, didn't you?' though the lady seemed to have missed the whole point of *Under the Rainbow*.

Often our circumstances are allowed to define who we are, although they are only part of the full story. Hannah and Peninnah knew all about that. Eight words marked out their identities: 'Peninnah had children, but Hannah had no children.' But there was so much more to tell. Peninnah may have had children, but she was far from happy. Being a baby-making machine for the man who loved another woman was no fun at all. Consequently, Peninnah is remembered for the cruel way she treated Hannah because of her childlessness.

Hannah may have known how much Elkanah loved her (verse 5), but the burden of scorn both inside her home and in the community was becoming too much to bear. She seemed powerless to have the only thing on earth her heart longed for – a child. But, with the benefit of hindsight, this is not what marks Hannah out for us; rather, it's what she did in those difficult circumstances.

Hannah and Peninnah clearly teach us that our true identity is not in our circumstances, but in how we respond to them. The circumstances of life can make us bitter or better, and, remarkably, the choice is entirely ours.

Lord, life is often complicated, disappointing and even painful. Help me to realize that circumstances need not define me if I react in a way that honours You. Amen.

15 May

And she was in bitterness of soul,
and prayed to the LORD and wept in anguish.
1 Samuel 1:10

Reading: 1 Samuel 1:4–7

Pain is a universal problem of life. Yet it is often the very place where God meets with us, and where we experience His presence in ways rarely felt when all is well with the world.

Little did Hannah know how the future of the nation would be affected by how she reacted to her circumstances when she wept at the door of the Tabernacle. Her pain drove her to God in anguished prayer. This decision resulted in her becoming the kingmaker's mother, and providing the nation with a godly prophet in place of Eli and his godless sons. We cannot see God's plans when our circumstances intertwine with His purposes, as we place them back into His hands. But know this – He wastes nothing.

Unfortunately, Peninnah's secret distress sent her the other way, and we find her choosing bitterness. This choice impacted not only Hannah, but undoubtedly also Peninnah's large family, for children learn by example, and we read of no redeeming features in Elkanah's second wife.

The root of bitterness spoken of in Hebrews 12:15 grows easily in the fertile soil of a hurting heart. Our anger can feel so justified when we have been devastated by disease, hurt by others or even disappointed by God. But bitterness soon grows. This particular weed will choke our Christian growth, destroy our testimony, sap us of needed strength and blot out the sun of God's comfort and peace – at the time we need it most. Life can indeed be unfair, illness cruel, and sometimes people unkind. That's why we need to weed the flower bed of our souls often, taking note of that bitter thought or angry word and plucking it out quickly before it really takes root. The consequences will be devastating if we don't.

Lord, You see my pain. Better still, You see what could be accomplished in my life and in others if I give it back to You. Help me quickly uproot any bitterness in my heart. Amen.

147

16 May

Draw near to God, and He will draw near to you.
James 4:8

Reading: 1 Samuel 1:8–11

The journey from Ramathaim Zophim to Shiloh for the annual sacrifice was sheer torment for Hannah. As other families joined them on the way, Peninnah used the yearly get-together to show off the latest addition to her family, while Hannah walked behind her husband with empty arms. Peninnah's public taunting only magnified Hannah's personal feelings of shame.

The religious feasts were also used as occasions to party, but Hannah was in no mood for festivity. Instead, she left the revelry behind and headed to where she knew she would find God. As a woman, she was only permitted to go a certain distance into the tented Tabernacle, but she knew that beyond was the Most Holy Place. It was here that the Ark of the Covenant was housed – the symbol of God's presence with His people. And in her despair, Hannah longed to be where God was, knowing He alone could help her.

How privileged we are. We don't have to wait for a once-a-year opportunity to approach God. We don't have to travel a long distance to be near Him. Because of Jesus we can, as James 4:8 says, 'Draw near to God', and we are promised that in return, 'He will draw near to you'. Yet when life throws difficulty our way we often run everywhere else looking for help, instead of heading for His presence.

For Hannah, the place to be near God was the Tabernacle. For us, it is the cross: the place where atonement was made for our sin, reminding us of God's love for us. It's at this place we can leave our burdens, recognizing that He can carry what we cannot. And we can visit this very place in prayer.

Perhaps we need to develop a little bit of Hannah's thinking: to develop a longing to be where God is.

Lord, forgive me for the times when I've seen prayer as a place of last resort. Instead, may I learn to seek You first, for You always reciprocate with Your presence. Amen.

17 May

'Go in peace, and the God of Israel grant your petition which you have asked of Him.'

1 Samuel 1:17

Reading: 1 Samuel 1:12–18

Hannah's name suited her well – 'woman of grace'. Grace never gives what we deserve, and the text leaves the impression that Hannah suffered in silence, sparing the family further dissention by not giving in to retaliation. Yet the very one who should have encouraged her added to her pain by jumping to the wrong conclusion. Eli, the old priest, totally misunderstood what was going on when he saw her slumped at the Tabernacle door. The feast was over, but with the noise of partying all around, he reckoned Hannah had fallen in a drunken state, and he rebuked her fiercely for her behaviour. Oh, if only he had taken the trouble to get his facts straight first, he would have seen a woman in deep distress seeking God's help.

A cautionary note to each one of us: conclusions can only be drawn when we are in possession of all the facts.

How sad that Hannah had to explain herself when she was already suffering. Eli offered no apology, but thankfully he got one thing right, and responded as God's priest with exactly what Hannah needed to hear: 'Go in peace, and the God of Israel grant your petition which you have asked of Him' (verse 17).

In spite of being wrongly accused, Hannah left it at that. She hadn't gone to ask Eli for anything – her request was made to God. But she was more than delighted to receive God's reply through His servant and to accept God's blessing. Afterwards, 'the woman went her way and ate, and her face was longer sad' (verse 18). It was done. She was prepared to leave the burden of her heart with God, and be content. And God honoured not only her request, but also her willingness to trust Him with the answer.

Heavenly Father, forgive me for the times I've jumped to the wrong conclusion without first checking the facts. May I pray like Hannah, content to wait for Your answer. Amen.

18 May

'O LORD of hosts, if You will . . . then I will . . .'
1 Samuel 1:11

Reading: 1 Samuel 1:19–23

Hannah isn't out of the woods just yet. Her prayer is still frequently misunderstood. At first glance it looks like a bargaining prayer. *God, if You do this for me, then I'll return the favour and do such-and-such.* Isn't it preposterous to think we have something to exchange with God!

On closer examination, Hannah's prayer is not bargaining, but a prayer of sacrifice. The vow she made with God was unbelievably difficult: 'O Lord Almighty,' she prayed, 'if you will look down upon my sorrow and answer my prayer and give me a son, then I will give him back to you. He will be yours for his entire lifetime' (verse 11, NLT). What? Ask for a son, and then return the child into God's service for his entire life? If this is a bargaining prayer then it sounds to me like Hannah isn't gaining much from it.

God kept His promise and gave Hannah a son (1 Samuel 1:20), allowing her to experience the joy of motherhood. Her arms would no longer feel empty, nor would her heart ache. Perhaps you have prayed as fervently for children as Hannah did, and God has not answered your prayers in the same way. To others, like myself, God gave children for only a few short years. What we need to understand is that Samuel's birth was about more than meeting Hannah's longings. It was important in God's bigger plan for the nation, for Samuel became God's prophet and priest, and eventually kingmaker: a kingly line that would one day produce the Messiah. The day did come when Hannah was called upon to keep her promise, and she did it willingly.

God's answers to our prayers always involve His greater plan. By faith, and with God's peace, we can learn to rest in how He answers.

God of the big picture, help me to accept the answers You give to my heart's longings, however hard that might be. Amen.

150

19 May

A PASSAGE TO PONDER

And the LORD called to Samuel again the third time.

So he arose and went to Eli, and said, 'Here I am, for you did call me.'

Then Eli perceived that the LORD had called the boy.

Therefore Eli said to Samuel, 'Go, lie down;

and it shall be, if He calls you, that you must say,

"Speak, LORD, for Your servant hears."'

So Samuel went and lay down in his place.

Now the LORD came and stood and called as at other times,

'Samuel! Samuel!'

And Samuel answered, 'Speak, for Your servant hears.'

1 Samuel 3:8–10

Read the passage slowly and let the Author speak to you. As you ponder, ask yourself these questions:

- What does it say?
- What does it mean?
- What is God saying to me?
- How will I respond?

20 May

For all the promises of God in Him are Yes,
and in Him Amen, to the glory of God through us.
2 Corinthians 1:20

Reading: 2 Corinthians 1:20–22

Cheerleading has never quite taken off here in the United Kingdom: not the pom-pom-shaking variety usually engaged in by beautiful young women at American sports events. But go to any school sports event and you'll see frantic parents shouting and encouraging their offspring to do great things on the field of play. Arm-waving and jumping up and down are also par for the course. We all need encouragement, after all, and that can come in various ways.

I like to think of God's promises as cheerleaders He has placed along the road of life for us. I have this beautiful picture in my mind of our Heavenly Father cupping His hands around His mouth and shouting in our direction:

- 'I will be with you' (Isaiah 43:2), when the way ahead seems impossible.
- 'I will strengthen you' (see Philippians 4:13), when you feel weak.
- 'I will never leave you' (Hebrews 13:5), even when it seems like everyone else has.
- 'I will hear when you call to Me . . .' (see Isaiah 65:24), and even before your mouth forms the words.
- 'I will come again and receive you to Myself' (John 14:3), for not even death will take you from Me.
- 'I will wipe away every tear' (see Revelation 21:4), for one day there will be no more sorrow or pain.

And my heart swells and beats with enthusiasm as I run this race of life, knowing that I am not alone. There is One cheering for me, whose encouragement knows no bounds. I'm going to make it to the finishing tape . . . and I'm going to win!

Lord, thank You for the promises in Your Word that encourage me to keep on going, especially when the way is tough. Amen.

152

21 May

So encourage each other, and build one another up,
just as you are already doing.

1 Thessalonians 5:11, NLT

Reading: Colossians 1:1–6

Encouragement, like plant food, not only helps us grow, it also makes us blossom.

In his letters, the apostle Paul often had tough stuff to say to the believers, yet he always included a word of encouragement, especially that he was praying for them.

- His first letter to the Corinthians starts by thanking God for them (1 Corinthians 1:4), and his second letter finishes by praying that they would 'do no evil' and 'be made complete' in Christ (2 Corinthians 13:7, 9).
- In his letter to the Galatians, he prays a blessing over them (Galatians 6:16).
- To the Philippians he is exuberant in his prayers, thanking God for them with joy, thanks and confidence, praying that their 'love may abound still more and more' (Philippians 1:3–6, 9).
- He told the Colossians that he was 'praying always' for them (Colossians 1:3).

I could easily go on, because Paul was masterful with encouragement. What a thrill it must have been for those believers in far-off places to hear what Paul was praying for them through the letters he wrote. Some of those recipients may have met Paul in person, but others never had that privilege. Yet they all discovered that in their difficulties and their joys someone else was carrying them to God in prayer. Knowing that brought the encouragement their souls needed.

If you're like me, I'm sure there are many people you pray for, and for the most part they probably have no idea that we do it. Often that's appropriate, but sometimes telling someone that you are praying for them can give them the encouragement they just might need today.

Heavenly Father, thank You for the people who pray for me. May my prayers encourage others, and please show me whom I should tell that I'm praying for them. Amen.

22 May

That He would grant you, according to the riches
of His glory, to be strengthened with might
through His Spirit in the inner man.

Ephesians 3:16

Reading: Ephesians 3:14–21

One of our young people from church produced a prayer letter when she was leaving on a short-term mission trip to Kenya. In it she mentioned all the things you'd expect in such a letter. But how she finished the letter touched me deeply. She used Paul's powerful prayer in Ephesians 3 to tell us how she would be praying for us back at home as we prayed for her. Although still in her teens, she had grasped the importance of encouragement by praying for each other.

The first thing the apostle prayed was that these believers would be granted strength for their weakness (verse 16).

Do you ever feel weak – ill-equipped for the task God has given you to do? Are you tired in the journey; do you feel like giving up, wish someone else would carry the load for you? Is fear in today's circumstances, or of what tomorrow might bring, wearing you down? Has your strength been sapped? If so, then you can be sure that others feel the same way. Why not pray the words of Paul's prayer for others, that they might receive strength for their weakness.

Remember, we are not praying for that person to be strong in themselves, but for God's strength to be given to them, 'according to the riches of His glory' (verse 16). It's nothing to do with us 'pulling our socks up' or 'getting on with it'. It's a swap. God takes what is crippling us in exchange for what will empower us for life's challenges. He doesn't ask us to live the Christian life in our own strength – He has plenty to go round. In fact, His resources are unlimited. Wow! Now that's something special to pray for others.

Lord, I'm always so quick to bring my own needs to You. Help me to pray for others with the same enthusiasm, recognizing that You can exchange our weakness for Your unlimited power. Amen.

154

23 May

Think of ways to encourage one another
to outbursts of love and good deeds.

Hebrews 10:24, NLT

Reading: Acts 15:30–33

I realize that I am blessed with friends who have encouraged me by their prayers over many years. One friend occasionally sent me letters, which I have to this day. A poem or song would grace the page, written with love, and void of a sermon. She simply wanted me to know I was on her heart. As in Paul's prayer for the Ephesian believers, my friend's communications reminded me that God would replace my weakness with His strength – like this old song says:

> He giveth more grace when the burdens grow greater;
> He sendeth more strength when the labours increase.
> To added affliction He addeth His mercy;
> To multiplied trials, His multiplied peace.
>
> His love has no limits, His grace has no measure,
> His power no boundary known unto men,
> For out of His infinite riches in Jesus
> He giveth and giveth and giveth again.[8]

You can imagine what this did for my heart the day it arrived in the post. To realize that God cannot stop giving assured me that there would never be a day when my need was bigger than His provision. And my friend made sure this encouragement reached me.

Thank You, Lord, that Your grace and love are constantly poured into my life. Your giving is unending. Help me to develop the same attitude in my own heart, that I might bless others. Amen.

155

24 May

That Christ may dwell in your hearts through faith.
Ephesians 3:17

Reading: Ephesians 3:14–21

Paul didn't only pray for the Ephesian believers to have their weakness exchanged for God's strength. His desire for them was also that 'Christ may dwell in [their] hearts through faith' (verse 17).

My husband worked as an evangelist for more than twenty years. During that time he travelled extensively, which necessitated many nights sleeping away from home. The church he was working with would provide hospitality, usually in the home of a church member.

Invariably his host would tell him, 'Please make yourself at home.' This was easier to accomplish in some places than others. Making himself 'at home' was not quite what they meant when they showed him to his room, however much they wanted him to feel welcome. You see, back at home Philip had access to what was behind every door and in every drawer: there was nowhere he couldn't go. But as a guest, he stayed at a certain address for a time, but he didn't live there; some places were strictly out of bounds.

In his prayer for the believers at Ephesus, Paul asked not that they would experience what it was like to have Christ stay with them for a while, but that they would let Him remain there – permanently. Only then would Christ have access to what was behind every door. The New Living Translation renders it, 'that Christ will be more and more at home in your hearts as you trust in Him'. It takes a lot of faith in someone before you hand over the keys to your house – the same goes for your heart. But only then will we really discover what Jesus was talking about when He said in John 15:5, 'He who abides in Me, and I in him, bears much fruit; for without Me you can do nothing.' Christ permanently resident changes everything.

Lord Jesus, I want You to have free access to every part of my life – to be permanently resident. I pray that for my friends also. Amen.

25 May

May you have the power to understand,
as all God's people should, how wide, how long,
how high, and how deep His love really is.

Ephesians 3:18, NLT

Reading: 1 John 4:7–11

I've discovered a science show on the radio that I listen to occasionally while driving. I especially like it when they discuss medical advances. One afternoon I caught an interview with the author of a book about mathematics. The reason she wrote the book was to show people with no interest in the subject how very easy and exciting maths could be. This was something I needed to hear. But after fifteen minutes of careful listening I still didn't understand what she was talking about! I won't be buying the book.

The apostle Paul recognized that understanding the enormity of God's love was beyond some people. Their concept of God was of a distant entity who needed to be appeased, and certainly not interested in them personally. Understanding God's love for them was key if they were to continue in the faith, which would undoubtedly bring challenge and even persecution. That's why Paul prayed that they would grasp God's love in all its fullness. It was an essential component in their relationship with God – and is in ours too.

Everything else hangs on this truth. God's love reveals His plan for us when nothing else makes sense. God's love shows us that we are precious when circumstances, other people, and even our own hearts, try to say otherwise. God's love, revealed in Jesus, shows us that 'while we were still sinners, Christ died for us' (Romans 5:8). What a powerful, mind-blowing fact. How can we get our heads around it? Thankfully, Paul explained that in the following verse in Ephesians 3: 'May you experience the love of Christ, though it is too great to understand fully' (verse 19, NLT).

Experiencing God's love personally is the only way to understand it. It's not a head-thing: it's a heart-thing.

Heavenly Father, I will never fully understand Your great love for me, but thank You that in Jesus Christ I can experience it. Amen.

157

26 May

A PASSAGE TO PONDER

Is there any encouragement from belonging to Christ?

Any comfort from His love?

Any fellowship together in the Spirit?

Are your hearts tender and sympathetic?

Then make me truly happy by agreeing wholeheartedly
with each other,

loving one another,

and working together with one heart and purpose.

Philippians 2:1–2, NLT

Read the passage slowly and let the Author speak to you. As you ponder, ask yourself these questions:

- What does it say?
- What does it mean?
- What is God saying to me?
- How will I respond?

27 May

He led me along the stream for 1,750 feet and
told me to go across . . . it was up to my ankles . . .
another 1,750 feet . . . up to my knees . . . another
1,750 feet . . . up to my waist . . . another 1,750 feet,
and the river was too deep to cross without swimming.

Ezekiel 47:3–5, NLT

Reading: Ezekiel 47:1–12

I live some fifteen minutes' drive from three beautiful beaches. I've walked those golden strands on balmy summer days and windy winter mornings. I've even dared to dip my toes into the sea, but only briefly. The icy chill of northern waters always sends me scurrying back to the sand with a gasp.

The sea around Tenerife is altogether different. There I was able to wade out knee deep in warm water – until, that is, a wave too large for my liking unsteadied the hold my toes had on the seabed, causing me to dash for the beach.

You may have guessed it. I can't swim! Therefore the sea commands more from me than respect; it holds fear. I have to stay on the shore. I can only watch with admiration those who ride the surf, paddle canoes, skim across the waves on jet skis or simply squeal with delight atop a banana boat, unconcerned that they will inevitably land in the water.

Therefore, as I help my grandchildren build a sandcastle, I gaze beyond the shore-line with jealousy, wishing I had the skills and courage to launch into the deep. I know I'm missing so much.

Ezekiel's watery vision took him to places where he was shown the power of the deep. He was told to go across this river that eventually was so deep that he had to swim in it. But if he'd stayed only in the shallows he would have missed seeing what God had for Israel: the sight and experience of the healing of the nations; the power of life over death. I'm sure he was glad he plunged in.

Powerful God of wind and wave, give me the courage to step off the shore and experience the spiritual deep with You. Amen.

28 May

Set your mind on things above,
not on things on the earth.

Colossians 3:2

Reading: Colossians 3:1–5

There's an old saying that goes something like this: 'He (or she) is so heavenly minded that he (or she) is of no earthly use.' It conjures up images of people running around with their heads in the clouds, hopeless with the nitty-gritty of life but able to quote Bible verses to order.

It's absolute nonsense, of course, because if we have immersed ourselves in God's Word, and are knowledgeable about His big plan, then we'll be very aware of what's needed in our families and communities. To be heavenly minded makes us perfect for earthly use.

So the big question is, how heavenly minded are we as those who claim to have been 'raised with Christ' (Colossians 3:1)? What is it that naturally holds our attention? What do we think about most often? Has God, or His Word, even reckoned in our thinking today? In our busy lives, have we managed to fit Him in somewhere? We can totally immerse ourselves in relationships, hobbies and work, and neglect to put first things first.

Paul isn't telling us here to forget about the things we need to see to on earth, but rather to set our thinking above it. We may spend eight hours a day at our place of employment, but does our work reflect our relationship with God? We have to keep the house clean, and do the laundry, but what's my attitude like while I'm mopping the floor? We enjoy meeting up with friends, but does our conversation with them honour God? Is there a natural connection with God hour by hour in our lives that demonstrates to others that He is with us wherever we happen to be? Are we in fact heavenly minded enough to be of earthly use?

Lord, forgive me for thinking that fitting You into my day somewhere is enough. Teach me to set my mind on the realities of heaven, and everything else will fall into place. Amen.

160

29 May

Finally, brothers and sisters, whatever is true,
whatever is noble, whatever is right, whatever is pure,
whatever is lovely, whatever is admirable – if anything is
excellent or praiseworthy – think about such things.

Philippians 4:8, NIV

Reading: Romans 8:5–8

It's one thing to say, 'Set your minds on things above' (Colossians 3:2), but how do we do it? Is this another one of those impossible requests from Paul – a tough ask for already busy lives? On the contrary, Paul looks at the whole subject of focusing our minds rightly as a spiritual discipline with great rewards. 'The things which you learned and received and heard and saw in me,' he challenges them in Philippians 4:9, 'these do, and *the God of peace will be with you*' (emphasis mine).

Turning our thoughts God-ward always brings rewards. It's difficult to be anxious when you are filled with God's peace. Making plans is so much simpler when we know God's heart on certain matters. It's also easier to reject what's not of God when we focus on what is true, noble, just, pure, lovely and admirable.

The practicalities involve forming habits which quickly become a delight, one of which I've added to this book to help you on your way. As you may have noticed by now, each Sabbath I've included a 'Passage to Ponder' to encourage you to 'set your mind on things above'. Reading slowly and asking simple questions of a Bible passage helps to reset our focus on God and what He wants to say directly to us. Developing a consistent prayer life opens the door to God's throne room, and when we catch a glimpse of Him we won't want to drop our eyes to anything Satan may want to tempt us with. And remembering that we have been 'raised with Christ' (Colossians 3:1) adds the eternal dimension to it all, and helps us recognize that this earth is temporary – we are heaven-bound!

Lord Jesus, I want to reset my focus heavenward. I want to see You, Lord, to hear You speak, and to make my life count for eternity. Amen.

30 May

Now when He had spoken these things, while they
watched, He was taken up, and a cloud
received Him out of their sight.

Acts 1:9

Reading: Acts 1:9–11

Today is Ascension Day. We rightly make much of Christmas, Good Friday, Easter Sunday and even Pentecost, but not enough of us give thought to Ascension Day. Why is it important to commemorate this day, to acknowledge that Jesus' ascension – His return to Heaven – was both bodily and visible? Does it really matter?

When Jesus arrived on earth as a little baby, we recognized Him as God incarnate. Yet, while both God and man in equal measure, Jesus was restricted to one place in one time because of His bodily limitations. The Ascension removed that limitation for ever. No longer do we have to seek Him out, as the people did during His thirty-three-year life span. The ascended Jesus is now available to us wherever we are, and whenever we choose to meet with Him, through the Holy Spirit that He left behind to reside in us.

The Ascension allowed Jesus to return to His rightful place at the Father's right hand. Once there, He took His place as both advocate and mediator for us. His redemptive work on earth was finished; the work of mediation on our behalf was able to begin (Hebrews 8:1, 6). So when the Father looks on us flawed human beings, He sees His glorified Son instead, and He is satisfied.

The rulers of Israel and Rome knew nothing of the power of Christ when they nailed Him to the cross. Neither did they understand that His death and resurrection were but a step towards the power He would wield once ascended. Jesus is 'far above all principality and power and might and dominion, and every name that is named, not only in this age but also in that which is to come' (Ephesians 1:21).

Lord, there is none like You: crucified, risen and ascended. May the very thought of the power of the glorified Saviour strengthen me today. Amen.

31 May

'Men of Galilee, why do you stand gazing up into heaven?
This same Jesus, who was taken up from you
into heaven, will so come in like manner
as you saw Him go into heaven.'
Acts 1:11

Reading: 1 Thessalonians 4:15–18

What a roller coaster of a ride the disciples had experienced since that evening in the Garden of Gethsemane. They'd watched Jesus die; yet, miraculously, it wasn't the end, for Jesus rose again. Afterwards, He not only showed Himself to them, but also spent time with them, eating, and teaching them once more.

Just when they thought He had returned for good, perhaps even to take Israel back from the Romans (Acts 1:6), Jesus gave them the command to return to Jerusalem. Finally, while standing on the Mount of Olives with Jesus, His followers witnessed the incredible: the feet of Jesus left the ground and He started to lift into the air – right before their eyes, finally disappearing into the clouds . . . and He was gone! (Acts 1:9) They were transfixed! Shocked! Unable to take it in . . . until the angels spoke: 'What are you looking at! This very same Jesus has gone back to heaven, but He will come again. And He's coming back exactly how He went – visibly and bodily – He will return!' (Acts 1:11, my paraphrase).

Jesus had to leave in order to prepare that promised place for them (John 14:3). He had to leave in order that He could be with them in more than one place at a time – only possible when the Spirit would come, indwell them and give them the power they needed for all that lay ahead. He had to leave in order to represent them before the Father in heaven as both their advocate and mediator.

But He would return . . . to take them to where He was. That's what they had to focus on. Not past failings, nor present disappointments . . . but future hope. One day, we too will be glorified. What a promise . . . what a hope!

Lord Jesus, one day You will return. May that truth hold my focus as I set my heart on You. Amen.

163

June

1 June

One of the two who heard John speak, and followed Him, was Andrew, Simon Peter's brother.

John 1:40

Reading: John 1:35–42

Fishing may have been the family business, but Andrew's mind was set on higher things. This young man was a truth searcher, or, perhaps I should say, a Messiah seeker.

He was already a disciple of John the Baptist when Jesus came along. It only took John to declare Jesus as 'the Lamb of God' (John 1:35) in his hearing for Andrew to leave the Baptist and go after Jesus. Andrew was the first recorded follower of Jesus, later to become one of the disciples. The disciples were the men who followed Jesus for the three years of His earthly ministry; they were taught by Him, observed His miracles, watched Him die, met with Him after He was resurrected and witnessed His ascension.

But recognizing Jesus as the Messiah was not something Andrew kept to himself. He immediately set about bringing people to Jesus. Andrew was a bringer. 'He first found his own brother Simon, and said to him, "We have found the Messiah" (which is translated, the Christ). And he brought him to Jesus' (John 1:41–42).

Peter was only the first. We read in John 6:8–9 that it was Andrew who brought to Jesus the boy with his lunch of two small fish and five little loaves when the crowds following Jesus needed to eat. Jesus went on to increase the gift into enough food to feed five thousand and more. It was Andrew, along with Philip, who introduced some Greeks to Jesus when they came looking for Him (John 12:21–22). Andrew may have been in his brother Peter's shadow, but he still did what he could to bring people to Jesus. Surely that's what is most important – for it is Jesus who changes lives.

Lord, throughout history You have used the witness of quiet men and women to bring people to Jesus, some of whom turned out to be Moodys or Grahams. I want to be a bringer! Amen.

2 June

A PASSAGE TO PONDER

And Jesus walking by the Sea of Galilee, saw two brothers,

Simon called Peter, and Andrew his brother,

casting a net into the sea; for they were fishermen.

Then He said to them, 'Follow Me,

and I will make you fishers of men.'

They immediately left their nets and followed Him.

Going on from there, He saw two other brothers,

James the son of Zebedee, and John his brother,

in the boat with Zebedee their father,

mending their nets.

He called them, and immediately they left the boat

and their father, and followed Him.

Matthew 4:18–22

Read the passage slowly and let the Author speak to you. As you ponder, ask yourself these questions:

- What does it say?
- What does it mean?
- What is God saying to me?
- How will I respond?

3 June

So He said, 'Come.' And when Peter had come down out
of the boat, he walked on the water to go to Jesus.

Matthew 14:29

Reading: Matthew 14:22–33

Jesus probably knew something about boats . . . up to a point. As a carpenter living
twenty miles from the Sea of Galilee it is possible that Joseph & Sons were called
in to make or mend the odd boat. Boats were made of wood, after all.

Peter, on the other hand, knew just about everything there was to know about
boats. Structure was one thing, but sailing them in the unpredictable waters of
Galilee required skill. Peter's strength of body and character was undoubtedly
forged working in the family's fishing business. It took courage on many nights to
bring in a catch.

Courage was something the first disciple called by Jesus had in bucketloads. Peter
was spokesman for the twelve, unwise at times, but no-one could question the
fisherman's passion for the Lord or his courage in following Him. The normal
reaction of any fisherman weathering a storm on Galilee would be to stay on board
at all costs, praying that the wooden structure between him and the turbulent deep
would remain in one piece.

When Jesus walked on the water, towards the men struggling in the storm, Peter
wanted to get out of the boat and walk to Him. Brave? Mmmm. Foolish? 'Probably,'
is our likely reaction. Yet when Jesus eventually had to rescue the struggling Peter
from the waves, He reprimanded the disciple not for getting out of the boat, but
for his lack of faith in not believing that he too could walk on water. Jesus admired
the disciple's courage. Everyone else on the boat was absorbed in staying alive,
while Peter wanted to please the Master. After all, it's not possible to walk on
water unless you actually get out of the boat. And that takes more than courage. It
takes faith.

*Lord Jesus, help me to follow You into the extraordinary with courage based on faith.
For nothing is impossible with You by my side. Amen.*

4 June

Then He appointed twelve . . . James the son of Zebedee and John the brother of James, to whom He gave the name Boanerges, that is, 'Sons of Thunder'.

Mark 3:14, 17

Reading: Mark 3:13–19

Do you have a nickname? Or do you remember giving one to a teacher at school? Unfortunately, nicknames can sometimes be cruel, but they can also be a sign of affection – a term of endearment.

I love that Jesus gave James and John a nickname. He obviously knew all about their explosive characters, which were clearly confirmed when they wanted to call down the fire of judgment to destroy a Samaritan village that wasn't welcoming to the Saviour (Luke 9:54), an attitude the Lord rebuked them for. But Jesus undoubtedly had a special affection towards them, as they became two of the three closest companions He had on earth. They were the ones, along with Peter, whom Jesus took with Him up the Mount of Transfiguration where His divinity was displayed (Matthew 17:1–2). John was the disciple who ran with Peter to see Jesus' empty tomb for himself (John 20:3ff). James was the first of the twelve disciples to be executed for following Jesus (Acts 12:2). John was the disciple to whom Jesus committed the care for His mother after His crucifixion (John 19:27).

In spite of their frowned-upon fiery temperaments, the passion of James and John was harnessed by the Saviour and channelled into following Him when He was alive, and for the benefit of the church after Christ's ascension. And what is remarkable is that nicknames can be changed. John lived longer than any of the other original twelve, living his later years not as a 'Son of Thunder', but as an 'Apostle of Love'. Forty times in his letters he speaks on the subject of love. But then a passionate man knows that love is not soft, but strong.

Lord Jesus, thank You that You can take my dispositions, refine them and use them for Your glory. May my passion for You be obvious to all, yet characterized by the strong love of Jesus. Amen.

5 June

The following day Jesus wanted to go to Galilee,
and He found Philip and said to him, 'Follow Me.'
John 1:43

Philip found Nathanael.
John 1:45

Reading: John 1:43–51

The reality TV show, *The Apprentice*, brings together a group of highly motivated entrepreneurs. Although bent purely on personal success, they are expected to work together as a team. They soon learn that not everyone can be the boss. Good teamwork requires differing skill mixes, including a plodder – someone who will get on with the menial while others do the planning.

The team Jesus was building around Him would have faced the 'You're fired!' of Lord Alan Sugar long before they'd left the starting blocks! Not enough whizz-kids among them – too ordinary to get noticed.

We are told very little about either Philip or Nathanael, apart from the fact that Jesus sought Philip out (John 1:43), and Philip brought Nathanael to meet Jesus. Philip was one of the practical guys on Jesus' team (John 6:5–7). But Philip was also a seeker, asking Jesus in John 14:8–9 to show them the Father. Yes, his knowledge had gaps, but he was in the right place for answers – he was on Jesus' team.

We know even less about Nathanael – sometimes called Bartholomew – except that he was Philip's friend. But Jesus saw the genuineness in Nathanael's soul and the integrity of his character before He saw his face (John 1:47). Jesus called him 'an Israelite indeed, in whom is no deceit!'. Nathanael had the kind of character you'd expect Jesus to call. Perhaps he was there to help the team with their moral choices? In truth, we are not told.

Knowing so little about these disciples is quite comforting. Jesus wasn't always looking for front people. He added those to His team who got on with what He asked them to do: men who remained faithful, quietly making a difference, and willing to be taught.

Lord Jesus, thank You that You don't always look for the super-skilled to be included in Your team. It's faithfulness that really matters. Amen.

6 June

As Jesus passed on from there, He saw a man named
Matthew sitting at the tax office. And He said to him,
'Follow Me.' So he arose and followed Him.

Matthew 9:9

Reading: Matthew 9:9–13

To this growing group of pupils, Jesus added a man who was despised by all and sundry: Matthew, also known as Levi, the tax collector.

A few days later, Matthew and the others packed a little bread in the pouches hanging from their belts. They were going on a journey – for a rest, Jesus had said. Matthew couldn't help but wonder where they could possibly go and not be found by the needy poor.

The group had started out before darkness had said its daily farewell. Matthew cringed as they passed the tax booth situated on Capernaum's main highway. His successor had caught on to the tricks of the trade very quickly, Matthew thought. Opening at this hour he could catch the fishermen returning after a night's work and tax their catch. There was a day when that thought would have made him chuckle, but not any more.

The official, sitting under the same spreading branches where Matthew once sat, raised his hand in greeting as the former tax collector walked by. Only the slightest inclination of the head in response identified Matthew as an acquaintance. Even the neat rows of coins no longer tempted the man who had instantly followed the rabbi, Jesus, when He passed his booth one day and called Matthew to follow Him: a decision the tax collector didn't regret.

Matthew chuckled quietly as they walked, surveying the group of men who were now his daily companions. A strange, eclectic mix of fishermen, revolutionaries, tradesmen and, yes, even a tax collector: the loved and despised of society, all drawn together by the teachings of a most unusual rabbi. But, in the seclusion of his private thoughts, Matthew believed Jesus was very much more.[9]

However we come to You, Lord, loved or despised, You accept us. Thank You. Amen.

172

7 June

And He went up on the mountain and called to Him those He Himself wanted. And they came to Him.
Mark 3:13

Reading: Matthew 10:5–14

Have you ever stood with a group of people, longing that you'd be chosen for something special? I remember our son's first week at grammar school. I prayed fervently that he'd make friends, only to discover later that he'd wandered around the playground on his own yet again. Eventually someone invited him to the music room at lunchtime, and at last he had found his happy place!

Jesus' public ministry hadn't long started before crowds were following Him everywhere. It's no wonder, really, because the news about Jesus' ability to heal the sick spread like wildfire. People travelled for miles to experience the miraculous. They'd never seen the like before. Many simply wanted to hear this new rabbi teach, for it was unlike anything others were saying.

Among those following Him were twelve men. Only a few of them knew each other, but each was drawn by what was happening in front of their eyes. On one particular day, Jesus began to call out the names of individuals whom He wanted to be His disciples. I can't help but wonder whether Thomas and James, the son of Alphaeus, longed that Jesus would call their names? Or did they imagine that the Master would pass them by, once they'd seen the ones He'd already asked to follow Him? They felt less worthy. He would never choose them. Then it happened: *their* names were called above the clamour of the crowd. Jesus asked *them* to join Him. They were chosen! Immediately they responded, and followed Jesus.

Interestingly, Jesus still calls for men and women to follow Him today. 'Behold, I stand at the door and knock,' He says. 'If anyone hears My voice and opens the door, I will come in to him and dine with him, and he with Me' (Revelation 3:20). Let's not keep Him waiting for our reply.

Thank You, Lord, that You are still calling today. May my response be immediate. Amen.

8 June

Judas (not Judas Iscariot, but the other disciple with that name) said to him, 'Lord, why are you going to reveal yourself only to us and not to the world at large?'

John 14:22, NLT

Reading: Luke 9:1–6

Bible names can be confusing. Some people were also known by different names depending on who was using them, and when. Thaddeus was one such. That particular name is used in Scriptures listing the calling of the twelve (Matthew 10:1–4), but Bible scholars confirm that he is referred to by three other names, including Judas (not Iscariot). Complicated explanations aside, Thaddeus, aka Judas (not Iscariot), was one of the privileged twelve called by the Master to follow Him: something he did gladly and faithfully.

This little cameo of him in John 14:22 reveals something special about the man with four names: he had a heart for mission. He questioned Jesus as to why He taught the disciples while so many other people needed to hear. In His reply to Thaddeus Judas, Jesus explained that soon the Holy Spirit would come, and then they could tell the world all they had learned from Him. Thaddeus Judas was being taught the difference between a disciple and an apostle, the former being a student, the latter a messenger: a sent-out-one with a mission. This disciple's heart was already warming to his calling.

Another of the twelve whose name causes some confusion is Simon the Zealot. The Zealots were a political sect that would happily have used violence to end Roman rule. They were always up for a fight. The term 'Zealot' was also used at the time to describe those who were extreme in their commitment to Judaism. They were zealous Jews. So which was Simon? We are not told, but my guess is that whichever 'tribe' he belonged to before he heard Jesus' call, Simon quickly became zealous after Christ. No other cause was more important than Christ's.

Heavenly Father, it's easy to be passionate about many things. May my heart's desire be that others hear Jesus, fired by zeal for Your glory. Amen.

9 June

A PASSAGE TO PONDER

When the day of Pentecost came,

they were all together in one place.

Suddenly a sound like the blowing of a violent wind

came from heaven and filled the whole house where they were sitting.

They saw what seemed to be tongues of fire that separated

and came to rest on each of them.

All of them were filled with the Holy Spirit

and began to speak in other tongues

as the Spirit enabled them . . .

'In the last days, God says,

I will pour out my Spirit on all people.

Your sons and daughters will prophesy,

your young men will see visions,

your old men will dream dreams.'

Acts 2:1–4, 17, NIV

Read the passage slowly and let the Author speak to you. As you ponder, ask yourself these questions:

- What does it say?
- What does it mean?
- What is God saying to me?
- How should I respond?

175

10 June

But Jesus said to him, 'Judas, are you betraying the Son of Man with a kiss?'
Luke 22:48

Reading: Acts 1:21–26

In spite of being one of the twelve, Judas never got to experience Pentecost with the others. The indwelling Holy Spirit was not for the man who had betrayed the Messiah. He'd seen the miraculous, felt Jesus' love at close quarters and heard Him teach. He'd even held the trusted position of treasurer within that specially chosen group. But eventually money was his downfall.

Yet what dreadful loss he exchanged for those thirty pieces of silver. He lost the privilege of seeing the resurrected Christ. He never got to spend those final days with the risen Jesus, and he missed the Saviour's ascension. Was it purely greed that sent Judas astray, or could there have been some other altruistic motivation for his madness? We'll never know, but his actions shout a warning to us from the grave: 'Therefore let him who thinks he stands take heed lest he fall' (1 Corinthians 10:12). They were Paul's words, but they might as well have come from the mouth of Judas Iscariot.

It's easy to point an accusing finger at Judas. What we need to remember is that we too are privileged to walk with Jesus. And the enemy of our souls seeks a weak spot in us to tempt us to treason against the King of kings. Oh, how we need the Holy Spirit's power to help us stand against Satan's lies.

Judas was replaced in the twelve by Matthias, one of those who had followed Jesus for the full three years of His ministry and had witnessed His power and resurrection (Acts 1:21–22). We know little about him, other than that his appointment teaches that God can raise up others to take our place. God doesn't ask us to be successful, but He does expect us to remain faithful.

Lord Jesus, I realize that I am weak, but thankful that You intercede on my behalf. May my heart always be loyal to the King of kings, for You alone are worthy. Amen.

11 June

'You have skirted this mountain long enough: turn northward.'
Deuteronomy 2:3

Reading: Deuteronomy 1:3–8

There comes a time when we have to stop treading old ground and move on.

There are mountains God will have us climb, and He will give us the strength to scale them when we must. Other mountains we skirt around, unwilling to move beyond the blockage they cause in our lives. Often they are of our own construction, perhaps a longing for something that we believe is right for us. So we keep on praying about the same thing over and over again until it becomes an obsession. Time, energy and peace are sacrificed by constantly hugging the same old mountain. Could it be that God wants us to leave it with Him, and move on?

Or perhaps we face a mountain built by the transgression of others. It's not our fault, but we can't get away from it because the boots of hurt, anger and an unforgiving spirit march us round and round in a circle of pain and self-pity. Might it be time to take those boots off and leave that mountain behind? Forgiveness, and choosing to let go, will soon set us on a different path.

'You have skirted this mountain long enough,' God told the wandering Israelites. Forty years they'd meandered in the wilderness after leaving Egypt, when all the time the Promised Land was waiting for them. It was time to change direction, time to leave what was holding them back and trust God for what lay ahead. It was a move that required action on their part – they had to get up and go.

'Rise, take your journey, and cross over …' (Deuteronomy 2:24). Freedom, fulfilment and joy await us if only we'd stop skirting around the same old mountain. It's time to move on.

Lord, I'm tired of skirting around this mountain. I long to leave it behind and cross over into whatever You have for me. May courage lift my feet and allow me to follow a different path. Amen.

12 June

I look up to the mountains –
does my help come from there?
My help comes from the Lord,
who made heaven and earth!

Psalm 121:1, NLT

Reading: Psalm 121

The sun was already shining brightly when we entered the kitchen for breakfast. The forecast was for thirty degrees Celsius, and we were dressed for the weather. Two old rucksacks sat on the table, and a collection of sturdy winter shoes littered the floor. Our hostess muttered, 'Morgen,' as she handed me a woollen sweater to try on. I doubted we would really need all the things she stuffed into the rucksacks, but thought better not to argue. 'You can't go into the mountains unprepared,' she told us in broken English.

Jungfraubahn is the feat of Swiss engineering that transports you up Europe's highest mountain, bearing its name. The red train had the ability to climb steep gradients, overlooking sheer drops, while at the same time scaring the wits out of this particular height-phobic woman. Up we went, stopping first at Kleine Scheidegg to picnic on the grass opposite the majestic north face of the Eiger. The heat was stifling, the view breathtaking.

An announcement was made in many languages when we reboarded the train for the summit: 'Please add clothing and footwear suitable for disembarkation.' All over the train, travellers struggled to pull on jumpers, trousers, mountain boots, hats and gloves. Our full rucksacks didn't seem so foolish now as we layered up to meet the eternal snow. And boy, were we glad we weren't like the two young women who stepped off the train in skimpy shorts and tops. Their journey lasted mere minutes as they scurried back from the snow to board the train again. They missed the experience of a lifetime: beauty beyond imagination, all because they didn't prepare for the journey.

Life's mountains aren't leisure trips, but the preparation of knowing God helps us to experience all He intends for us at the top.

Lord, life's mountains are inevitable, but Your strength is available for the climb. Help me to know You better before I face the mountain. Amen.

13 June

'Now therefore, give me this mountain
of which the LORD spoke in that day.'
Joshua 14:12

Reading: Joshua 14:10–15

Ask any mountaineer why they put their lives at risk to climb the world's highest mountains and the standard reply is, 'Just because it's there.'

The sun shone hot on our skin as we picnicked on the grass opposite the north face of the nearby Eiger mountain. My husband trained his binoculars on the 1,800-metre rock face opposite in an unsuccessful attempt to identify climbers. As we munched our sandwiches, we had no idea that that piece of vertical rock had claimed at least sixty-four lives since the first attempt to scale it in 1938. So dark is its reputation, it is nicknamed 'Mortwand' – 'Murder Wall'; yet it continues to magnetize those with a burning desire to conquer it.

Forty-five years after visiting the giant-inhabiting hill-country of Hebron, Caleb's desire to claim it for God persisted. It was something that the fears of the wilderness-wandering Israelites had previously prevented him from doing. Significantly, Joshua 14:15 declares that it was only after Caleb's capture of that particular mountain that 'the land had rest from war'.

Do you have a burning desire to conquer a certain 'mountain', or to see it moved, in order that God's kingdom is extended? That's very different from wanting to do something big that gets us noticed, for that kind of climb can end in disaster. But once tested with prayer and the clarity of God's leading through His Word, there comes a time when it is right to leave base camp and begin the ascent. But remember, sensible climbers always follow their Guide. God already knows the pitfalls, and the best way to conquer the 'mountain'. We need to follow Him closely, and not head off on our own. Then perhaps, like Caleb, we'll discover the endeavour life-changing for more than ourselves.

Heavenly Father, Caleb waited patiently for forty years to conquer his 'mountain'. Whatever You are asking me to do, help me to do it according to Your plan, following Your lead. Amen.

179

14 June

They wandered in the wilderness in a desolate way;
They found no city to dwell in.

Psalm 107:4

Reading: Psalm 107:4–9

The highest mountain in Northern Ireland is Slieve Donard, which rises to the giddy heights of 850 metres. The mountain is hidden as you journey along the main road into the area until you turn round one particular bend when it suddenly comes into view, sweeping all the way down to the sea.

In spite of its paltry height, compared to the Jungfrau's whopping 4,158 metres, Slieve Donard has its own dedicated Mountain Rescue Team. People flock to the mountain at every season of the year to enjoy the beauty of the area. At times, mist can rapidly cover the peaks, changing the landscape unrecognizably. You can quickly get lost in an environment that has suddenly become dangerous. It's a frightening thing to lose your way, not to be able to see familiar points of reference or to know whether your next step will land on level ground or over a precipice. That's when you're glad of the Mountain Rescue Team, for they know every inch of the mountain.

Losing our way in life can also happen unexpectedly. Circumstances change. Disappointment fogs our thinking. Hurt renders us powerless to respond in ways that previously were clear cut. Before we know it we've lost the beauty of walking with God and our souls become as barren as the mountain on which find ourselves. We need a rescuer. The psalmist reminds us in Psalm 107 of how the Israelites, God's own people, had lost their way both physically and spiritually. Eventually, 'They cried out to the LORD in their trouble, and He delivered them out of their distresses. And He led them forth by the right way' (verses 6–7). However lost we feel, when we call for help, He will find us and lead us out.

Lord, sometimes I find myself lost in the circumstances of life. Thank You that I can cry for You and be sure that You will find me and bring me to a place of safety. Amen.

15 June

The fear of the LORD is the beginning of wisdom,
and the knowledge of the Holy One is understanding.
Proverbs 9:10

Reading: Proverbs 9:9–12

Fear is a very healthy emotion that can prevent us from falling into all kinds of danger. Fear evokes risk assessment, even at an unconscious level.

Go to any mountaineering or trekking website and you'll find a list of recommendations for planning a safe experience on the mountain:

- Choose the right equipment, clothing and food for the journey.
- Tell someone where you are going and your planned time of return.
- Check the weather.
- Pack a map and compass: know how to use both.
- Take advice from the locals: they'll know the problem spots.

Fear is not merely worry but involves developing proper respect for the very thing we may have to face. Respect the mountain and you'll find the journey more enjoyable and safe.

There are many reasons why we should actually fear the God before whom we will all give an account one day, but respecting Him first and foremost is where wisdom starts. Godly wisdom is the foundation on which we can build, adding knowledge that leads to understanding who God really is. To fear God is simply to be in awe of Him – His majesty, justice, mercy and the love He has shown to us through salvation's plan. Developing an exalted view of God confirms that I can trust Him with my soul – in fact, with everything in my life.

That's the kind of fear I am happy to live with. It's a win-win situation.

Heavenly Father, God of heaven and earth, You alone are ruler of the universe and I am privileged to be Your child. I stand in awe of Your glory yet humbled by Your love for me. Be glorified in my life, Lord. Amen.

181

16 June

A PASSAGE TO PONDER

The crown of the wise is their riches,

But the foolishness of fools is folly.

A true witness delivers souls,

But a deceitful witness speaks lies.

In the fear of the LORD there is strong confidence,

And His children will have a place of refuge.

The fear of the LORD is a fountain of life,

To turn one away from the snares of death.

Proverbs 14:24–27

Read the passage slowly and let the Author speak to you. As you ponder, ask yourself these questions:

- What does it say?
- What does it mean?
- What is God saying to me?
- How should I respond?

17 June

And Elijah came to all the people and said,
'. . . If the LORD is God, follow Him; but if Baal,
follow him.' But the people answered him not a word.

1 Kings 18:21

Reading: 1 Kings 18:20–24

It's that time of the year when the DIY stores across the country are at their busiest. The summer sun invades our homes, exposing the repairs and redecorating that need to be done. However, starting one job often leads to another. Scraping off the old wallpaper invariably reveals the reason why you didn't paint the wall in the first place . . . cracks!

Elijah's contest with Ahab and the prophets of Baal is often seen as the reason he went to Mount Carmel in the first place. But it was only one of the jobs God had in mind for him. Turning up for that one revealed another of greater importance. If Elijah were only to defeat the prophets of Baal, it would have been a bit like 'papering over the cracks' in the spiritual life of the nation. The cracks needed to be dealt with, and pointing them out was Elijah's first task.

The Children of Israel had been happy casually worshipping the Baals, while believing they could have Jehovah in their pockets as well. They had obviously forgotten the first commandment: 'You shall have no other gods before Me' (Exodus 20:3), as well as the second and third to boot! When he pointed out their folly, Elijah was met with silence. I think those words, 'But the people answered him not a word' (verse 21), are particularly sad. I want to believe it was an embarrassed silence but I can't be sure.

Israel's challenge is one we also face. Too often we amble along, happy to have God as some sort of eternal insurance policy, while worshipping our own self-made deities of career, possessions, leisure and, yes, even family. Maybe it's time to identify the cracks in our own spiritual lives?

Heavenly Father, there should be no other gods in my life. Help me to look for any cracks in my devotion. Amen.

18 June

Then Elijah said to all the people, 'Come near to me.' . . .
And he repaired the altar of the LORD
that was broken down.

1 Kings 18:30

Reading: 1 Kings 18:30–35

The odds were crazy – 450 prophets of Baal versus one lone prophet of Jehovah! The challenge set by Elijah seemed even more ridiculous – take a bull, set it on an altar of wood and call on your god to burn up the sacrifice. He'd do the same, and then they'd witness that 'the God who answers by fire, He is God' (1 Kings 18:24). The contest was accepted, but first Elijah had to repair the altar.

This was no new altar, but rather the place where the sin-offering was once made. It was the place where the people had once met with God: the place of sacrifice, and of surrender to God's rule over the nation and their personal lives. But God's own people had been so busy worshipping false gods that they'd neglected this place of meeting and forgiveness, allowing it to fall into disrepair. What was broken must be repaired before Elijah dared ask God to send the fire.

So the man of God took twelve stones, representing the twelve tribes of Israel, and made the altar of sacrifice ready for when God would answer his prayer. By choosing twelve stones, Elijah reminded the gathered crowd who they were, where they'd come from and who had made them into a nation in the first place (verse 31). They also needed to remember what God required of them, if they were ever to renew fellowship with Him. Repairing the altar was the first sign of repentance: the first step in giving God His rightful place.

Have we forgotten who we are? Where we've come from? Does the memory of the price paid for our redemption cross our minds less than it did before? Has our altar fallen into disrepair? Does it need to be rebuilt?

Father, simple neglect can break what's good in my relationship with You. Lord, if my altar needs to be repaired, point out what's broken, that we might rebuild together. Amen.

19 June

For we are God's fellow workers.
1 Corinthians 3:9

Reading: 1 Kings 18:36–39

God doesn't need us to accomplish His purposes, but He does choose to work with us. That way, we get to witness first-hand what God's heart is like, as well as to experience His power.

God could have struck Mount Carmel without Elijah's help, but He chose to use the solitary prophet, along with twelve big stones, to give His wayward people a visual aid of His love for them, before finishing it off with the spectacular. God loves teamwork.

I once worked as the 'team nurse' in the Cardiac Ambulance, answering emergency calls direct from the ward to places all over Belfast. The team included the driver of a specially fitted out ambulance, plus a doctor and a nurse, all trained in cardiology. I had a very specific role, which included making sure all the drugs and equipment potentially required for a call-out were available the instant they were needed. If something was used in a call-out it had to be replaced before the next call was taken.

What would have happened if we arrived to help a patient who needed an intra-cardiac drug and the nurse before me hadn't replaced the special needle required to administer the drug directly into the heart? The opportunity for recovery would have slipped away. Teamwork was vital. Lives were at stake.

We may not feel that walking closely with God, or even keeping our altars in good repair, is all that important, but it is. For as we work with Him in obedience He gives us the opportunity to have heaven touch not only our lives, but perhaps even to transform the lives of others – for eternity. When Elijah repaired the altar, it resulted in the fire falling and the people declaring, 'The LORD, He is God! The LORD, He is God!' (1 Kings 18:39). What a result!

Lord God, I feel inadequate, yet You choose to allow me to be Your fellow worker. May I keep my altar repaired and my heart willing for whatever You ask of me. Amen.

20 June

Elijah was as human as we are, and yet
when he prayed earnestly that no rain would fall,
none fell for three and a half years!

James 5:17, NLT

Reading: James 5:16–18

Yeah, right! Elijah is nothing like me! When he prayed the rain stopped, the dead were raised, fire fell from heaven, and then it rained again after three and a half years of drought! That doesn't happen to me.

Yet, surely, answered prayer is all about the One who does the answering, not the one who does the praying. Yes, there may be altars to repair. Yes, God often chooses to work with us and through us to accomplish the answers He sends. But God doesn't need superheroes. Answering prayer is His prerogative alone. He only asks that we communicate with Him, however inadequately, and leave the outcome with Him.

I grew up in a church that was strong in prayer. I was privileged to listen to the fervent praying of godly men and women. I was also foolish enough to imagine that the angels were impressed by the apparent power in their words. They were the Elijahs of our day as far as I was concerned. But as I grew older in years and faith I realized that impressing others was the furthest thing on their minds. Everyone and everything else simply disappeared when they spoke to the One whom they were absolutely convinced could answer their prayers. God could make the fire fall – that's why they prayed as they did. And often He did just that in those days of special blessing.

When we wonder how to form our words in prayer, struggle while waiting for the answer, feel condemned by others for lacking faith, let's remember that we are not responsible for the answers – God is. But as our Father, He loves to hear our voice, and He understands what is behind our words.

Heavenly Father, may faith rise in my heart as I wait for Your power to be displayed in answered prayer. I believe that Elijah's God still lives today. Be glorified. Amen.

21 June

'What are you doing here, Elijah?'
1 Kings 19:9

Reading: 1 Kings 19:1–8

Sometimes the distance from the mountaintop to the desert place isn't very far. One minute we are on a spiritual high, and the next we wonder if God is there at all. Our perceptions demonstrate our ability to swing effortlessly in either direction. And it seems that Elijah is after all as human as we are when we read about what happened to him shortly after the victories on Carmel.

It would also be easy to feel a failure when we reach places like the one Elijah did in that wilderness, wailing, 'It is enough! Now, LORD, take my life' (1 Kings 19:4), were it not for the response of the One he thought he had failed. God didn't ask the question at the top of the page until much later in the story. Rather, on discovery of His exhausted prophet, the Lord responded with deep kindness. There was no wagging finger of blame for running away from Jezebel's threats. Instead, the God of heaven let His burnt-out servant sleep, and then He made him breakfast!

And after another nap, we read, 'And the angel of the LORD came back the second time, and touched him, and said, "Arise and eat, because the journey is too great for you"' (1 Kings 19:7). Imagine – God knows when the journey is too much for us to handle. He also knows what lies ahead, and exactly what we need to face it, and so He meets us in our desert place in order to give us the strength to leave it behind.

Sermons don't help on those giving-up-days. But love does. Yes, there'll come a day when we have to answer the question, 'What are you doing here?' but for now, we hear Him say, 'I know ... the journey is too great for you.' And His loving touch will lighten our load.

Lord, there are days when I feel that I can't go on. Thank You for meeting me in the desert place. Please give me the strength to leave it behind. Amen.

187

22 June

'He said to them, "An enemy has done this."'
Matthew 13:28

Reading: Matthew 13:24–30

I couldn't believe my ears.

'Two fourteen-year-olds planned the murder of a mother and daughter while they sat eating burgers in a McDonald's restaurant,' the news reporter announced as I munched on my cornflakes.

Only this wasn't some crazy fantasy where teenage bravado made threats that would never be put into action. No, this was a cold, calculating plan to murder, simply because the girl didn't like the woman in question. So one day that mother and her daughter were viciously knifed to death.

Surely 'an enemy has done this', I whispered, shell-shocked.

Fast-forward two weeks, and our little province reels at the ruling of an appeal court stating that a gracious young couple were guilty of discrimination when they acted according to their Christian beliefs in business. The judgment stated that no longer do we have rights if a customer wants us to do something against our religious beliefs or conscience.

Surely 'an enemy has done this', I shouted, dumbfounded.

Yet do we who own the name of Christ recognize this enemy any more? Or are we afraid to look foolish if it were to be discovered that we actually believe in Satan? Could it be that we are so caught up in our own busy lives that we haven't taken time to pray for the wayward teenagers of our land, or our lawmakers in Parliament? 'As long as me and mine are all right' is an attitude that has infiltrated the church, resulting in an inability to be more than merely shocked when we hear such news.

'What can we do about it?' you may well respond.

For me, it has been a case of, 'Lord, teach me how to pray.'

Lord Jesus, we read in Your Word that we are in a spiritual battle. Help us to recognize the enemy of our souls, and that 'the weapons of our warfare are not carnal but mighty in God for pulling down strongholds' (2 Corinthians 10:4). Amen.

23 June

A PASSAGE TO PONDER

So then neither he who plants is anything,

nor he who waters, but God who gives the increase.

Now he who plants and he who waters are one,

and each one will receive his own reward

according to his own labor.

For we are God's fellow workers;

you are God's field, you are God's building.

According to the grace of God which was given to me,

as a wise master builder I have laid the foundation,

and another builds on it.

For no other foundation can anyone lay

than that which is laid,

which is Jesus Christ.

1 Corinthians 3:7–11

Read through the passage slowly and let the Author speak to you. As you ponder, ask yourself these questions:

- What does it say?
- What does it mean?
- What is God saying to me?
- How will I respond?

24 June

It is good to give thanks to the LORD,
And to sing praises to Your name, O Most High.
Psalm 92:1

Reading: Psalm 92:1–4

The littlest hand at the table shot up immediately in response to the question, 'Who'd like to give God thanks for the food today?' As our two-year-old grandson clasped his hands under his chin and squeezed his eyes tightly shut in concentration, his dad quietly whispered, 'And remember to thank God for one more thing as well as the food.' Training in righteousness requires the occasional hint!

'Thank you God for the food,' was spoken with great passion, and we all waited patiently for the 'additional' piece of thankfulness to be added. I have to confess sneaking a peek at our little grandson as he tried hard to think of something else to be thankful for. One of his eyes remained tightly closed while the other scanned the table frantically . . . 'And for the sausages!' he shouted triumphantly. And who isn't thankful 'for the sausages'?!

With our prayer lists bulging and a passion for God to step into the lives of those we care for, we can easily forget to stop and be thankful. For some reason it seems to be difficult to spend time only in praise, with thanksgiving drawing the short straw, before returning to petition in our prayer times.

Why the predicament? Thanking God should be as natural as the air we breathe. Should we need to scan the surroundings like a two-year-old to find one more thing to thank God for? As I examine my own heart I wonder if the problem is that, while I've formed the habit of petition, I haven't formed the habit of praise. Perhaps it's down to practice. I don't do it often enough for it to become a part of me. So . . . can we find one more thing to thank God for today?

Thank You, Lord, for Your loving kindness and Your faithfulness towards me. You deserve the praise of my heart, and so much more. I love You, Lord. Amen.

190

25 June

The LORD watches over you –
the LORD is your shade at your right hand.

Psalm 121:5, NIV

Reading: Exodus 13:17–22

Shadows are fascinating. Whichever direction the sun is coming from, when it reaches us it produces an attachment that we can't run away from. It's always there. We cannot be parted from it. In fact, light of any strength will produce a shadow when it comes in contact with an object. Even in almost pitch darkness it is possible to find the slightest of shadows. It's with us wherever we go.

What a deep truth these words carry: 'The LORD is your shade at your right hand.' As our shade He protects us from what might do us harm, all the while attaching Himself to us. God has promised to be with us at all times; He accompanies us. However, when we walk in the Light He is more visible, easily seen, always near. We can't escape His presence, cannot run away from Him – His very shadow becomes part of who we are. We are attached – one and the same. The darkness of sin and suffering may try to blot out the Light, but as the commentator Matthew Henry says, 'The God of Israel is sometimes a God who hides Himself, but never a God who absents Himself; sometimes in the dark, but never at a distance.'[10]

He is known as the invisible God (Colossians 1:15), yet He is always present. As close as at our right hand, in fact. In the light and in the dark, 'The LORD watches over you.'

Lord God, thank You that the shadow of Your Son is forever attached to my mortal frame as I walk in the light. I need not fear, for You are watching over me. Amen.

191

26 June

'Therefore choose life, that both you
and your descendants may live.'
Deuteronomy 30:19

Reading: Deuteronomy 30:15–20

I'm sure someone has researched how many choices the average human being makes every day. Sweater or tee shirt? Coffee or tea? Pasta or rice? Bath or shower? Bus or train? Hardly stretching choices, are they?

However, it was only when a young Eastern European man came to stay with my parents that I realized how much we take for granted. His first visit to a supermarket resulted in full-blown culture shock. 'How do you decide what to buy?' he stammered. 'You have so much to choose from.' Later, he tearfully told my mum how his own mother, a university professor, would visit the market early each morning to see what food was available. Sometimes they'd eat carrots for days simply because there was nothing else to choose from. We are so very privileged, even on the days we feel our choices are limited by our resources.

God frequently puts choices before us that are of far more importance than what we might have for dinner:

- Life or death . . . 'that you may love the LORD your God' (Deuteronomy 30:20).
- God or money . . . 'you cannot serve God and mammon' (Luke 16:13).
- Relationship or rules . . . 'you ignore God's law and substitute your own tradition' (Mark 7:8, NLT).
- Secular or spiritual . . . 'Mary has chosen that good part' (Luke 10:42).
- Love or hate . . . 'love your enemies' (Matthew 5:44).

These choices are not tests that God uses to check our spiritual scores. Neither are we pre-programmed always to do what's right. Within the freedom to choose what is right, God refines our character and draw us closer to Himself.

Father, there are times when I don't make the best of choices, yet You know my heart. May my will be wrapped in Yours as I seek to follow You. Amen.

192

27 June

As you therefore have received Christ Jesus the Lord, so walk in Him.
Colossians 2:6

Reading: Colossians 2:6–9

Dog owners walk whatever the weather. My dad certainly did – sunshine or rain, snow or blow. But it's the long June days that undoubtedly increase the numbers of walkers passing our home each evening. Some people saunter, enjoying talking with a companion as much as the exercise, while others push the word 'walk' to its limit, forging ahead at a serious speed.

Interestingly, the English dictionary defines the word 'walk' in a variety of ways. 'Walk' means 'to move on foot' – pretty predictable. It also means 'to move a large object by rocking'. What picture comes to mind when you read that? I like this definition: 'to be freed from jail or acquitted'. I think the dictionary is being kind here, as 'walk' in this context does not usually evoke thoughts of justice having been served.

For those of us who enjoy a walk, especially when the sun is shining and the days are long, the word simply means going at a measured pace – not rushed, but consistently moving along. That's exactly what Paul was encouraging the Colossians to do. Christ now lives in us, the apostle reminded them, so walk in Him.

We are to take a measured pace, becoming firmly established in what the Saviour wants us to learn. That way we can recognize those trying to cheat us 'through philosophy and empty deceit ... and not according to Christ' (Colossians 2:8). Don't try to rush on ahead of Christ's guidance. He knows exactly where the potholes are, knows the places where we might fall. We can't impress Him. He's not in a hurry. Walking means we will consistently make progress and head in the direction He wants us to go. And we will no doubt be blessed by our conversation with Him along the way.

Lord Jesus, I want to walk with You each and every day. May I never rush ahead, but enjoy each step of the journey with You by my side. Amen.

193

28 June

Walk in the Spirit, and you shall not fulfill
the lust of the flesh.

Galatians 5:16

Reading: Galatians 5:16–18

O for a closer walk with God,
a calm and heavenly frame,
a light to shine upon the road
that leads me to the Lamb.

Where is the blessedness I knew
when first I saw the Lord?
Where is that soul-refreshing view
of Jesus and His word?

Return, O Holy Dove! Return,
sweet messenger of rest!
I hate the sins that made Thee mourn,
and drove Thee from my breast.

The dearest idol I have known,
what'er that idol be,
help me to tear it from Thy throne,
and worship only Thee.

So shall my walk be close with God,
calm and serene my frame;
so purer light shall mark the road
that leads me to the Lamb.[11]

This is my prayer, Lord. Amen.

29 June

'You are worthy, O Lord,
To receive glory and honor and power;
For You created all things,
And by Your will they exist and were created.'
Revelation 4:11

Reading: Revelation 4:8–11

Walking and worshipping should be interchangeable. As we walk with Christ we cannot help but worship Him. Unfortunately, methods of praising God in church can sometimes cause division. How different from places where God's children face persecution for daring to worship their Lord at all.

The woman our friends met in the coffee shop barely raised her head the whole time they spoke together. Where she lives, looking someone in the eye is seen as challenging authority. She had bravely left her country on a short visitor's visa, with the threat of imprisonment for her family if she didn't return at the allotted time. In a voice barely above a whisper she told them how her father had disappeared one day, never to return. It was only years later that she discovered he was taken from them because the authorities discovered he was a Christian – a crime against the state punishable by death or imprisonment in a labour camp. They still do not know if he is alive or dead.

What little they could see of her eyes lit up as she talked about the church meeting in her home. A hole has been dug under her tiny house, where eight believers can squeeze in, shoulder to shoulder, to worship together and learn from God's Word. But they daren't sing, in case someone hears them and reports them to the authorities. This sister in Christ knows more about worship than we ever will, for hers is truly 'the sacrifice of praise', spoken of in Hebrews 13:15, that undoubtedly delights the Father's heart.

Lord of the universe, worthy of all my praise, forgive me for wanting to do it my way. Please bless and protect Your children around the world today who truly worship You in spirit and in truth. Amen.

195

30 June

A PASSAGE TO PONDER

To you, O LORD, I lift up my soul;

in you I trust, O my God.

Do not let me be put to shame,

nor let my enemies triumph over me.

No-one whose hope is in you

will ever be put to shame,

but they will be put to shame

who are treacherous without cause.

Show me your ways, O LORD,

teach me your paths;

guide me in Your truth and teach me,

for You are God my Saviour,

and my hope is in you all day long.

Remember, O LORD, your great mercy and love,

for they are from of old.

Remember not the sins of my youth

and my rebellious ways;

according to your love remember me,

for You are good, O LORD.

Psalm 25:1–7, NIV

Read through the passage slowly and let the Author to speak to you. As you ponder, ask yourself these questions:

- What does it say?
- What does it mean?
- What is God saying to me?
- How should I respond?

July

1 July

There are diversities of gifts,
but the same Spirit.
There are diversities of ministries,
but the same Lord.

1 Corinthians 12:4–5

Reading: 1 Corinthians 12:1–6

The conference had been going well. The large church was filled to capacity but I felt unusually alone in the crowd. The evening worship was a lot livelier than I was used to, but the preacher was excellent. Then he asked those within the gathering who had the gift of tongues to lead us in singing. I rolled my eyes at the thought of what might come next.

For about twenty seconds I felt vindicated in my unspoken criticism as a cacophony of noise filled the building. Then, quite suddenly, much of the noise disappeared, and what remained was the most beautiful sound I have ever heard. The harmony was breathtaking and the sound moved through the space like a welcome gentle breeze. The sense of God's nearness was such that this cynical soul was first convicted of her arrogance, and then humbled to have been given the opportunity to experience God's presence in this way. What was it that happened that evening?

I can only explain what happened that evening as the Spirit's gift to some in the gathering to lead us in praise through the use of music and words that were supernatural. I guess the next time I will experience similar worship will be in heaven.

Gifts often come to us because of birthdays or Christmas – the best arriving unexpectedly. But a gift is useless unless it is accepted, and of little value if left unused. The gifts of the Spirit are also given for a purpose – primarily to empower the receiver to do something to bless the church, but always, ultimately, to bring glory to God. While we are also personally blessed, gifts are not given to make us look spiritual, but to point to the gracious God who gives them.

Lord, forgive me when I'm critical about what I don't understand. May I accept Your gifts to bless others and glorify Your name. Amen.

2 July

A spiritual gift is given to each of us as a means of helping the entire church.

1 Corinthians 12:7, NLT

Reading: 1 Corinthians 12:7–11

Many of our churches are filled with very talented people who have a natural, or even an inherited, ability to perform certain tasks or roles that undoubtedly are extremely useful to the family of God. However, we need to be careful not to mistake natural ability with the specific gifting of the Holy Spirit. Churches merely filled with clever people and well-organized programmes will neither empty hell of lost souls nor produce changed lives. That's the work of the Holy Spirit, a work He often chooses to do through gifting individuals. How can we recognize the difference?

That's not easy to answer, but the bottom line is that spiritual gifts are all about service. They are given not as a sign of special favour, but rather as a special ability to serve Christ and the church. To ensure a believer didn't become proud over the gifts he was given, the apostle Paul told him 'not to think of himself more highly than he ought to think' (Romans 12:3). As we look at others, we sometimes see them as more valuable to the church than we are. That's not the case, for in Romans 12:6ff Paul goes on to list the spiritual gifts, and I love that in these verses there is no hierarchical structure included. Each gift is seen to be as important as the others, whether it is the gift of encouragement, giving, praying, preaching, teaching, or meeting the physical and emotional needs of others. The only proviso is that what God gives us to do we should do 'with cheerfulness' (Romans 12:8). That becomes much easier when we realize that the focus is not on us, but on Him, and the benefit not for us, but for others.

Is it any wonder that Paul says, 'desire spiritual gifts' (1 Corinthians 14:1)?

Lord, my desire is to be the person You want me to be. Fill me, Lord, and equip me for whatever You have planned. Amen.

3 July

Having then gifts differing according to the grace that is given to us, let us use them.

Romans 12:6

Reading: Romans 12:6–13

My husband loves to try to guess what's inside a gift before getting down to opening it, but me – I just rip the paper off!

How can we use our spiritual gifts if we don't know what they are? If, as 1 Corinthians 12:7 says, we have each been given a gift, how can we unwrap it and discover not only its identity but also what it is God wants us to do with it? The clue for me is in the prefix – 'spiritual' gifts. You can't receive or unwrap such a thing unless the 'spiritual' is already present in your life. To be more accurate, a spiritual gift can only be given to you if the Holy Spirit already lives within you through salvation in Christ.

In Samaria there was a man called Simon who wanted the gift of power that the apostles displayed, and offered them money for it. Rebuking him for his folly, Peter said, 'You can have no part in this, for your heart is not right with God' (Acts 8:21, NLT). Some today also have an interest in the Holy Spirit, and are especially curious for the more unusual gifts of speaking in tongues, prophecy and healing. But an interest in the supernatural is not the same as having a relationship with the supernatural God. Beware of modern-day Simons.

Discovering our gifts only comes from walking with Him, who is the Giver. Lives given completely to Christ allow His Spirit free course to work in us. As God transforms our lives, the gift will be unwrapped and we will know His will for us (Romans 12:1–2). There is no magic formula. Yes, others can pray for us and with us, but ultimately it is God – the Power Source – who gifts us when and how He chooses. But remember: 'To whom much is given, from him much will be required' (Luke 12:48).

Holy Spirit, my life is Yours. Access all areas and change me from within. Amen.

4 July

But earnestly desire the best gifts.
And yet I show you a more excellent way.
1 Corinthians 12:31

Reading: 1 Corinthians 13:4–10

In many ways, the Corinthians were just like us. They were interested in what we might term the 'showy' gifts, especially speaking in tongues. Paul appeared to think the gift of prophecy to be of the greatest importance to the church (1 Corinthians 13:2), but he wanted the Corinthians, and us, to look for a more excellent way of handling the gifts given to us. It doesn't matter what gift you have if it is not underpinned with love, so Paul reminds us that love:

- is patient and kind;
- is not jealous nor boastful nor proud nor rude;
- does not demand its own way;
- is not irritable;
- keeps no records of when it has been wronged;
- is never glad about injustice but rejoices when the truth wins out;
- never gives up;
- never loses faith;
- is always hopeful;
- endures through every circumstance.

(1 Corinthians 13:4–7, NLT)

In fact, 'Love will last forever . . . but when the end comes, these special gifts will all disappear' (1 Corinthians 13:8, 10, NLT).

Is it any wonder that Paul calls this 'a more excellent way' (1 Corinthians 12:31)?

Lord Jesus, Your Word says that if I don't have love, I have nothing. While I desire Your gifting, may I never seek it without craving for love first and foremost. Amen.

5 July

And now abide faith, hope, love, these three;
but the greatest of these is love.

1 Corinthians 13:13

Reading: Hebrews 11:1–6

It's very interesting to see how people react when my husband tells them he is a Christian minister, usually in answer to the question, 'What do you work at?'

One gentleman immediately responded with, 'I'm sure you'd like to hear this story about faith', and proceeded to share it with him.

> I was driving down past our local train station recently when I noticed this African woman standing on the footpath outside, one big suitcase perched either side of her on the ground. So I stopped and went to speak to her.
>
> 'You look lost,' I remarked. 'Can I help you?'
>
> The woman smiled a big smile and replied that she wasn't lost. Remarkable, considering she told me she'd just arrived from Africa for her first ever visit to Ireland to visit her son. It transpired she'd got off the train a stop too soon. She had no idea where she was.
>
> I repeated myself, saying that I'd thought she'd looked a bit lost, which was why I'd stopped. Once more she denied her predicament. 'No, I'm not lost,' she continued. 'I was just standing here, praying that the Lord would send someone along to help me. And look,' she continued, tapping her watch, 'it took Him just fifteen minutes to send you. I'm not lost. He knows exactly where I am.'

How remarkable! This lady had crossed continents and arrived in a country she'd never visited before, yet was totally unfazed when her travel plans went wrong. Faith was her natural default setting. It had become as natural as breathing. The God who made the universe knew exactly where she was, so she didn't need to worry about it. Instead she waited until He sorted out her problem. And it only took Him fifteen minutes!

Lord of the universe, how easily I fret over things that are already under Your control. Help me to choose faith over worry, trust before fear. Amen.

6 July

Let us hold unswervingly to the hope we profess,
for he who promised is faithful.

Hebrews 10:23, NIV

Reading: Hebrews 10:19–23

There are some things that naturally go together, like fish and chips, strawberries and cream, pen and paper, hot and cold. Think of one, and the other quickly follows.

What follows after 'faith' at the close of Paul's unforgettable 1 Corinthians 13 discourse doesn't quite roll off the tongue in the same way. Faith and hope together? Surely not? Faith is absolute trust in something or someone – certain they will come through for us. Hope appears to express the complete opposite – uncertainty. We can wish and dream, but nothing is sure. Yet in the Bible the two are inseparable. As the old song says, 'You can't have one without the other!'

We tend to think of hope with a cross-your-fingers mentality, but in biblical terms the emphasis is on certainty. A certainty that has its confidence in God's faithfulness. A belief that what has been promised will come true. God always comes through on what He says – a hundred times out of a hundred. Therefore hope is an essential component of faith. While faith can refer to the past, present and future, hope focuses our minds on the future. What God promises, He delivers. That's why we can be confident about whatever lies ahead, why we can be bold in our declaration of who God is, and why we are sure of Heaven one day. 'Hope is faith in the future tense'[12] (John Piper).

Our hope rests on certainty . . . 'for he who promised is faithful'. This is what keeps us going through all that life throws at us. Is it any wonder that Paul tells us that hope along with its bedfellows faith and love are what will remain long after the gifts are gone?

Lord Jesus, faith in You is essential for traversing life's journey, while hope provides the certainty I need for the future. Love should be the response of my life for all I receive through You. I pray it will be so. Amen.

204

7 July

A PASSAGE TO PONDER

And yet I show you a more excellent way.

Though I speak with the tongues of men and of angels,

but have not love, I have become sounding brass or a clanging cymbal.

And though I have the gift of prophecy,

and understand all mysteries and all knowledge,

and though I have faith, so that I could remove mountains,

but have not love, I am nothing.

And though I bestow all my goods to feed the poor,

and though I give my body to be burned,

but have not love, it profits me nothing.

1 Corinthians 12:31 – 13:3

Read through the passage slowly and let the Author speak to you. As you ponder, ask yourself these questions:

- What does it say?
- What does it mean?
- What is God saying to me?
- How will I respond?

8 July

Continue earnestly in prayer, being vigilant in it with thanksgiving; meanwhile praying also for us.
Colossians 4:2–3

Reading: 2 Corinthians 13:7–10

What do you pray about most of all? My guess is that much of our praying is focused on those closest to us – family and friends in particular. Nothing wrong with that, of course, but Paul demonstrates a passion and commitment in praying for others that is enormously challenging. While he encourages earnestness, vigilance and thanksgiving in their prayers, Paul asks the Colossians to pray for him and for his companions in addition to the things already preoccupying them. It seems that praying for others was as important to Paul as evangelism, teaching and leadership. Whatever he had to say in his letters to the churches, Paul invariably told them how, and what, he was praying for them:

- **To the Corinthians:** In his first letter Paul starts by thanking God for them. He finishes his second letter to them by praying that they 'do no evil', and 'be made complete' in Christ (2 Corinthians 13:7, 9).
- **To the Galatians:** He prays a blessing over them (Galatians 6:18).
- **To the Ephesians:** He asks that the Lord Jesus 'may give to you the spirit of wisdom and revelation in the knowledge of Him' (Ephesians 1:17). And that's after affirming that he never ceases to pray for them!
- **To the Philippians:** He is exuberant in his prayers for them with joy, thanks and confidence, while longing that their 'love may abound still more and more' (Philippians 1:9).
- **To the Colossians:** He tells them he is 'praying always' for them (Colossians 1:3).

What a thrill and encouragement that must have been for those struggling believers. Paul was praying for them. And what an example to follow.

Lord Jesus, forgive me if my praying is self-obsessed. Touch my heart for those of the household of faith who need encouragement today, that I might bring their needs before Your throne. Amen.

9 July

Bear one another's burdens,
and so fulfill the law of Christ.
Galatians 6:2

Reading: 2 Corinthians 1:8–11

The great William Booth, founder of the Salvation Army, was due to address a large convention in London. The building was full of excited people eagerly anticipating what the great man would have to say.

However, at the last minute he became ill and was unable to travel to the meeting, so instead he quickly sent a telegram to be read to the disappointed crowd. The telegram was opened on stage with not a little pomp and ceremony. The gathered throng hushed to listen. The reader of the message carefully opened the telegram, cleared his throat, and spoke the contents loud and clear.

'Others!'[13]

That was it! The entirety of William Booth's message was one word. No mini-sermon had been enclosed. No Bible reference for them to flick through the pages of their Bibles to find and study when they arrived home. Just one word – Others!

In many ways William Booth did turn up at the huge gathering that evening, for the word he sent was more than a message: it summed up the man himself. His life was completely devoted to others. There was nothing more for him to say. His burden for others, especially those without hope in this life and the next, consumed him completely. The words of Galatians 6:2 ran through his being much like the name of a seaside town runs through a stick of rock.

The church of Jesus Christ should be forever grateful for those who have taught us the vital importance of social action. Bearing the burdens of others is a direct command, one that ought constantly to engage us physically, emotionally and spiritually. However, Paul's example taught us the importance of bearing one another's burdens in prayer. His 'telegrams' were also full of the word 'others'!

Lord, the time for action is now. A hurting, lost world needs me not only to think of them but to act on their behalf. Teach me to pray for others, Lord. Amen.

10 July

That He would grant you, according to the riches
of His glory, to be strengthened with might
through His Spirit in the inner man.

Ephesians 3:16

Reading: Ephesians 3:14–21

So how can we pray for others? Where do we start? We are privileged to learn from a master. Paul has left us some wonderful examples of exactly how to go about praying for others – even for those we have never met.

In his prayer for the Ephesian believers, the apostle starts by asking that they would receive strength to replace their weakness: 'That God will give you mighty inner strength' (verse 16, NLT). Do you ever feel weak, or tired in the journey? Are you feeling ill-equipped for something God has asked you to do? Do you feel like giving up, wishing someone else would carry the load instead of you? Has your strength all but gone? If so, you can be sure others feel that way too. Someone right now needs us to pray that God will replace their weakness with strength.

Thankfully, we are not praying for mere human strength for others but rather for God's strength to be granted, 'according to the riches of His glory' (Ephesians 3:16). Imagine, God can replace our weakness with His strength, and that will never run out. God's strength comes directly out of His unlimited resources, and His heart is so generous towards us that He can't stop giving.

Paul prayed for tired, persecuted believers, that their inevitable weakness would be exchanged for God's strength. He knew they couldn't face life without God's enablement, which would never be exhausted, even when they were. What would happen if we were to pray for each other in the same way? God's strength in exchange for our weakness? That's an exchange with no losers.

Time to get praying, Lord. So many of us are tired of struggling through the day. Please complete that exchange in the life of the person who is on my mind right now. Amen.

208

11 July

That Christ may dwell in your hearts through faith.
Ephesians 3:17

Reading: Ephesians 3:14–21

Having prayed first of all about what he recognized as the most common condition afflicting believers – weakness – Paul turned his prayers for them in a different direction. It was the apostle's deepest desire that followers of Jesus might truly experience Christ abiding in their hearts. A mere head knowledge of Jesus wouldn't do; Paul wanted them to live every day in the reality of the Saviour constantly with them.

This was an entirely new concept for the members of this fledgling church. Worshipping a god had always been about bringing stuff to *him*, providing sacrifice, doing what the priests told you would please the deity. There was never a possibility of the deity actually being with you in the true sense of word, even if a little carved image jingled in your pocket. Therefore, God 'in your hearts' was as foreign to the Ephesians as bringing the stars inside. That's why Paul prayed for them, that they might be convinced of Christ dwelling in them ... through faith. Another exchange had already taken place to reach that point. Christ had come to live in their hearts in exchange for allowing Him to deal with the sin and the selfish nature that once had houseroom. The transformation had begun, but Paul asked for more.

In the end, Christ making Himself 'more and more at home in your hearts' (verse 17, NLT) all came down to trusting Him to do just that. Simple faith. Problem is, faith isn't always simple to us today. We like to have things explained before we believe them. As we pray for each other, let's ask for the simplicity to believe that Christ really can make Himself more and more at home in our hearts, as we trust Him. The answer to this prayer will be transformative.

Lord Jesus, I cannot hold You in my hands, but I can experience You dwelling in my heart by faith. As I pray that others might experience this truth, please transform my heart too. Amen.

209

12 July

May you experience the love of Christ,
though it is so great you will never fully understand it.
Ephesians 3:19, NLT

Reading: John 3:14–17

She should never have left the house. At least Donna's heart didn't race when she stayed inside. Why had she promised to go to the hall that day? The argument subsided when she reached a door that needed a lick of paint as much as her own did. She was glad it wasn't fancy. She couldn't cope with fancy. The little 'un enjoyed playing on the toy-strewn floor. It kept him happy while Donna calmed her nerves with a strong brew, complete with two heaped spoonfuls of sugar. Seemed a friendly enough place. And they had biscuits.

'God so loved the world' was all Donna heard before her hackles rose. She'd liked the young woman who was speaking until she said that. She'd always hated liars, and this girl wasn't telling the truth. God couldn't love her. No-one had ever loved her. Not even her own mother and father. She'd enough broken bones and belt marks to prove it to anyone who doubted her. Every man she'd ever known had used her as a punchbag . . . and she'd learnt to hit back nearly as hard. No – God couldn't love the likes of her.

The young woman nervously held her ground, even with Donna's accusing finger in her face. As they sat on the floor together Donna argued, then listened, as the young woman showed her from the Bible that God really did love her . . . no matter what anyone else had told her. He'd even loved her enough to send His Son to die so that her sins could be forgiven. It was overwhelming. Donna testifies that 'the first person to ever tell me He loved me was Jesus'.

And the young woman thanked God that her prayer for Donna to experience His love had been answered in the most amazing way.

Lord Jesus, thank You for showing Donna that You love her. Teach me to pray that others might discover the extent of Your love for themselves. Amen.

13 July

The Lord will keep you from all harm – he will watch over your life.
Psalm 121:7, NIV

Reading: Psalm 91:11–16

I'm very grateful for those who pray for me as I travel many miles each year to speak at engagements. I thought I knew who they were, until one night I found myself in hospital after an accident on the motorway. The weather had been atrocious on the journey home. The visibility was poor because of the heavy rain. Suddenly the car was hit by an out-of-control vehicle from the fast lane and we were shunted off the carriageway. It was both scary and painful.

The next day I received a private message on social media from a lady who was very distraught about my accident, and particularly disappointed that God had not answered her specific prayers that night to keep me safe. I was deeply touched, but recognized that God had indeed answered her prayers. That was one message to which I happily replied.

You see, my friend and I were to travel to Belfast in my little C3 as her car was in for a service that day. At the last minute she had her car returned and we made our journey in her substantial 4X4. While being attended to after the accident, I mentioned the car swap to the paramedic. His immediate response was, 'If you'd been travelling in a C3 we wouldn't be having this conversation right now. This car likely saved your life.'

So God had answered that lady's prayer that night. She'd seen the weather forecast and stopped to pray for Catherine Campbell's journey. God had not let her, or me, down. I couldn't help but smile as I also told her that the vehicle travelling directly behind us was an unoccupied ambulance! God had it all under control.

Thank You, Lord, for Your hand of protection on my life. Thank You also for the prayers of others. Amen.

14 July

A PASSAGE TO PONDER

For this reason we also, since the day we heard it,

do not cease to pray for you,

and to ask that you may be filled with the knowledge of His will

in all wisdom and spiritual understanding;

that you may walk worthy of the Lord,

fully pleasing Him, being fruitful in every good work

and increasing in the knowledge of God;

strengthened with all might, according to His glorious power,

for all patience and longsuffering with joy;

giving thanks to the Father who has qualified us

to be partakers of the inheritance of the saints in light.

Colossians 1:9–12

Read through the passage slowly and let the Author speak to you. As you ponder, ask yourself these questions:

- What does it say?
- What does it mean?
- What is God saying to me?
- How will I respond?

15 July

And it happened when He was in a certain city,
that behold, a man who was full of leprosy saw Jesus;
and he fell on his face and implored Him, saying,
'Lord, if you are willing, You can make me clean.'
Luke 5:12

Reading: Luke 5:12–16

Meeting Jesus is always life changing. Some people turn away from Him, unwilling to respond to His challenge, yet unaware of how that will affect every day of the rest of their lives, and beyond. Others will discover that for the remainder of life's journey Jesus' presence will provide more than they ever dreamed.

Some will even experience a miraculous touch, like the man we read about in Luke 5:12. This man had life-changing words spoken to him on two occasions. The first time was when the local priest declared him unclean when skin lesions were first visible on his body. We can't imagine what it was like for him suddenly to be treated as an outcast: losing his home, family, community, employment and even the opportunity to worship at the synagogue.

By the time he met Jesus he was 'full of leprosy'. His deformities at this stage of the disease, mixed with the smell emanating from his torso, would have made him totally repulsive. Yet Jesus 'put out His hand and touched him' (Luke 5:13). That touch, never mind the immediate healing, must have been overwhelming. No-one had touched him in years. Then in response to Jesus' life-changing words, 'I am willing; be cleansed' (verse 13), he felt the nose growing on his face again, and his limbs receive back their toes and fingers. Soon, he'd be able to run back home. For this man, meeting Jesus was something he would never forget.

Ostracism of a different kind can touch any of our lives. But meeting Jesus still has the power to confirm who we really are: people of worth – people He wants to touch. People He loves. That is truly life changing.

Thank You, Jesus, that You still touch the lives of the ostracized in our society, and even in our churches. Amen.

16 July

'Daughter, your faith has made you well.
Go in peace, and be healed of your affliction.'
Mark 5:34

Reading: Mark 5:25–34

Jesus knew that power had gone out of Him, and Reumah had the sneaking suspicion that He already knew it was she who had touched him, as His eyes met hers in the crowd. Moving forward to own up, she trembled visibly with fear. Now it was her turn to be on her knees before the only One who could heal – the One who had changed her life. And she simply told Jesus all about it.

She told Him about her sickness, her helplessness, her attempts at cures, and how, when she had heard about Him, she knew, finally, that she only had to touch the edge of His garment and she would be healed. As she spoke to Him, the crowds seemed to disappear, and she knew for that moment she was His only concern. Hearing Jesus' first word, her fear melted away.

'Daughter,' He said, 'your faith has made you well.'

Suddenly it struck Reumah that it wasn't superstition about some piece of magical cloth that had healed her. Rather, it was faith in this man – this Jesus, who was like no other she had ever met.

His captivating words held her gaze: 'Go in peace, and be free from your suffering.'

She didn't want to leave the ground where she was kneeling before Jesus, but as she watched Jesus turn back to speak to Jairus, Reumah knew that meeting Jesus had changed her life for ever.[14]

Lord Jesus, I am deeply moved by Your tenderness when people fall at Your feet. Whether sick, sad or sinner, You reach out to each one of us with such compassion that our lives are forever changed. Amen.

17 July

'One thing you lack: Go your way, sell whatever you have and give to the poor, and you will have treasure in heaven; and come, take up the cross, and follow Me.'

Mark 10:21

Reading: Mark 10:17–22

Not everyone who met Jesus went away happy. But everyone who met Him went away changed.

Jesus was on His way out of the city when the young man caught up with Him and His travelling companions. He was out of breath by the time he got to Jesus; clearly he had something serious on his mind. 'Good Teacher,' he asked, kneeling in the dust, 'what shall I do that I may inherit eternal life?' (Mark 10:17). Not a question Jesus was often asked by the wealthy religious. It appeared that this young man was aware that something wasn't right with his soul. Maybe this rabbi could give him the one piece of advice he needed to make that unsettled feeling disappear. He'd do anything to gain eternal life. Well, almost anything.

He thought he'd done everything the Law had asked of him up to that point, and as Jesus looked at him, He had a tender spot in His heart for him (verse 21). Rehearsing his spiritual pedigree to Jesus didn't give him what he wanted. Instead of the 'Great, what a good boy you are; keep up with the good works', he had longed to hear, Jesus pointed out the flaw the young man hadn't detected in his religiosity. He didn't love the Lord God with all *his* heart, or his neighbour as *himself* (Matthew 22:37, 39), for that matter after all. Jesus quickly identified his idol – the one thing he loved more than God.

It turned out the young man preferred the treasure in his pocket to the kind he could lay up in heaven, and so 'he was sad at this word, and went away sorrowful, for he had great possessions' (Mark 10:22).

Lord, I can't imagine meeting with Jesus and going away sad. May I choose the real treasure every time. Amen.

18 July

Now when Herod saw Jesus, he was exceedingly glad;
for he had desired for a long time to see Him,
because he had heard many things about Him, and
he hoped to see some miracle done by Him.

Luke 23:8

Reading: Luke 23:6–12

There were many people who wanted to see Jesus during His life, just as there are those who are fascinated by Him today. He had become rather famous after all. A miracle-worker. An orator. Anti-establishment. A troublemaker. Herod Antipas even wondered if Jesus might be John the Baptist back from the dead to haunt him (Matthew 14:2).

Pilate had declared Jesus innocent on three occasions (Luke 23:4, 14, 22) but still couldn't convince the Jewish leaders to release Him, so he sent Him to Herod Antipas – local ruler, adulterer and murderer. Herod was hoping that some excitement might ensue after struggling out of bed early that morning at Pilate's request. Perhaps this Jesus he'd heard so much about might perform some magic trick or miracle? After all, Herod did have the power to kill Him or to let Him live. That fact alone should make for an interesting show. This despicable king mocked Jesus, scorned Him and threatened Him, but Jesus didn't respond to the man who had murdered His cousin John, and Herod couldn't find Him guilty either.

So Herod sent Jesus back to the Roman governor robed like a king, hoping Pilate would find it funny. But God is not mocked by our attempts at trying to ridicule His Son. A few years later Herod himself was falsely accused of treason. He lost all his money, land and power, and eventually died in exile.

He'd come face to face with Jesus but wasted his opportunity to have his life changed, his sins forgiven or his eternal destiny secured. What a waste!

Heavenly Father, You give us opportunities to come face to face with Your Son, yet Jesus is still scorned by the very ones He came to save. Have mercy, Lord. Forgive us, Lord. Amen.

19 July

Then they came to Jesus, and saw the one who had been demon-possessed and had the legion, sitting and clothed and in his right mind.

Mark 5:15

Reading: Mark 5:1–15

Those whose tombs he shared for sleeping called him to death, but his masters wouldn't even let him go there. And the swineherds working nearby could never know the torment behind his screams. He truly was a man possessed.

There was no sleep to be had that night. As the dawn started to push back the night skies, the tormented man crept out of the tombs. Walking up the hill, he trembled, the air cool and clear against his skin after the storm of the previous night. Some distance below, in the small harbour, Legion watched the activity surrounding a small fishing boat. Fishermen with their tunics tucked up around their waists secured the vessel to the wooden pier with ropes.

He began to experience something new – fear. Until now, his life had been marked by anger, strength and violence, his possessors ensuring that everyone he encountered was afraid of him. Yet what remained of the real him sensed that they were afraid – of what, or of whom, Legion didn't know.

A battle of immense magnitude was raging inside his mortal frame. In a split second of time, Legion saw the cause of his tormentors' fear. It was the Man who was stepping off the boat on to the shore. He was the one hell had tried to drown in the storm the night before – the one whom Legion's possessors recognized immediately. And, deep inside his real self, Legion knew that the Man on the boat had come through the storm just for him.[15]

Lord, there is little more frightening than feeling out of control. Thank You for this beautiful truth that You came through the storm for just one man. Thank You that You are the One who can liberate me from whatever holds me prisoner. Amen.

217

20 July

But Jesus said, 'Let the little children come to Me.
Don't stop them! For the Kingdom of Heaven belongs
to those who are like these children.'

Matthew 19:14, NLT

Reading: Matthew 18:1–6

Wherever Jesus went, the crowds followed. Where the mothers went, the children were brought along. Little ones hung on to their mamas' skirts, while the older ones played around the edges of the gathering with whatever they could find. Imagine what it was like to watch Jesus work miracles without the suspicions of the adult mind, wondering was Jesus a fake, a magician, a conman? Children eagerly believed what they saw and heard. The innocence of their faith was what Jesus said was needed to belong to the kingdom of heaven.

But when mothers brought their children to Jesus to receive a blessing, the boys and girls were pushed back by the disciples. The whole experience must have been very frightening, until Jesus spoke up, rebuking the disciples for their behaviour. For Him, children weren't merely a good illustration to use about faith. Each individual child was important to the Saviour. He warned the listening crowd that if anyone caused a child to sin, then it would be better to have a millstone tied to them before being drowned in the sea. Serious rebuke, or what?! And I've seen those Middle Eastern millstones strewn about the ruins of Capernaum. They're huge.

Jesus undoubtedly loves children to meet with Him. Boys and girls can trust in Jesus for themselves, and how wonderful to know that He will stand against those who dare to lead astray a little one who believes in Him (Matthew 18:6, NLT). We have been warned.

Lord Jesus, thank You that it is possible for children to meet You, and to trust in You as Saviour. Help me to encourage those little ones who are following You. Amen.

218

21 July

A PASSAGE TO PONDER

Now when Jesus had entered Capernaum,

a centurion came to Him, pleading with Him, saying,

'Lord, my servant is lying at home paralyzed, dreadfully tormented.'

And Jesus said to him, 'I will come and heal him.'

The centurion answered and said,

'Lord, I am not worthy that You should come under my roof.

But only speak a word, and my servant will be healed.

For I also am a man under authority, having soldiers under me.

And I say to this one, "Go," and he goes;

and to another, "Come," and he comes;

and to my servant, "Do this," and he does it.'

When Jesus heard it, He marveled, and said to those who followed,

'Assuredly, I say to you,

I have not found such great faith, not even in Israel!'

Matthew 8:5–10

Read through the passage slowly and let the Author speak to you. As you ponder, ask yourself these questions:

- What does it say?
- What does it mean?
- What is God saying to me?
- How will I respond?

219

22 July

'I appeared to Abraham, to Isaac, and to Jacob,
as God Almighty [El Shaddai], but by My name
LORD [Yahweh] I was not known to them.'
Exodus 6:3

Reading: Exodus 3:13–15

There are occasions in the Bible when God changes a person's name, usually to denote the transformation they experienced after a specific encounter with Him. Abram became Abraham, Jacob became Israel, Saul became Paul, and so on.

However, the names God uses for Himself are intended to reveal who He is and what He intends to do. They reinforce His character to us, which should evoke worship, reverence and trust in return. Knowing someone's name is the first step in building relationship. God is a relational God. He not only wants us to know who He is, He also wants us to know Him.

God calls Himself by the name 'Yahweh' in the Old Testament more often than by any other name. It is regarded as so sacred by the Jews that they don't speak it, and only write it without the vowels: YHWH. In our English Bible versions, the word LORD (in small capitals) is the translation of YHWH. While the Bible writers use this name for God from the very beginning of Genesis, God first introduces Himself as YHWH to Moses when He meets with him at the burning bush (Exodus 3:13–15).

The runaway prince was to return to deliver God's people from the Egyptians, and to tell them 'I AM' – which is interchangeable with YHWH in the Hebrew – had sent him. 'I AM', 'YHWH', signifies that God's self-existing nature cannot be separated from His eternal presence. He is, and will be, there with them and for them. He is alive, and none can rival His power, as they would soon discover.

Centuries later, God speaks through Malachi to remind His ancient people that even today He remains the unchangeable 'I AM': 'For I am the LORD [YHWH], I do not change' (Malachi 3:6). He is still with us, and for us.

Unchangeable One, thank You that I can have confidence in Your great name. Amen.

23 July

'I am the LORD, that is My name;
And My glory I will not give to another.'
Isaiah 42:8

Reading: Genesis 22:11–14

I was distressed as I listened to a group of ladies complain about how a nearby church was changing their pew Bibles to a newer translation. I interjected, asking if any of us present spoke Hebrew, Aramaic or Greek? Didn't they know that the Bible was neither handed through the clouds in English, nor in a certain translation? My sanctification was tested. Translations of the Bible still cause dissention among believers, and sometimes a particular word caused problems for those who painstakingly translated God's Word in order that we might have it in our own language today.

The word YHWH is a perfect example. The original biblical text was first translated into Latin, and when it was further translated into English a German translator had difficulty with the letters Y and W and replaced them with J and V. Vowels were added to make the word readable for us, and the final word that came from the Hebrew YHWH was JEHOVAH. Today, many translations simply use the capitalized LORD to cover up this apparent error.

Yet, when suffixed by other words, the term 'Jehovah' produces beautifully descriptive names for the LORD – YHWH.

- **Jehovah-Jireh, The-Lord-Will-Provide**, was the perfect name for Abraham to give to the place where God provided a substitute sacrifice in place of Isaac (Genesis 22:14).
- **Jehovah-Nissi: The-Lord-Is-My-Banner**. Banners and flags symbolized unity and strength, so when Moses built a commemorative altar signifying Jehovah's victory over the Amalekites, he declared the LORD as their strength (Exodus 17:15).

Lord, thank You that Your name covers it all. Be glorified in my life. Amen.

24 July

'And the name of the city from that day shall be:
THE LORD IS THERE.'
Ezekiel 48:35

Reading: Revelation 21:1–3

There have probably been many times when you, like me, have asked someone to explain what they've just said. It's important to know exactly what the person is saying, so that we can make an appropriate response.

It appears that Ezekiel was using one of God's titles by which to name a city. 'Jehovah-Shammah' is translated as 'THE LORD IS THERE'. What was the prophet talking about? Prophets deal with future things, particularly by conveying what God is saying. Their words are not their own – they are delivery boys.

When you've been using the 'Passages to Ponder' each week, I've suggested you ask yourself some questions as you read. This verse is perfect for such examination.

What does it say? The book of Ezekiel is about delivering God's message of judgment, and also God's promises of what will happen when the Israelites return from exile in Babylon. In context, Ezekiel is telling them about the rebuilt Jerusalem.

What does it mean? The meanings are layered. God is addressing the Israelites, through the prophet, as Jehovah-Shammah – always present. He will be in Jerusalem when they return, and will never leave them.

What is God saying to me? Peel back another layer and you discover that this prophecy travelled the centuries where God declares Himself Jehovah-Shammah to His church. THE LORD IS THERE in every believer, as promised in Matthew 28:20: 'I am with you always.' Scholars also explain that this will not be completely fulfilled until we dwell in the New Jerusalem where He (Jehovah-Shammah) 'will dwell with them' (Revelation 21:3).

How will I respond? You fill in the blanks!

Jehovah-Shammah, thank You that You have been true to Your word in my life. Thank You for always being there for me. I look forward to the rest. Amen.

25 July

The LORD is my shepherd;
I shall not want.

Psalm 23:1

Reading: Psalm 23

There seem to be charts for everything. The Top Ten most popular tourist destinations. Top Ten Movies. Top Ten Investment Solutions. Top Ten Singles Charts. There are even charts for the Top Ten Hymns . . . and the Top Ten Bible Verses. It will not surprise you to know that Psalm 23 is always rated as one of the Top Ten Favourite Bible Passages.

And right at the start of the Psalm we find one of God's most beautiful names: Jehovah-Rohe . . . Jehovah my Shepherd. Many of God's names in the Old Testament can be identified in the New Testament, and this is one that Jesus publicly used of Himself in John 10 when He said, 'I am the good shepherd. The good shepherd gives His life for the sheep' (verse 11).

Many theologians have recognized in Psalm 23 a picture of God's identity through His names as expressed in each verse. It's wonderful!

- Verse 1: Jehovah-Rohe – The LORD My Shepherd
- Jehovah-Jireh – The LORD Will Provide
- Verse 2: Jehovah-Shalom – The LORD Is Peace
- Verse 3: Jehovah-Tsidkenu – The LORD Our Righteousness
- Verse 4: Jehovah-Shammah – The LORD Always There
- Verse 5: Jehovah-Nissi – The LORD Our Banner
- Verse 6: Jehovah-Qadesh – The LORD Who Sanctifies

What we lack, He will provide. When we are troubled, He gives us peace. He covers our sin with His own Son's righteousness. We are never alone, for He is always there, even in death. In the face of our enemies, He gives us victory. And His mercy gives us entry through heaven's gate.

Jehovah-Rohe, my Shepherd, my Saviour, I bow down with thankfulness at Your provision for me. Amen.

26 July

For all people walk each in the name of his god,
But we will walk in the name of the LORD our God.

Micah 4:5

Reading: Psalm 115:1–4

We climbed the steep steps along with the faithful and the curious. Yet the moment we crossed the threshold from the sunshine of God's beautiful creation into the Buddhist temple, darkness enveloped us unlike that of nature's night. No amount of shiny golden figurines or lighted candles could diminish the oppression in that place dedicated to the pantheon of visible 'gods' surrounding us. Although the Buddhas said there is no god, it appears that millions of their followers across the world need a deity to help them reach the afterlife.

Following Adam and Eve's exclusion from the Garden of Eden, humankind needed something to worship, and eventually they built their own gods (Psalm 115:4). In ancient times the names of these gods often included the word El – The Strong One – but there was only One who could own that name in its full meaning. He was, and is, the One named Elohim, a plural form of the word El, alluding to the triune nature of His being. Elohim was the name God used when He spoke of Himself as Creator. After all, none could be more powerful than One who created something from nothing, spoke light into the darkness and breathed life into the lifeless.

While the gods of wood and stone are given the best food by the hungry, and those covered in gold require everything from the poor, our God – Elohim – is the Lord we worship. He is the giver of life, and He makes it easy to find the enlightenment millions seek, because He has told us where to find it: 'You will show me the path of life; in Your presence is fullness of joy; at Your right hand are pleasures forevermore' (Psalm 16:11).

Elohim, Strong One of Creation, bring Your light to those who walk in darkness. Show them the path of life, and give me a heart to pray for them. Amen.

27 July

The LORD appeared to Abram and said to him,
'I am Almighty God; walk before Me and be blameless.'
Genesis 17:1

Reading: Genesis 17:15–19

The name 'El Shaddai' was first used in the Old Testament when God confirmed His promise to Abraham that Sarah was going to have a baby in her old age (Genesis 17:1). Historically, the name is used in conjunction with statements of covenant promise. God was making a promise involving the continuation of the covenantal line, and so He referred to Himself as El Shaddai.

In simple terms, El Shaddai means 'Almighty God'. The English translation doesn't do it justice. If you peel back another layer in its Hebraic meaning, linguistic scholars have translated it as 'God who is sufficient', or simply 'God who is enough'.

Imagine God's perfect timing in revealing Himself as 'God who is enough' to Abraham for the very first time. Abraham was staring the impossible in the face: 'How could I become a father at the age of one hundred? Besides, Sarah is ninety; how could she have a baby?' (Genesis 17:17, NLT).

And God declared Himself as El Shaddai – 'God who is enough' – in the face of Abraham's mocking doubt. True to His word, the covenant-keeping God came through, making possible the impossible, when Sarah gave birth to Isaac.

There are times in our lives when we face the impossible, the immovable, the unchangeable. It is at those times that I like to whisper His name – El Shaddai.

For He is enough . . .

- . . . when we are weary;
- . . . when we are weak;
- . . . when we have reached the end of ourselves.

That name stretched all the way from Genesis to the cross, where we find He is enough for our sin. . . our salvation. . . and our eternal destiny![16]

El Shaddai, thank You that You alone are enough for all I need. Amen.

225

28 July

A PASSAGE TO PONDER

Praise the LORD!

Praise, O servants of the LORD,

Praise the name of the LORD!

Blessed be the name of the LORD

From this time forth and evermore!

From the rising of the sun to its going down

The LORD's name is to be praised.

The LORD is high above all nations,

His glory above the heavens.

Psalm 113:1–4

Read the passage slowly and let the Author speak to you. As you ponder, ask yourself these questions:

- What does it say?
- What does it mean?
- What is God saying to me?
- How will I respond?

29 July

'I and My Father are one.'
John 10:30

Reading: John 1:1–5

We all have numerous identities. Some of mine are: daughter, sister, wife, mother, grandmother, nurse, speaker, author. I've also been addressed as 'that woman with those children', 'the woman who writes the books' and 'the boss's Mrs'! But when someone uses my name, especially my first name, it makes the relationship personal.

The Trinity is not an easy concept to grasp. Each member of the Godhead displays certain identities specific to it while remaining at one with the others. Each has different names, yet the Son has embodied some of the Father's names, clothing them in human flesh for us to witness for ourselves.

In the New Testament we see Jesus as:

- Elohim – The Strong One of Creation. He was there with the Father when the stars were flung into space, 'and without Him [Jesus] nothing was made that was made' (John 1:3).
- El Olam – The Eternal God. In Revelation 22:13, Jesus testifies to the churches, 'I am the Alpha and the Omega, the Beginning and the End, The First and the Last.'
- El Roi – The God Who Sees Me. Peter affirmed that Jesus knew everything about him (John 21:17), just as Hagar had discovered in the wilderness that God knew exactly where she was (Genesis 16:13).
- El Shaddai – The God Who Is Enough. 'My grace is sufficient for you,' Jesus said, 'for My strength is made perfect in weakness' (2 Corinthians 12:9).

Jesus didn't appear out of nowhere when the angels announced His birth. He has always been there, with the Father, from the beginning of time. That's a fact to encourage our faith for sure.

Eternal God, thank You that each of Your names encourages me to trust You more. There is none like You. Amen.

30 July

'I have come that they may have life,
and that they may have it more abundantly.'
John 10:10

Reading: Ephesians 2:5–10

As I travelled to the ladies' service at which I was to speak that morning, I reached for the car radio. The morning service was being broadcast from a church whose pastor was a friend of ours. It was an inspiring service: full of energetic worship, testimonies of God's transforming grace and, to top it off, a challenging Bible message given by our friend. I couldn't help but smile as I thought of the change in my friend today, as pastor of a thriving church, from the time I first knew him at school.

Back then he used to sit behind me in Latin class and conjugate Latin verbs into my ear when the teacher asked me to recite them while he chalked them on the board. Pity I couldn't remember them for the exams! My clever classmate considered me and my Christian friends foolish when we tried to explain the gospel to him. To say he wasn't interested is an understatement. Yet today hundreds flock into his church to hear him speak about the very thing he ridiculed all those years ago. What changed?

In answer to the prayers of some friends, he had a personal encounter with Jesus. Jesus, Elohim – the Strong One who gives life – gave this reluctant teenager life in all its fullness when he stopped resisting Him and trusted Him for salvation.

As I reached for the off button I thanked God for my friend, but I thanked Him more that He still gives abundant life to all who come to Him in faith. And I prayed for all the reluctant listeners, that they too might hear the Giver-of-Life call them by name, just as my friend did all those years ago.

Thank You, Lord, that You came to give us life. I pray today for family and friends who continue to hold out against Your call to salvation, that they will experience new life for themselves. Amen.

31 July

'Peace I leave with you,
My peace I give to you.'
John 14:27

Reading: John 14:25–28

I was glad of the rain hitting my face. It meant the passers-by couldn't distinguish between the raindrops and the tears streaming down my face. Anyway, most of them dashed past, vision obscured by umbrellas. They neither knew nor cared that I'd had my heart broken once again by the thoughtless words of a doctor.

Thankfully Cheryl was finally asleep in her buggy when I reached my husband's car. In the flurry of my getting into the back seat out of the rain, my husband was distracted by my soggy visage. It was the sobbing that gave me away.

'What did they say?' was all he could manage, as my weeping reached crescendo-force.

And it all tumbled out . . . how the eye clinic was packed, and Cheryl screamed with the pain of the drops . . . and how we were seen behind a curtain so everyone else could hear what the consultant said – not to me, but to his entourage of medical students. 'It's obvious this child is blind' – he didn't even use her name – 'look at how small her head is . . . vision centres haven't developed.' Then he finally turned to me: 'Sorry, Mum, nothing we can do I'm afraid . . . no need to make another appointment.'

As the car splashed its way towards home, I squealed the unfairness of it all to God, all the while squeezing our little girl closer. But in an exceptional moment of Divine kindness, Jehovah-Shalom visited us in that confined place of anguish. It was as if a bucket of His peace was poured over my head, settling both heart and mind, while assuring me that whatever happened, no-one could rob me of His loving care. Perhaps Jehovah-Shalom is my favourite name for Jesus, because His peace has kept me sane in many of life's storms.

Thank You, Lord of Peace, that You have settled this heart of mine so often. I couldn't live a day without You. Amen.

August

1 August

The fear of the LORD is the beginning of knowledge,
But fools despise wisdom and instruction.

Proverbs 1:7

Reading: Proverbs 1

The TV camera panned along the giant poly-tunnel, filming row upon row of vine tomato plants. The tomatoes bedecked the branches like Christmas tree decorations, hanging in greens and shades of orange, with the deep reds among them shining like ruby globes against the green foliage. It was quite stunning for a television advertisement about the lowly tomato.

Beavering away, replete with smiling faces and happy conversation, the workforce carefully cut off the ripened vines. Then, for his brief moment of fame, a young man dressed in dazzling white held a perfect vine of sun-blushed tomatoes to the camera and said, 'I love growing vegetables. These tomatoes are perfect for any meal.'

I confess to releasing a little gasp at his mistake, more surprised that the producer of this very expensive advertisement for a leading supermarket didn't spot it before it hit the small screen. Tomatoes aren't vegetables! They're fruit. The common misperception is often used to explain the difference between wisdom and knowledge: *Knowledge is knowing that a tomato is a fruit. Wisdom is not adding it to a fruit salad!*

In essence, wisdom is applied knowledge. The book of Proverbs is packed full of pithy little statements to help us reach the goal of successful living by the path of wisdom – making the right choices with the knowledge we have. King Solomon, the writer and collector of these proverbs, doesn't make any gaffes when he starts his volume by teaching us that fundamental knowledge begins with a respectful fear of the Lord. It's a foolish builder who doesn't start with a firm foundation. If we want to be biblically wise, it starts here – with a right relationship with God.

Lord God, thank You that You have revealed Yourself to us in the Bible. May my actions always be influenced by my knowledge of You. Amen.

2 August

If you seek her as silver,
And search for her as for hidden treasures;
Then you will understand the fear of the LORD,
And find the knowledge of God.

Proverbs 2:4–5

Reading: Proverbs 2

A large jigsaw puzzle sprawled across the work surface in our son and daughter-in-law's kitchen. The unfinished puzzle of the London Underground dared onlookers to fit another tiny piece into the remaining gaps. In fact, there were very few gaps left, which was surprising, considering the few hundred pieces still in the box awaiting allocation.

The map of the network itself was complete, helped no doubt by the knowledge they both had attained riding the underground during the years they lived in London. The remaining pieces of the 1,000-piece puzzle were all white, and every single one unique in shape. I had a feeling that the puzzle's designer had a sideline in torture methods, which explained the vast surround of nothing but white. But our son was upbeat, extolling the virtues of working patiently at something until you get it right.

In our microwave age of 'if you're going to do it, do it fast', Solomon's words seem strangely out of place. Knowledge and wisdom are a bit like the jigsaw puzzle – it takes time to build the whole picture, which only comes together one tiny piece at a time. If we are going to 'understand the fear of the LORD, and find the knowledge of God', then we have to seek as if searching for precious hidden treasure. Rushing in and out of God's presence, or speed-reading through the Bible, will never thrill the way that discovering a gem of God's promise can. He wants us to find every tiny little piece of all that He has for us. It takes time, but finding the treasure is well worth the search.

God of Heaven, I want to gain the knowledge that comes from You, and the wisdom to apply it to my life. Give me the patience to seek for both. Amen.

3 August

Trust in the LORD with all your heart,
And lean not on your own understanding;
In all your ways acknowledge Him,
And He shall direct your paths.

Proverbs 3:5–6

Reading: Proverbs 3

My mother-in-law exercised the wonderful gift of encouragement through the dying art of letter-writing. For many decades her beautiful handwritten epistles traversed the world to bless the lives of missionaries.

If you ever received a birthday card from her, it was never only once – Annie never forgot. As one of those on her very long birthday card list, I was a grateful recipient, yet at times her postscripts made me chuckle. You see, she always used the same Bible verse to end each birthday greeting – Proverbs 3:5–6. Every year . . . there it was . . . just like the previous year! Privately I would smile, at times joking, 'Does she not know any other Bible verses?'

Shortly after her death, I affectionately turned to Proverbs 3:5–6 to examine the verses she constantly passed on to others, and I discovered not only the wisdom of Solomon, but also the heart of a woman who loved God.

- 'Trust in the LORD with all your heart': half-hearted trust is no trust at all. 'Give God your all' was Annie's advice to those she loved.
- 'Lean not on your own understanding': 'What little we know will never take us through the hard times,' her post-script whispered in my ear.
- Her voice was stronger in my head now. 'In all your ways acknowledge Him': 'Make sure He's the One who gets the credit for everything in your life.'
- Then came this amazing promise she wanted me to read every year: 'And He will direct your paths.' I could almost hear her say, 'Catherine, wonder of all wonders . . . He will be your guide . . . even down the darkest of paths.'[17]

Heavenly Father, I now recognize that there was no foolishness in Annie's annual postscripts. Help me display such godly wisdom. Amen.

4 August

A PASSAGE TO PONDER

Get wisdom! Get understanding!

Do not forget, nor turn away from the words of my mouth.

Do not forsake her,

and she will preserve you;

Love her, and she will keep you,

Wisdom is the principal thing;

Therefore get wisdom.

And in all your getting,

get understanding.

Proverbs 4:5–7

Read the passage slowly and let the Author speak to you. As you ponder, ask yourself these questions:

- What does it say?
- What does it mean?
- What is God saying to me?
- How will I respond?

5 August

For the lips of an immoral woman drip honey,
And her mouth is smoother than oil;
But in the end she is bitter as wormwood,
Sharp as a two-edged sword.

Proverbs 5:3–4

Reading: Proverbs 5

Among a small, but dedicated, following there's a worldwide fascination with domino toppling. The idea is to set the small bricks side by side, and by knocking down the first one the rest follow one by one, creating amazing displays. That's how we get the phrase 'the domino effect'.

I don't know if Solomon was aware of the Chinese dominoes that existed in his day, but he certainly knew about the domino effect of sexual sin that he warns about in this chapter.

Temptation to immorality starts by listening to the sweet words of enticement and flattery, even the kisses of a woman who is not your wife, Solomon warns (verse 3). Don't go near her in the first place, he advises (verse 8). The father teaches the son about the destination of this folly in an attempt to prevent the younger continuing down the road of unfaithfulness and sin. It might begin by tasting sweet, but it will soon poison your body and your life (verse 4). The excitement of illicit sex will quickly fade and you'll waken up one day to discover you've lost your reputation, your money and even your health (verses 9–11).

The wisdom he passes on in this father–son discourse is, 'Drink water from your own cistern.' Enjoy your own wife (verses 15–19)!

Fundamental to any domino toppling is the correct placing of the first domino. Getting that right increases the probability of success. Solomon identifies the key domino knocking down the immorality trail as ignoring your father's instruction and advice (verses 12–14). Hit that and the rest will fall.

We do well to listen to the wisdom of those who've been longer on the road of life than we have.

Heavenly Father, forgive me for the times I've wanted to ignore godly advice and go my own way. Amen.

237

6 August

There are six things the LORD hates,
seven that are detestable to Him:
haughty eyes,
a lying tongue,
hands that shed innocent blood,
a heart that devises wicked schemes,
feet that are quick to rush into evil,
a false witness who pours out lies
and a man who stirs up dissension among brothers.
Proverbs 6:16–19, NIV

Reading: 1 Corinthians 1:10–13

Centuries after Solomon wrote these words, Paul was told about division in the church at Corinth. Some people were stirring up dissension among the new believers and even daring to cite theology as the reason for their argument.

Was the teaching of Paul more correct than that of Apollos or Peter or – perish the thought – Christ (1 Corinthians 1:12)? The church was beginning to split into separate groups of Paul followers, Apollos followers and Peter followers. It seemed that doctrinal snobbery, rather than mere difference of interpretation, was the bad apple in the barrel, and Paul wasn't having it. 'Is Christ divided?' the apostle challenged. 'Was Paul crucified for you? Or were you baptized in the name of Paul?' (1 Corinthians 1:13). He followed on with, 'but we preach Christ crucified' (verse 23). He urged them to keep their eye on the ball, to keep the main thing the main thing!

Unfortunately, disagreement continues to be stirred up in the church today. A few, often those who speak loudest, lose their focus on what's really important. They draw others away from what they deem 'inferior' to what they believe is 'better', but with devastating consequences.

Interestingly, Solomon names six things God hates, but then adds a seventh, changing God's description of it from being hateful to detestable. That detestable thing in God's eyes is 'a man who stirs up dissension among brothers' (verse 19). A salutary warning for us all.

God in Heaven, may my words never cause disagreement in the church, or lead another down a wrong path. Amen.

238

7 August

Keep my commands and live,
And my law as the apple of your eye.
Proverbs 7:2

Reading: Proverbs 7

God always referred to the Children of Israel as 'the apple of His eye' (Deuteronomy 32:10). It's an idiom we understand well – it is still in daily usage, referring to having a special fondness, usually more for a person than for a thing.

In Psalm 17:8, King David asks the Lord to 'Keep me as the apple of Your eye; Hide me under the shadow of Your wings.' The imagery here is of God's power to protect David as His precious child. And what father wouldn't want to protect the child he loves?

It's protection for his own children that Solomon is speaking about in Proverbs 7. He longs that they would follow his wise advice and avoid the traps set for them by those wanting to lead them astray. Therefore he encourages them to approach his commands and wise advice as precious things, in the same way that they are precious to him. He wants them to see his instructions not as a rod for their backs, but rather counsel for their good.

However, Solomon's commands are primarily to prevent his children from doing evil, whereas 'The LORD our God commands us to obey all these laws and to fear Him for our own prosperity and well-being, as is now the case' (Deuteronomy 6:24, NLT). Obeying God is a two-sided coin. Choosing His way undoubtedly helps to keep us from sinning, but it also benefits and blesses our lives. Oh, how much more convincing an argument is when we accentuate the positive.

We are the apple of God's eye, after all.

How wonderful, Lord, to know that we are Your precious children, and Your desire is to protect us from evil. May Your Word be as precious to us as Your love is for us. Amen.

239

8 August

My gifts are better than the purest gold,
my wages better than sterling silver!

Proverbs 8:19, NLT

Reading: Proverbs 8

Wisdom has its rewards. That's a concept even the young can understand.

Our seven-year-old granddaughter always runs out of school with a smile on her face, and it's not because it's over for another day, but because she really loves school! As we chatted away about the happenings of the day I asked if everyone in her class was happy at school. Her tone moderated as she told me about one friend who 'hated' school.

'He just doesn't like work, Granny,' she said sadly, screwing up her little nose in sympathy. 'The only thing he likes to do is play, or draw, or do PE. All the fun stuff, but not the work.'

I commiserated, suggesting that hopefully as the year progressed he'd become more settled.

'I don't think so, Granny,' she muttered, shaking her head. 'I even had a talk with him in the playground and told him if he worked harder, and faster, then he'd get to the play table quicker . . . and then he'd enjoy school more.'

'What did he say?' I replied, buckling her seat belt.

'He said he'd try, but he didn't. He still works so slow that he gets less time to play than I do,' she said, hands raised to the ceiling in exasperation.

'Then we'll just have to pray that he takes your advice, sweetheart,' I commented as the car headed homeward.

'Yes, Granny,' she sighed deeply, 'but if he keeps working slow then he'll never enjoy school.'

Such wisdom from one so young: working smarter pays off. Exactly what Solomon said: wisdom delivers!

Thank You, Lord, for reminding me that following Your wisdom benefits me more than material rewards can. Help me to act on what You are telling me. Amen.

9 August

'Come, eat of my bread
And drink of the wine I have mixed.
Forsake foolishness and live,
And go in the way of understanding.'
Proverbs 9:5–6

Reading: Proverbs 9

We don't always get it right, do we? If we're honest, we haven't always chosen correctly. Unfortunately we can't put the clock back, but we can make another choice – to learn from our mistakes.

The book of Proverbs uses stark language to present the choices of wisdom and foolishness to us. Much of its teaching is good advice for life, if we're prepared to take it. But we shouldn't forget that the writers of these proverbs endeavour to underpin, with what some see as take-it-or-leave-it material, how God expects us to live our lives.

Proverbs 9 is set out as an invitation to two banquets, one prepared by Wisdom and the other by Foolishness. Always portrayed as a lady, Wisdom provides feasts which are good and wholesome, while the parties of Foolishness are aimed at enticing others towards the temporary delights of secret sin. Since the days of Eve, who was fooled into taking what seemed the more exciting option, choosing right over wrong has proved more difficult than at first sight.

Excuse after excuse was made in response to the invitation to the banquet Jesus speaks about in Luke 14:16–24, until, eventually, the Master sent out the invitation to society's lowliest instead. It seems that wisdom didn't accompany the wealthy in this story. They thought they had more important things to do. Oh, how wrong they were.

Wisdom's words here (verses 5–6) mirror those of Jesus in John 6:35, where He declares Himself 'the bread of life', assuring us that 'He who comes to Me shall never hunger, and he who believes in Me shall never thirst'. Let's choose to accept the invitation we can trust: 'Forsake foolishness and live.' No 'party' on earth can satisfy like Jesus can.

Lord Jesus, thank You that I never need to look elsewhere for satisfaction once I come to You. I choose Your invitation to life today. Amen.

241

10 August

He who keeps instruction is in the way of life,
But he who refuses correction goes astray.
Proverbs 10:17

Reading: Proverbs 10

The phrase 'self-assembly' is anathema to me. You find the exact piece of furniture you're looking for and think, *Job done!* It looks perfect in every way, until . . . you notice in the small print, 'Requires assembly.' Alarm bells ring as memories of slanting shelves and wonky drawers rocket to the surface.

That was the case recently when we bought a child's ride-on toy. When we went to pick it up from the store, those dreaded words were printed on the box. I pleaded with the staff member to build it for me – I was even prepared to pay him for doing so, but to no avail. Later, after hours of failing to construct this *easy-assembly* item, we gave up, and enlisted the help of someone who loves doing the very thing we hate. Not to be outdone, however, I insisted he talk me through the instructions, and managed to complete the task under the tuition of a person more experienced than I.

Following instruction is much easier when there is someone to explain the directives, and to help you understand the reasons behind them. The end result delivers an immense sense of achievement that increases your confidence for the next time. Sad indeed is the person who is too proud to seek out help.

God has left us instructions and principles for life in the Bible, but He doesn't expect us to understand them all by ourselves. The Holy Spirit 'will guide you into all truth' (John 16:13). The third person of the Trinity is standing by to guide and instruct. We don't have to do it alone. He's willing, and exceptionally able, to walk us through when the instructions are hard to follow. The question is, are we wise enough to let Him?

Lord, forgive me when pride gets in the way and I end up going astray by refusing to accept the help I need. Holy Spirit, teach me what I need to know. Amen.

11 August

A PASSAGE TO PONDER

He who earnestly seeks good finds favor,

But trouble will come to him who seeks evil.

He who trusts in his riches will fail,

But the righteous will flourish like foliage.

He who troubles his own house will inherit the wind,

And the fool will be servant to the wise of heart.

The fruit of the righteous is a tree of life,

And he who wins souls is wise.

If the righteous will be recompensed on the earth,

How much more the ungodly and the sinner.

Proverbs 11:27–31

Read the passage slowly and let the Author speak to you. As you ponder, ask yourself these questions:

- What does it say?
- What does it mean?
- What is God saying to me?
- How will I respond?

12 August

Wise words bring many benefits,
and hard work brings rewards.
Proverbs 12:14, NLT

Reading: Proverbs 12

Words. They're essential for everyday life, setting us above the rest of the animal kingdom. Written or spoken, words make up our language and form our primary means of communication. For some, like myself, words also form the main component of our work. But our words don't have to be in the public arena to have a powerful impact on the lives of others.

Solomon encourages us here to use our words wisely, and that in turn will benefit others, as well as ourselves. And one way to help us think before we speak, or write, is also to remember the wrong that words can accomplish.

'But what comes out of the mouth, this defiles a man,' said Jesus in Matthew 15:10.

'Their talk is foul, like the stench from an open grave. Their speech is filled with lies' (Romans 3:13, NLT).

'And the tongue is a fire, a world of iniquity . . . Out of the same mouth proceed blessing and cursing. My brethren, these things ought not to be so' (James 3:6, 10).

'Sharp tongues are the swords they wield; bitter words are the arrows they aim' (Psalm 64:3, NLT).

How will we use our words? As a stench, a raging fire, a curse, a destructive sword or a piercing arrow? Or will we choose to use them as 'honeycomb, sweetness to the soul and health to the bones' (Proverbs 16:24)?

Lord, forgive me when I allow foolishness to form my words. Teach me to speak to others with love and grace, adding sweetness that will bless their lives. Amen.

244

13 August

A wise son heeds his father's instruction,
But a scoffer does not listen to rebuke.
Proverbs 13:1

Reading: Deuteronomy 6:4–9

My friend discovered that her car had been broken into when she returned to the hospital car park after a long night shift. Later, at the police station, she gave a list of the stolen items to the officer on duty, but she doubted she'd ever see any of them again. The only truly personal thing taken was a cassette recording of favourite gospel songs that her husband had recorded for her birthday.

A few weeks later she received a phone call asking her to return to the station. It seemed they'd picked up a lad with some stolen property on him, and the officer thought some of it might belong to her. Along with her husband, she was taken into an interview room where a teenage boy sat beside his parents. Sure enough, on the table were a few of her stolen possessions. But the boy swore that the goods belonged to him. Challenged about the aforementioned cassette, my friend was shocked to hear not only the boy say it was his, but also his mother testify to the police that she had personally recorded the songs for him as a gift!

A wise son does indeed heed his father's instruction, but what kind of teaching are fathers giving to their sons? In that police station, the teenager's sinful behaviour was endorsed by his parents. Was he following in his father's footsteps, or did they foolishly believe they were helping him by lying for him?

Moses commands us to teach our children at every opportunity to 'love the LORD your God with all your heart . . . soul . . . strength' (Deuteronomy 6:5, 7). That's the wisest instruction any of our children can receive, but we need to heed it first ourselves.

Heavenly Father, how can my children and grandchildren follow wise instruction if what I teach them leads them to sin? Teach me to obey Your Law, that those coming after me might find it easy to do the same. Amen.

14 August

Godliness exalts a nation,
but sin is a disgrace to any people.
Proverbs 14:34, NLT

Reading: Proverbs 14

The psalmist in Psalm 139 reminds us that God 'made all the delicate, inner parts of my body and knit me together in my mother's womb' (verse 13, NLT). Yet 197,887 individuals were aborted in clinics in the UK in 2016 . . . 'Sin is a disgrace to any people.'

Genesis 1:27 tells us that 'God created man . . . male and female He created them'. Yet supermarket chains are refusing to display children's clothes as for boys or girls, for fear of gender labelling . . . 'Sin is a disgrace to any people.'

God initiated marriage when He said, 'Therefore a man shall leave his father and mother and be joined to his wife, and they shall become one flesh' (Genesis 2:24). Yet our government has redefined marriage to include those of the same sex . . . 'Sin is a disgrace to any people.'

'There will always be some among you who are poor,' Moses said (Deuteronomy 15:11, NLT). 'That is why I am commanding you to share your resources freely with the poor . . .' Yet the homeless lie in our city streets while the government appears to favour the wealthy in its policymaking . . . 'Sin is a disgrace to any people.'

'Do not exploit the foreigners who live in your land. They should be treated like everyone else,' we read in Leviticus 19:33 (NLT). Yet governments bribe voters with promises of initiating strict controls on refugees . . . 'Sin is a disgrace to any people.'

Thankfully, all is not lost, for God has promised, 'If My people who are called by My name will humble themselves, and pray and seek My face, and turn from their wicked ways, then I will hear from heaven, and will forgive their sin and heal their land' (2 Chronicles 7:14). Burying our heads in the sand over our nation's sin won't change anything, but prayer can. It's God's clarion call.

Lord, we can blame politicians for what is wrong with our nation, yet few of us are praying for the tide to turn. Forgive me, Lord. Amen.

15 August

Better is a little with the fear of the LORD,
Than great treasure with trouble.
Proverbs 15:16

Reading: Proverbs 15

Glancing around the dining room, I could see that I was surrounded by the rich and very famous. Seated at every table were men and woman from the worlds of sport, film, television and business. They had everything I hadn't: clothing from the finest designers, watches that cost more than my car, physiques honed by their very own personal trainers; and later they would drive their fabulous cars back to country mansions or exclusive London apartments. They also seemed to have a desire to outdo others in their company, a ploy the auctioneer used to great advantage when the charity auction started.

Without doubt, many of those present were kind and generous to the charity I had come to represent. They knew nothing about me, but the press had ensured that their personal lives were not so private. I felt saddened to observe the posturing of some attempting to gain acceptance from their peers after the latest media exposé, and I wondered how 'so-and-so' was surviving the pain of their latest very public broken relationship. For many of my fellow guests, 'great treasure' had indeed brought them trouble.

The following evening I sat in an altogether different dining room, having returned to the Christian conference centre where my husband was guest speaker for the week. No starched linen graced the table, nor did the waitresses wear white gloves to avoid smudging the silver. A little silk rose took the place of the ornate table centre, and the conversation was altogether different. I couldn't help but smile as a discussion started about the morning's talk, and soon another person's journey with God was shared over the coconut sponge and custard.

I knew my place. And this was it, for 'better is a little with the fear of the LORD, than great treasure with trouble' (Proverbs 15:16).

Heavenly Father, wealth may bring happiness of a kind, but it cannot give contentment that lasts. Help me find my treasure in You. Amen.

16 August

The silver-haired head is a crown of glory,
If it is found in the way of righteousness.
Proverbs 16:31

Reading: Luke 2:36–38

In the days following the creation, people often lived to a very old age. But in New Testament times, few people lived as long as Anna. She was already more than a hundred years old when she met Jesus on the day Mary and Joseph brought Him to the temple in Jerusalem.

Luke's brief record of Anna's life instantly reflects the heartache she'd experienced early on. Widowed after only seven years of marriage, while probably still in her early twenties, Anna's loss would have been great. But she was a woman who didn't waste her pain. She never remarried, but instead became a member of the resident staff at the temple, choosing to grow old in the service of the Lord. In return, God gave her more of Himself to replace her lost love. God is no man's debtor: 'For God is not unjust to forget your work and labor of love which you have shown toward His name' (Hebrews 6:10). Luke comments on Anna's devotion, including 'fastings and prayers night and day' (Luke 2:37) as she waited for the promised Messiah.

She held the title prophetess, although in fact it was Simeon who prophesied about Jesus' future (verse 34). But it was that very encounter which brought Anna to approach the family whose Son Simeon was holding in his arms. Instantly the old woman of the temple recognized Jesus as the One for whom all of Israel had waited. And she didn't keep it to herself, but 'spoke of Him to all those who looked for redemption in Jerusalem' (verse 38)! Anna the prophetess became Anna the evangelist the moment she met Jesus.

Aging may rob us of health, independence, mobility and much more, but it cannot remove the wisdom given by years of walking with God. Neither can it take away His presence, nor the opportunity to speak up for Jesus.

Lord, as I age, I want to do it with You, and for You. Let it be so. Amen.

17 August

Disregarding another person's faults preserves love;
telling about them separates close friends.

Proverbs 17:9, NLT

Reading: Proverbs 17

Do you remember the first time you were the focus of gossip? It might have been as far back as schooldays, when someone else revealed a secret you had entrusted to a friend. The problem was that by the time it had got around the playground it wasn't anything like what you had said in the first place. And it hurt.

Or the time you made a mistake and wronged someone, and thought your heartfelt apology would be the end of the matter? Only it wasn't the end. Instead, your mistake did the rounds, splitting friendships and resulting in even more pain.

None of us is guiltless when it comes to hurting others. We've all done it at some time or another, as well as being on the receiving end. Unfortunately, it's also true that gossip is difficult to stay clear of. Even listening to it can add validity to the words spoken. So obnoxious is gossip to God that Paul lists it alongside heinous sins such as murder and immorality (Romans 1:29)! A few verses later Paul declares, 'They are fully aware of God's death penalty for those who do these things, yet they go right ahead and do them anyway' (verse 32, NLT). Wow! Gossip? Can it really be that serious? Apparently so.

Betrayal is a terrible thing, but there comes a time when we need to leave it behind and choose love, for the sake of both our own heart and that of the person who has wronged us. After all, God 'will not constantly accuse us, nor remain angry forever . . . for he understands how weak we are; he knows we are only dust' (Psalm 103:9, 14, NLT). If God is prepared not only to forgive us, but also to stop accusing us, then perhaps it's time we laid down that burden too.

Lord Jesus, You know that person I'm thinking about right now. I choose to forgive them for hurting me, and to give up my accusing spirit. Amen.

18 August

A PASSAGE TO PONDER

The name of the LORD is a strong tower;

The righteous run to it and are safe.

The rich man's wealth is his strong city,

And like a high wall in his own esteem.

Before destruction the heart of a man is haughty,

And before honor is humility.

He who answers a matter before he hears it,

It is folly and shame to him.

The spirit of a man will sustain him in sickness,

But who can bear a broken spirit?

Proverbs 18:10–14

Read the passage slowly and let the Author speak to you. As you ponder, ask yourself these questions:

- What does it say?
- What does it mean?
- What is God saying to me?
- How will I respond?

19 August

Some people are so lazy that they won't even lift a finger to feed themselves.

Proverbs 19:24, NLT

Reading: Proverbs 19

My father-in-law grabbed the two young lads by their arms as they tried to run off. He'd interrupted their attempt to steal petrol from his car in broad daylight. Thinking it more of a boyish prank, he tried to pass on some advice to the wayward twosome. Before letting them go he asked what they wanted to do when they left school: the very place they should have been just then. The response shocked him more than the attempted theft.

'I'm going on the brew like me da!' replied the cocky one. 'I don't want to work.' (Translation: 'I'll take government benefits like my father does.') Of course, the greatest majority of people claiming unemployment benefit are desperately seeking work. This attitude does them a disservice.

But do those of us who have employment always have the right attitude towards our jobs? God instituted work at creation and declared it 'very good' (Genesis 1:31), while Solomon reminds us in Ecclesiastes 9:10, 'Whatever your hand finds to do, do it with your might.' We don't find a hierarchy of employment in Scripture, yet often we become dissatisfied with what we do because we think it unimportant. You'll not find that in the Bible either; instead, Paul tells us, 'Whatever you do, do heartily . . . for you serve the Lord Christ' (Colossians 3:23–24). That's all of us!

Rick Warren assures us that 'Work becomes worship when you dedicate it to God and perform it with an awareness of His presence'.[18]

Laziness brings God's displeasure, but we should also remember that our true worth lies in who we are, not in what we do. God says of us, 'I have loved you with an everlasting love' (Jeremiah 31:3). That's who we are, and it merits a response of worship, even in our work.

Lord, I praise You for what I have been given to work on today. May I do it with all my heart, in worship of You. Amen.

251

20 August

Who can say, 'I have made my heart clean,
I am pure from my sin'?
Proverbs 20:9

Reading: 1 John 1:5–10

In spite of some changes in the past few decades, Northern Ireland still has high levels of church attendance compared to the rest of the UK. Mostly this is a good thing. However, the ease with which we substitute regular church attendance with knowing Christ personally through salvation is indeed very sad.

Frequently, my husband and I meet people who have well-thumbed Bibles and an impeccable church attendance record who bluntly tell us they have no need of salvation – they go to church . . . they haven't done anyone any harm. Other people might be sinners, but not them.

Centuries after Solomon asked his rhetorical question, the apostle John responds with these words: 'If we say that we have no sin, we deceive ourselves, and the truth is not in us' (1 John 1:8). As the author of a book about the Bible, I take no pleasure in publicly declaring that I am a sinner, but the recognition of this fact is the only acceptable entrance to a relationship with God. Because of that I gladly own up to my sinfulness.

Thankfully, John continues with a promise that rescues us from the misery such an admission ought to bring: 'If we confess our sins, He is faithful and just to forgive us our sins and to cleanse us from all unrighteousness' (1 John 1:9). I cannot make my heart clean; neither can I make myself pure from sin. Only Jesus can do that.

Solomon and John were somewhat alike: they both called a spade a spade – a practice that is not well received in today's atmosphere of political correctness. But, however we see it, churchianity is not Christianity, and, 'If we say that we have not sinned, we make Him a liar, and His word is not in us' (1 John 1:10).

Lord, sometimes tough talk is needed to bring us to our senses, yet You always lace it with Your redemptive love. Thank You. Amen.

21 August

Whoever pursues godliness and unfailing love
will find life, godliness, and honour.
Proverbs 21:21, NLT

Reading: Proverbs 21

If we are honest, I wonder what we'd say our life goals are. What do we strive to achieve? Where do our priorities lie?

We are body, mind and spirit, so perhaps it's tempting to approach these questions individually. As far as our body is concerned, there are few of us who wouldn't admit to striving for comfort, and the resources to make that possible. For our mind, education is vital, and the opportunities for lifelong learning today are endless. We couldn't find fault with this particular goal.

As creatures of community we'd also like to be appreciated, respected and even liked by those we associate with. None of us wants to experience rejection.

We might even have spiritual goals. Establish a daily Bible-reading routine? Spend more time in prayer? Follow a missionary's progress and support them by financial giving and prayer? All very admirable.

The problem is, our body, mind and spirit can't be separated from each other. Each is essential for the others to function. While we'd like to box things separately, and therefore stay in control, Jesus clearly explains what our priority for all of life should be: 'But seek *first* the kingdom of God and His righteousness, and all these things shall be added to you' (Matthew 6:33, emphasis mine). Sounds a lot like what Solomon is saying, doesn't it?

Those who seek good things, or perhaps that should read, 'God' things, will always find more than they were seeking in the first place. And it's not our own spiritual goals that both Solomon and Jesus are talking about. It is seeking after God Himself – not that He can give us any more of Himself, but rather that we can give more of ourselves to Him. It's a priority that produces everything we need . . . life, godliness and honour.

Forgive me Lord, for wanting to set my own priorities. Help me to hand over my desires to You daily, and to trust You with the outcome. Amen.

22 August

For it is good to keep these sayings deep within yourself,
always ready on your lips.

Proverbs 22:18, NLT

Reading: Psalm 119:6–16

My Collins English dictionary explains a proverb as 'a short saying that expresses a truth or gives a warning'. In Hebrew thought, a 'mashal' (proverb) is conveyed as a brief saying that makes a comparison, which perfectly expresses Solomon's many contrasts between what is wise and what is foolish. However, he urges the reader to do more than read the proverbs; he urges the reader also to meditate on them for his or her own benefit, and to memorize them, so that their wisdom can be passed on to others.

God frequently instructs us to meditate on His Word (Psalm 119:11), and to memorize it so that we can declare it to others (Psalm 119:13). It's only by saturating our minds with God's Word that our hearts begin to understand His rebuke, correction, forgiveness, unfailing kindness and everlasting love for us. These words then take root, becoming part of us, enabling us to recall them to others when God wants to pass on the same encouragement He has given to us.

The eminent Christian philosopher Dallas Willard comments, 'If I had to choose between all the disciplines of the spiritual life, I would choose Bible memorization, because it is a fundamental way of filling our minds with what it needs.'[19]

Bible memorization is well named as a discipline. I for one don't find it easy, but what a thrill it is to have a verse ready on your lips when someone asks a question or needs an encouraging word from the Lord. And in the dark night of the soul, nothing is more precious than to hear God speak peace to your heart through a scripture you had hidden there years earlier. What God says we shouldn't forget, but when He speaks directly to our hearts, we will always remember.

Thank You, Lord, that You are a speaking God. Help me not to be selfish but to pass on this good news to others. Amen.

23 August

Don't weary yourself trying to get rich.
Why waste your time? For riches can disappear
as though they had the wings of a bird!

Proverbs 23:4–5, NLT

Reading: 1 Timothy 6:17–19

Remarkably, commentators say that in Scripture, more references are made to wealth than to salvation. Jesus devoted almost 50% of His parable-preaching time to money and how we use it. Solomon also takes up the topic in his many proverbs. Money matters to people. That's why the Bible addresses the issue so often. And why we need to pay attention to what it says.

Not that God is against money – a fact Solomon himself reminds us of in Ecclesiastes 5:19: 'As for every man to whom God has given riches . . . this is the gift of God.' However, both Solomon and Paul go to great lengths to explain that the misuse of money can cause all kinds of problems, even to straying from the faith (1 Timothy 6:10). While 'God . . . gives us richly all things to enjoy' (1 Timothy 6:17), Acts 20:35 instructs us to share what we have been given. Money is not ours to hoard selfishly or to spend thoughtlessly. God intends us to use what we have for His kingdom, and to bless those who have less than we have ourselves.

There are those to whom God has given great wealth, and some have recognized this as their ministry to mission, the church and the poor. Before opening his soap business in the early nineteenth century, William Colgate was deeply challenged by a Christian man who encouraged him to make the best soap he could, and to give God what was His due. The young businessman started tithing his company profits immediately, increasing it annually until he eventually was giving away between 50 and 90% of it to the work of God around the world. He also ensured his own workers were looked after properly – an uncommon practice in those days. God gave; William Colgate gave it away.

We don't have to be rich for that to be our regular, godly practice.

Lord, give me a generous heart. Amen.

255

24 August

Through wisdom a house is built,
And by understanding it is established;
By knowledge the rooms are filled
With all precious and pleasant riches.
Proverbs 24:3–4

Reading: Proverbs 24

Home means different things to different people. For most of us it is the place where we feel safe and loved, where we kick off our shoes and tuck our feet under us, where the stress of life is shut outside with the turning of a key. Sadly this is not the case for others. Stress, contention and even fear might very well lodge at your address. Some of this we can change; some we cannot, but Solomon cites principles here to help us to engage in building a home that will be filled with 'precious and pleasant' things.

The things he doesn't mention include what some might feel essential for happiness at home. While the aesthetics of carpets and curtains might appeal to the eye, they are no substitute for acceptance and love.

Instead, Solomon lists three basics for building a happy home:

- **Wisdom.** Family is at the heart of happiness in the home. Love, kindness, understanding and consideration towards each other come from applying what God says about how we ought to live our lives. How we behave, especially at home, is quickly copied by our children.
- **Understanding.** Often described as discernment, understanding is the ability to see beyond what appears obvious to what is going on behind a word or action. 'A soft answer turns away wrath, but a harsh word stirs up anger' (Proverbs 15:1).
- **Knowledge.** If we want our homes to be filled with the 'precious and pleasant riches' of loving relationships and contentment, then the knowledge that serves us best is of God.

Lord, I want my house to be a home where You are honoured. Grant me the wisdom, understanding and knowledge I need for that to happen. Amen.

25 August

A PASSAGE TO PONDER

A word fitly spoken is like apples of gold

In settings of silver.

Like an earring of gold and an ornament of fine gold

Is a wise rebuker to an obedient ear.

Like the cold of snow in time of harvest

Is a faithful messenger to those who send him,

For he refreshes the soul of his masters.

Whoever falsely boasts of giving

Is like clouds and wind without rain.

Proverbs 25:11–14

Read the passage and let the Author speak to you. As you ponder, ask yourself these questions:

- What does it say?
- What does it mean?
- What is God saying to me?
- How will I respond?

26 August

Fire goes out for lack of fuel,
and quarrels disappear when gossip stops.
Proverbs 26:20, NLT

Reading: Proverbs 26

Gossip may be defined as casual conversation or a bit of banter, but more often than not it is full of inaccuracies. Half-truths, misinformation or deliberate lies might be used to 'juicy-up' a chat between friends, but there should never be room in our conversations for such talk. Someone always gets hurt. And the 'no smoke without fire' excuse is the lamest of all, especially when the arsonist is sitting right there.

C. H. Spurgeon was right when he said, 'A lie travels round the world while truth is putting on her boots.'[20] How sad that we could be faster to listen to, believe and even pass on a falsehood, rather than first seeking out the truth. Solomon tells us to give that kind of fire no fuel, and it will soon go out. The best way to start fire-dousing is not to listen in the first place. Refuse to be another log on someone's fire. If you can't get away from the conversation, then challenge the information – pour cold water on it.

Whatever happens, let's keep our own conversation sweet. 'Let no corrupt word proceed out of your mouth, but what is good for necessary edification, that it may impart grace to the hearers' (Ephesians 4:29). Or, as my husband would say, 'If it isn't true, isn't kind or doesn't build up, then don't say it.' Don't stoke a fire that never should have been lit; worse still, don't use religion as kindling. 'If anyone among you thinks he is religious, and does not bridle his tongue but deceives his own heart, this one's religion is useless' (James 1:26). Don't repeat in the prayer meeting what has been told in confidence. Instead, let's use our words to bless, and not to harm.

Gossip devastates lives, ruins ministries and dishonours God. We can choose not to be part of it.

'Set a guard, O Lord, over my mouth;
Keep watch over the door of my lips (Psalm 141:3). Amen.

27 August

Do not boast about tomorrow,
For you do not know what a day may bring forth.
Proverbs 27:1

Reading: James 4:13–15

Simon excitedly clapped his friend's shoulder as the city came into view. They'd travelled more than 900 miles, battled heat and threats from desert marauders, all to be in this place at this time. Passover in Jerusalem was Simon's dream come true, and nothing, or no-one, was going to stop him from finally attending the evening sacrifice in the temple.

Fellow travellers had warned that there might be trouble ahead, even Roman crucifixions, so Simon determined to stay clear of likely trouble spots.

'You, dark skin!' The Cyrenian couldn't mistake whom the Centurion was calling as he tried desperately to bypass an angry crowd. He also heard weeping as soldiers dragged him to the front of the crowd. A man had fallen on the road . . . what was left of him. Simon had never witnessed such horror before. The criminal's back was torn in pieces, his hair matted with blood from . . . a crown of thorns?! The bloodstained forty-pound crossbar intended for a wooden Roman cross lay on the ground beside what was more like a dying man.

'Pick it up!' the soldier yelled, pushing Simon to the ground. Revulsion, anger and fear gripped him, his mind whirling. He didn't come to Jerusalem for this! He'd never make the sacrifice now. He'd be unclean! Yet the man on the road picked up His bruised and battered body without saying a word. Peace seeped from His torn body. Simon's young, strong shoulders lifted the load, and he walked quietly beside the One someone from the crowd called Jesus. What had He done to deserve this? And as their eyes met, Simon knew this was exactly why he'd come to Jerusalem. On that day, Simon attended the final sacrifice ever to be made for man's sin, and it didn't include a temple. Instead, the man from Cyrene got to walk alongside the Sacrificial Lamb. Something he hadn't planned. (Adapted from Mark 15:21.)

Lord, if changing my plans means meeting You, then change them. Amen.

28 August

He who covers his sins will not prosper,
But whoever confesses and forsakes them
will have mercy.

Proverbs 28:13

Reading: Psalm 32

Uriah the Hittite showed more moral principle than the king he served. King David thought he could cover up his adulterous liaison with Uriah's wife, Bathsheba, by first recalling him from the frontline, feigning the need for a battle report. Afterwards he encouraged the soldier to rest at home, roughly translated, 'Go and sleep with your wife' (2 Samuel 11:8, 11). With any luck, her husband could claim Bathsheba's illicit pregnancy, and she and David could cover their sin and get away with the consequences.

However, the honourable Uriah, knowing the rule about soldiers refraining from sexual intimacy during war, could not be tempted to do wrong. The cornered King David then sent Bathsheba's husband back to the battlefield with his own death warrant in his pouch. Once he had been deliberately positioned in the heat of battle, the Ammonites finished off Uriah for David's benefit.

Bathsheba may have wept at the news of her husband's death, but King David breathed a sigh of relief. They'd got away with it. Their sin; their secret. Or so they thought. Not so, for we read in 2 Samuel 11:27, 'But the thing that David had done displeased the LORD.' David had forgotten the words of Moses: 'Be sure your sin will find you out' (Numbers 32:23), but God hadn't. Nothing is hidden from Him. Remarkably, the second son of David and Bathsheba is the author of the words at the top of the page. How wonderfully Solomon speaks of God's mercy for sin that is confessed. A lesson surely learned directly from his father's mistake.

'I said, "I will confess my transgressions to the LORD,"' David says in Psalm 32:5, '"and You forgave the iniquity of my sin."'

Lord, no matter how hard I try, I can't hide my sin. Thank You that Your mercy is waiting when I own up. Amen.

29 August

The fear of man brings a snare,
But whoever trusts in the LORD shall be safe.
Proverbs 29:25

Reading: Matthew 10:27–31

Fearing God and fearing man are poles apart.

In a violent world, some fear physical injury above all else, even in their own home. Peer pressure, school and workplace bullying, relationships with strings attached: each in different ways causes us to fear. Yet here Solomon says that if we trust God more than we fear men, then we will be safe. Yes of course we need to do something about the bully or the assailant who seeks to harm us, but remember, 'we may boldly say, "The LORD is my helper; I will not fear. What can man do to me?"' (Hebrews 13:6).

I've heard missionaries tell of standing before firing squads and how God delivered them, while others speak of seeing colleagues slain before their eyes. It happens every day across our world. This verse does not provide Christians with immunity from suffering, but it does remind us that we should 'not fear those who kill the body but cannot kill the soul. But rather fear Him who is able to destroy both soul and body in hell' (Matthew 10:28). Thankfully, now is not all there is. While sin remains, our race continues to do harm to its members, sometimes with catastrophic effect, but God will avenge the wrongdoer – a fearsome thing indeed.

Most of us are not subject to physical or emotional assault. Our fear often comes from worrying about what others think of us. We don't want to appear foolish, especially when it comes to declaring our faith in God and our belief in the Bible. We are worried about our self-image. Sadly, it's a pride issue. The fear, we bring on ourselves. Jesus gives us a stern warning about such prideful behaviour: 'Whoever denies Me before men, him will I also deny before My Father who is in heaven' (Matthew 10:33). That's something to be truly afraid of, especially when trusting God delivers what is infinitely better.

Lord, may trusting You always trump my fear of men. Amen.

30 August

There is a generation that curses its father,
And does not bless its mother.

Proverbs 30:11

Reading: 2 Samuel 13:1–22

The Bible doesn't cover anything up. Man's best and worst is laid bare in these pages. We thought the David and Bathsheba debacle was bad enough, but the story of Amnon, David's eldest son, makes our skin crawl.

Amnon's lust after his half-sister Tamar resulted in her rape. Once he'd used and abused her, he threw her out of his home in disgrace, condemning her to a life of humiliation and seclusion in their brother Absalom's home. And what did her father, the king, do? We're told he was angry, but he took no action against his rapist son. Two years later Absalom killed his brother Amnon in revenge for what he'd done to their sister.

Rape. Incest. Murder. Some might argue that while Amnon committed this horrific act, it was his father's fault for lack of moral leadership. After all, the young man grew up in the home of a known adulterer. You might even argue that Absalom wouldn't have had to resort to murder if his father had done the right thing by Tamar in the first place.

The blame culture is still rife today. It seems that what we do is often seen as someone else's fault. If only we'd been brought up differently, or had more money, or better job opportunities, then we might not have chosen to do what we did. Yet multitudes in similar circumstances successfully made it through the tough stuff. 'It wasn't my fault' is an excuse used too often.

The Bible tells us, 'The one who sins is the one who dies . . . righteous people will be rewarded for their *own* goodness, and wicked people will be punished for their *own* wickedness' (Ezekiel 18:20, NLT, emphasis mine). Yes, Solomon reminds us that our sin shames our parents, but ultimately it should shame us, and lead us to repentance.

Heavenly Father, forgive me for the times I've blamed others for my own wrongdoing. Thank You that Jesus makes forgiveness freely available. Amen.

31 August

Whenever I am afraid,
I will trust in You.
Psalm 56:3

Reading: Psalm 56

Proverbs 31 speaks of finding an excellent wife (verses 10ff), but I want to turn that on its head, because for forty years I've had by my side the man I fell in love with as a teenager. My husband is gentle, kind and quiet. God knew exactly whom I needed to walk beside me during the many difficult years we've had to face as a family. He's been God's embrace in my life.

Yet yesterday I was more afraid than I have been in a long time as I listened to a doctor explain that my husband needed surgery for a very serious medical condition. And I wanted to run away. Not from him. I went into what used to be my failsafe mode during the years when our daughters faced yet another emergency: I'd ask to take them home from hospital. I always believed that if I could just wrap them up and take them home then everything would be all right. Home represented what was safe in my life – my place of escape. It added a peace that I couldn't find when surrounded by doctors, no matter how much I knew we needed them. Yesterday was like turning back the clock.

As I drove home from the hospital, the Lord gently dropped a thought into my heart. 'Catherine,' I heard Him whisper, 'I won't take this beyond what you can bear.' When I finally dropped into bed, exhausted, I looked across at my night-time devotional book, wondering whether I had the energy to concentrate on reading. I lifted it, and there they were – the words from earlier: 'God is faithful, who will not allow you to be tempted beyond what you are able' (1 Corinthians 10:13). And I realized that, after all these years, running for home really means running into the Father's arms. That's where I am truly safe.

Thank You, Lord, that You are my safe place. Thank You that behind the heartache Your plan is secure. You will carry me through. Amen.

263

September

1 September

A PASSAGE TO PONDER

Oh, magnify the LORD with me,

And let us exalt His name together.

I sought the LORD, and He heard me,

And delivered me from all my fears.

They looked to Him and were radiant,

And their faces were not ashamed.

This poor man cried out, and the LORD heard him,

And saved him out of all his troubles.

The angel of the LORD encamps all around those who fear Him,

And delivers them.

Oh, taste and see that the LORD is good;

Blessed is the man who trusts in Him!

Psalm 34:3–8

Read through the passage slowly and let the Author speak to you. As you ponder, ask yourself these questions:

- What does it say?
- What does it mean?
- What is God saying to me?
- How will I respond?

267

2 September

Then Jesus was led up by the Spirit into the wilderness
to be tempted by the devil.

Matthew 4:1

Reading: Matthew 4:1–11

The engine groaned as the coach advanced up the steep climb. Galilee was now some distance behind us. The beauty of the lake was no longer visible, the lush greenery of its fertile valley a cherished memory. But now, Jerusalem lay ahead.

Suddenly, the most unusual landscape I'd ever seen came into view. Undulating rock bleached a greyish-white by the heat of the eastern sun filled the expanse in wave-like formation. Not a tree in sight; only stone, shaped by hot winds and devoid of the tiniest blade of grass, stretched to the horizon beyond. Behind my fixation on the miles of nothingness I heard our guide say, 'Welcome to the wilderness – the place of Jesus' temptation.' Instantly, I understood why turning stones into bread would have looked so appealing to Jesus when Satan tempted Him to do so. The word 'barren' took on new meaning for me that day.

The Hebrew term for our word 'wilderness' was another eye-opener. It is translated as 'the place where God speaks'. How perfect! It's always easier to hear God speak more clearly when there's nothing else to distract – no other voices clamouring for our attention. When everything else is stripped away we are able to focus more sharply on Him. It is more than possible to hear God speak in life's 'wilderness', but which of us wants to walk voluntarily into this kind of desolate terrain?

We're told it was the Spirit who led Jesus into this inhospitable place. It was God's final preparation for the ministry, and sacrifice, that lay ahead. We might think that life is what brings us to 'the place where God speaks', but make no mistake, the Spirit has His part in it. And when we emerge we will be forever changed.

Lord, when You take me to walk where I do not want to go, help me to listen to what I need to hear to complete the journey. Amen.

3 September

How long, O Lord, must I call for help? But you do not listen! 'Violence!' I cry, but you do not come to save.

Habakkuk 1:2, NLT

Reading: Habakkuk 1:1–5

There are times when God seems distant. There may even be times when we wonder if He is there at all. Habakkuk's pleading certainly seems to suggest that the prophet wondered what God was doing. The nation was in a dreadful state, embroiled in sin and rebellion against God. To make matters worse, an international crisis was developing on their doorstep. The Babylonian empire was poised to strike. All seemed lost. Disaster awaited them. And Habakkuk's prayers were going nowhere. The prophet even challenged whether God was listening to his cries for help at all.

I understand Habakkuk's confusion. I've asked those very same questions. Are You there, Lord? Don't You hear me? I need Your help! When are You going to answer? We can easily be perturbed by God's seeming inactivity, but while God may at times remain quiet, He is never inactive, as Habakkuk was to discover.

Mind you, the prophet was probably something like us. As he prayed, he knew exactly how God could best solve the problem: punish the people for their sin, and send the Babylonians packing. That would solve everything. Or would it? Often our own prayers are more of a recitation of answers rather than a genuine appeal for God to step in and do what's best. When trouble is at our door – or worse still, already resident – praying becomes telling God what we think He should do.

In spite of getting it wrong, the important thing is that Habakkuk didn't stop praying. He was on a journey of learning to trust God even when he didn't understand what was happening, or what God was doing. Habakkuk didn't give up. And neither should we. Because God is at work – the answer is on the way.

Lord, forgive me for my impatience. As I pray, teach me to wait, thankful that You are already setting Your plans in motion. Amen.

4 September

The Lord replied, 'Look at the nations and be amazed!
Watch and be astounded at what I will do!'

Habakkuk 1:5, NLT

Reading: Isaiah 43:1–3

When Habakkuk heard these words he must have felt really excited. But God hadn't finished speaking. When He had, the response Habakkuk had received to his prayers shocked him. It was neither what he wanted nor what he had expected. God was sending the ruthless Babylonians to invade the land of Israel! Instead of rescue, the Israelites were facing devastation and exile: a situation that would also bring personal suffering to Habakkuk (Habakkuk 1:5–7).

Sometimes God surprises us with an answer to our prayers that we neither want nor expect. When our first child was born with profound multiple disabilities, we prayed fervently for her healing. Others joined our quest that God would grant us the miraculous; some even laid hands on her. I believed God could answer those prayers. Instead, He chose to surprise me one night with what I didn't want to hear. God's presence felt very real as He reminded me of some Bible verses I'd read previously, but they weren't what I expected.

'When you pass through the waters,' I heard Him say to my heart, 'I will be with you; and through the rivers, they shall not overflow you. When you walk through the fire, you shall not be burned, nor shall the flame scorch you. For I am the Lord your God, the Holy One of Israel, your Savior' (Isaiah 43:2, 3).

I had wanted God to tell me that the doctors were wrong and that Cheryl would be fine. Instead, He spoke of troubled waters, rivers of disappointment and the flame of suffering ahead for our lives. It wasn't what I wanted to hear; yet softening that bitter blow was an accompanying promise: 'I will be with you, Catherine.'

God never intends us to make wilderness journeys alone. Instead, He walks right beside us.

Lord, there are times when I find Your answers to my prayers difficult. But thank You that You walk with me through every testing step. Amen.

5 September

O Lord my God, my Holy One, you who are eternal –
is your plan in all of this to wipe us out? Surely not!

Habakkuk 1:12, NLT

Reading: Habakkuk 1:12–17

God's reply produces a crisis of faith in the prophet Habakkuk. It was his job to deliver to the people what God told him. But initially this was too much for Habakkuk. Instead of compliance with God's will, he responded with anger, questioning God's choice of using a pagan nation to bring Israel to repentance. In today's parlance, he replied, 'You can't do that, Lord! That's not fair!' And Habakkuk's use of the righteous indignation chant, 'You are of purer eyes than to behold evil' (Habakkuk 1:13), didn't change God's decree. Trouble was on its way.

We all struggle with the question of fairness, whether it's the fallout from natural disasters, or friends suffering from cancer. But when heartache strikes at home, we develop the need to blame someone – frequently, God. The fact that we live in a world damaged by the Fall quickly escapes us, and God's sovereignty, at times, adds to our pain. He knew all along, and didn't stop it.

Soon, the 'That's not fair' chant falls from our own lips. It certainly did from mine when our third child was born with the same disabling condition as her sister. This time we knew exactly what that would mean for her, and for us. Habakkuk was my friend during those difficult days. We thought alike, and asked God the same questions. But I learned, like Habakkuk, that it is never right to be angry with God, and always good to seek Him in confusion's darkness.

To all of our questions, and of the desire to be free from pain, God says, 'My grace is sufficient for you, for My strength is made perfect in weakness' (2 Corinthians 12:9). This imperfect world will invariably throw pain our way, but God has a plan to transform it into strength – perfect strength. All delivered by grace.

Lord, when my heart is full of questions, help me to rest in Your grace. Amen.

271

6 September

'For I know the plans I have for you,' says the Lord.
'They are plans for good and not for disaster,
to give you a future and a hope.'
Jeremiah 29:11, NLT

Reading: 1 Corinthians 13:1–12

Pain, loss, disappointment, betrayal, loneliness. It's hard to see how any of these things could possibly be good for us, let alone give us a future worth looking forward to. But God sees a much bigger picture than we do, and often the dark threads He adds give a clarity and meaning to our lives that would otherwise be missing. It's a bit like tapestry.

On my first attempt at such a craft, our instructor had laid out dozens of coloured strands of wool for us to choose from. Among the bright and beautiful were quite a number of dark threads. I didn't want my bookmark to be drab so I went for the reds and yellows.

'You might want to use some black,' she said. 'It'll help the other colours to stand out – give your pattern definition.'

I'd always thought life was better without black. It was a colour rarely found in my wardrobe, but I was there to learn so I begrudgingly picked up a long black strand of wool.

Cross-stitch seems simple enough, I thought, as I laboriously went in and out through the holes with my needle, all the time endeavouring to set out a recognizable pattern. It looked okay to the uninitiated – as long as you didn't look underneath! Reluctantly, I threaded the needle with the black wool and began work on the finishing border the instructor had suggested. Back and forward went the needle in a flurry of activity. I was totally convinced the black would spoil all the work I'd completed up to that point . . . until I cut the thread and held it out to examine. You could almost say it was beautiful. And I had to admit – it was the black border that showed off the pattern! The darkness made everything else I was trying to do stand out, clear and distinct.

Master Weaver, I am a work in progress. Teach me to trust You with the dark threads when I long more for the gold. One day I look forward to seeing the finished product. Amen.

272

7 September

'But the just will live by his faith.'
Habakkuk 2:4

Reading: Habakkuk 2:1–4

In spite of his disappointment, Habakkuk chooses well what to do with his unsettled feelings and nagging questions.

In response to God's message he replies, 'I will climb up into my watchtower now and wait to see what the Lord will say to me and how he will answer my complaint' (Habakkuk 2:1, NLT). The time to be angry was over. The prophet chooses instead to wait on the Lord, to listen instead of arguing.

Arguing is never productive – especially where God is concerned. And sitting in God's waiting room is perhaps one of the hardest things we will do, especially if we are there because of pain. We want answers and we want them now. Yet nothing can calm our souls the way that time in God's presence can. For there we find Him waiting to deliver the peace we so desperately need, and soon we'll even experience the beginnings of strength rising, for we are promised that 'those who wait on the LORD shall renew their strength' (Isaiah 40:31).

What did Habakkuk do as he waited? In the quietness he reminded himself of who God really is: of all that He had done for His people up to this point in history, and that the solution to his heartache was to trust the God who'd always got it right in the past (Habakkuk 3). We forget so easily, don't we? 'Wilderness' waiting gives us time to put our memory into gear and recollect what God has done for us before now. In turn, confidence rises, enabling us to live by faith (Habakkuk 2:4).

Faith is not a shot in the dark, hoping that everything will turn out okay. Rather, faith is a reasoned choice because of the One whom we are trusting. Waiting time reinforces that choice, ridding our hearts of anger, and readying us for the journey ahead.

Teach me to wait, Lord Jesus. Remind me of Your greatness as I place the broken pieces of my life into Your hands. Amen.

273

8 September

A PASSAGE TO PONDER

Have you not known?

Have you not heard?

The everlasting God, the LORD,

The Creator of the ends of the earth,

Neither faints nor is weary.

His understanding is unsearchable.

He gives power to the weak,

And to those who have no might He increases strength.

Even the youths shall faint and be weary.

And the young men shall utterly fall,

But those who wait upon the LORD shall renew their strength;

They shall mount up with wings like eagles,

They shall run and not be weary,

They shall walk and not faint.

Isaiah 40:28–31

Read the passage slowly and let the Author speak to you. As you ponder, ask yourself these questions:

- What does it say?
- What does it mean?
- What is God saying to me?
- How will I respond?

274

9 September

Though the fig tree may not blossom,
Nor fruit be on the vines;
Though the labour of the olive may fail,
And the fields yield no food;
Though the flock may be cut off from the fold,
And there be no herd in the stalls –
Yet I will rejoice in the LORD,
I will joy in the God of my salvation.

Habakkuk 3:17–18

Reading: Habakkuk 3:16–19

What a declaration of faith!

Habakkuk had travelled a long way – from questioning and anger to absolute trust in the One who was about to unleash disaster in his life. This is no reluctant acceptance of God's will. This is a pronouncement of joy-filled, absolute confidence in the Lord. Paraphrased, this verse says, 'Lord, even if I lose everything – my food, my employment, my health and my home – I choose to trust You.'

How did he come to accept the circumstances he'd previously railed against? I believe it was because he'd spent enough time with God to discover that He was bigger than the problem. And more than this: ultimately, He is a God of justice who would rescue them when the time was right. After taking a good look at God, Habakkuk concluded that He was more than sufficient for his loss and his heartache, right down to holding him steady on the wild mountain-terrain of life (Habakkuk 3:19).

This kind of faith doesn't come easily. Ultimately, it's a matter of choice – a choice that hangs on two important things: catching sight of the awesome nature of God, and believing that He cares deeply for us. Before declaring his faith, Habakkuk is filled with awe by the amazing things God has done (Habakkuk 3:2, NLT). Yet we today have something more than Israel's history to speak to us of God's love for His people – we have the cross. When I sit there, I'm soon overwhelmed by His deep love for me. And, like Habakkuk, I am awestruck.

This is a God I can trust.

Awesome God of heaven and earth, I choose to trust You completely today. Amen.

10 September

Jesus answered, 'Neither this man nor his parents sinned, but that the works of God should be revealed in him.'

John 9:3

Reading: John 9:1–7

Why? One question with the power to break hearts, but Jesus has the answer.

Years had passed since that first day on Herodian Road in Jerusalem. Dan had eventually given in to his plight and learnt to shout as loudly as any of the neighbouring beggars sitting on the temple approach. But it was the conversations that Dan heard that frequently made his day more interesting. It was on one such day that Dan himself became the object of such a conversation.

With ears fine-tuned like those of a bat, Dan noticed that one group of footsteps hadn't continued its journey away from the temple. They had stopped directly in front of him. He was rather surprised when he heard a man question a rabbi – about him!

'Rabbi?' the voice questioned. 'Who sinned, this man or his parents, that he was born blind?'

Dan felt his face flush, embarrassed that his sin should become the topic of such a public discussion. He was weary of the times his blindness was mocked. 'Neither this man nor his parents sinned,' came the reply, before the blind man had time to interrupt.

Is he saying that it wasn't my fault?! Dan's mouth dropped in amazement. Frozen in time, he could not utter a word.

'He was born blind so that the power of God could be seen in him.'

It wasn't my fault!

He didn't recognize the voice whose words, he felt, came wrapped in an otherworldly tone. It wasn't his fault. That's all he heard. And it wasn't his mother's fault . . . nor his father's fault! It wasn't sin that had made him blind![21]

Lord, I want the works of God to be revealed in my life. I give up my 'whys'. Be glorified in me. Amen.

11 September

'But He knows the way that I take;
When He has tested me, I shall come forth as gold.'
Job 23:10

Reading: Philippians 1:12–14

So, does God send suffering or does He merely allow it?

The theologians have been working on this particular debate for centuries, but in my study of God's Word I try to remember a simple principle: *don't allow what you don't understand about God to destroy what you already know about Him.*

Read in a contextual vacuum, Psalm 135:6, 'Whatever the LORD pleases He does, in heaven and in earth, in the seas and in all deep places,' paints God as unconcerned about the results of His actions. After all, He can do whatever He likes! Yet 'whatever the LORD pleases He does' cannot be separated from His divine character. The more we learn about His character, the more we realize that what God does in His sovereignty is always tied up in who He is.

Therefore, the God who numbers the very hairs on our head (Matthew 10:30) and collects our tears in a bottle (Psalm 56:8); the God 'who did not spare His own Son, but delivered Him up for us all' (Romans 8:32): this is the same God of Psalm 135:6!

The difficulties we may experience in understanding the doctrine of the sovereignty of God in human suffering are tempered by the knowledge and evidence of the divine character. Our God is loving, caring, holy and just. Because of who He is, we need not be afraid to trust Him . . . even with the tough stuff.

Pain, with its related suffering, is undoubtedly a result of the Fall . . . but we are also part of a much bigger picture in which God is working out His sovereign plan. Individual strands of suffering, woven together with those of God's providence and grace, make the whole become both beautiful and useful, in spite of the complexity of their source, or their effect on our lives.[22]

Lord, there are no easy answers. I leave the questions with You. Amen.

277

12 September

. . . looking carefully . . . lest any root of bitterness springing up cause trouble.
Hebrews 12:15

Reading: Ephesians 4:26, 30–32

The problem with the questions that pain throws our way is their ability to seed destructive attitudes when we are already suffering. In fact, one particular weed of destruction grows particularly well in the fertile soil of hurting hearts. The writer to the Hebrews calls it the 'root of bitterness'.

Life can be so unfair, and illness so cruel; sometimes people are unkind, and even God may stay silent. Before long our hearts are no longer pliable, but hardened, and shoots of bitterness start to grow in the cracks. Rapidly, this weed begins to choke our Christian growth, sapping our strength, destroying our testimony and blotting out the sun of God's comfort and peace when we need it most. If we are going to stop its toxic spread, the only course of action is to pluck it out. We need to weed!

None of us is immune from trouble, but we can reduce its impact by deciding how we react to it. Will we choose denial or acceptance? Anger or forgiveness? Bitterness or loving trust? We make the choices. Choices that will either unlock the door to God's resources and enable our pain to be turned into gain, or that will shut out the only One who can make sense of the seeming senselessness in our lives. Weeding is difficult work, but it has to be done.

So take back some control. Watch for that bitter thought. Silence that angry word. Don't let bitterness take over. Pluck it out quickly before it takes root. Then give God the broken pieces and watch what He will do, for 'The Lord is close to the brokenhearted; He rescues those who are crushed in spirit' (Psalm 34:18, NLT).

However we might feel, know this – God is for us (Romans 8:31).

Heavenly Father, help me choose peace over pain today by weeding my hurting heart. Then take the broken pieces, Lord, because I don't know what to do with them. Amen.

13 September

'Shall we indeed accept good from God, and shall we not accept adversity?'

Job 2:10

Reading: Job 2:7–10

Job's response to personal tragedy is legendary, and a tribute to his faith in God. However, he did question God, and frequently lamented, but in it all he never accused God of wrongdoing.

His wife suffered the same horrendous loss of seven sons and three daughters, along with material wealth and position. Yet, because of twelve ill-chosen words, she has been berated over the centuries. Some have labelled her foolish, thoughtless, uncaring, while others have gone as far as to describe her as 'the devil's accomplice' (Augustine)! 'Do you still hold fast to your integrity?' she said, when she saw her husband suffering in such agony. 'Curse God and die!' (Job 2:9). Which of us has not uttered words we have later regretted, especially when our heart is broken?

Job's response to his wife's grief-stricken tirade is critical, but only up to a point: 'You speak as one of the foolish women speaks,' he said (verse 10). Someone paraphrased it beautifully: 'You don't sound like yourself.' She was mistaken in what she said, but Job recognized that it wasn't like her to speak in such a way. After all, this was the woman who brought up his ten children, and who stayed with him through all of this horror. In fact, while God rebuked Job's friends for what they said to him (Job 42:7–8), there is no record of God rebuking Job's wife. God was silent. He understands our questions, and cares about our broken hearts.

In spite of her pain, Mrs Job was still wrong in what she said. Yet it appears she engaged in 'weeding' once her husband pointed out the problem, for God later blessed her, along with Job, with ten more children.

God is good . . . all the time.

God, forgive me for the times when I've said the wrong thing, especially when speaking about You. Thank You that You see my heart, and are willing to forgive. Amen.

14 September

'The LORD gave, and the LORD has taken away;
Blessed be the name of the LORD.'

Job 1:21

Reading: Psalm 63

I admire people whose first response to pain is Job-like. They publicly and instantly declare their absolute trust in God whatever happens, and respond with praise. They ask no questions of their Maker. They have no weeds to deal with in their souls. Peace has no roadblocks to navigate before it reaches its destination. Acceptance is never a struggle.

Thankfully, God understands us Habakkuk-types who question, and struggle, before reaching the place of acceptance. 'For He knows our frame; He remembers that we are dust' (Psalm 103:14). We grope for light on the darkest of days, wondering if the sun will ever shine again. The weeds blight our journey, filling the plot in our souls necessary for cultivating what is helpful and healing. But healing will come, because it is part of God's plan for us. I've discovered that praise is an excellent hoe with which to extract weeds, and prepare our soul's soil for what God wants to plant there.

Paul tells us to 'give thanks in all circumstances, for this is the will of God in Christ Jesus for you' (1 Thessalonians 5:18, ESV). He didn't say to be thankful *for* all circumstances, but *in* all circumstances. Praise diverts the focus from ourselves to God. It brings Him into the situation and reminds us who He is – especially that He is bigger than whatever is going on in our lives. His is the only light that can push back the darkness: His are the only words that can make any difference.

Even the whispering of His name, when we cannot form a word, is enough. Or using the words of others in a song when our hearts hurt too much to make up our own. Praise is like a boomerang. Its words always return to bless the sender.

Lord, You are worthy of praise whether we feel like it or not. I choose to worship Your great name today. Amen.

15 September

A PASSAGE TO PONDER

When I remember these things,

I pour out my soul within me.

For I used to go with the multitude;

I went with them to the house of God,

With the voice of joy and praise,

With a multitude that kept a pilgrim feast.

Why are you cast down, O my soul?

And why are you disquieted within me?

Hope in God, for I shall yet praise Him

For the help of His countenance.

Psalm 42:4–5

Read the passage slowly and let the Author speak to you. As you ponder, ask yourself these questions:

- What does it say?
- What does it mean?
- What is God saying to me?
- How will I respond?

16 September

But I will hope continually,
And will praise You yet more and more.
Psalm 71:14

Reading: Psalm 71:14–16

Praise is a choice, not a feeling.

When we choose to praise God, a number of things happen:

- **Our perspective changes.** The size of our problem can now be measured against the One who created the universe, 'who has measured the waters in the hollow of His hand, measured heaven with a span and calculated the dust of the earth in a measure' (Isaiah 40:12).
- **Our focus is redirected.** Although our circumstances may have changed in ways we cannot understand, praise reminds us that we trust a God who never changes, for 'Jesus Christ is the same yesterday, today, and forever' (Hebrews 13:8). His faithfulness towards us is unaltered.
- **Our memory is heightened.** Our hope is in the One who knows all about suffering, and we are persuaded that nothing 'shall be able to separate us from the love of God which is in Christ Jesus our Lord' (Romans 8:39).
- **Our reading of God's Word becomes real.** Nothing sends us to Scripture faster than suffering. It's where we hear God speak. Yet as we speak our praise to Him, the declaration of His power reverberates in our hearts, producing strength we didn't know we had.
- **Our understanding of His love for us increases.** 'Casting all your care upon Him, for He cares for you' (1 Peter 5:7).

It's a no-brainer really. The benefits of praise far outweigh any cost we might imagine exists, because 'Whoever offers praise glorifies [God]' (Psalm 50:23).

Lord, God of heaven and earth, there is no-one like You. May my praise rise to You like a fragrant offering, for You alone are worthy. Amen.

17 September

All the earth shall worship You
And sing praises to You.
Psalm 66:4

Reading: Psalm 19

For me, driving is purely the means to get me from A to B in the shortest time possible. I spend so much time behind the wheel these days that I rarely spend many minutes taking in the surroundings.

Yet while I desire the shortest journey possible, I dislike driving on the motorway, so there's one particular road I know very well. It's rarely busy so progress can be made fairly easily, unless a tractor trundles across your path or, someone is out for a gentle afternoon drive. This country road is undulating, with only a few straight stretches suitable for overtaking.

Dashing home one afternoon I got caught behind a tractor and was forced to take in the drama playing out in front of my very eyes. How had I not noticed this display six hours earlier? Or yesterday? Yet here in front of me was one of those jaw-dropping experiences that make you forget for a moment where you are. Mesmerized, I didn't notice the tractor turning into the farmyard, or care that other cars were now zipping past me in frustration.

All around me the earth was declaring the praise I had been too busy to give. Nature was experiencing the change in the seasons, yet it seemed determined to party in spite of losing the grandeur of summer foliage. Subtle greens were being transformed into the glorious colours of autumn, now catching the light of the sinking ball of fire in the sky. I felt I was looking into the treasure store of heaven, and God's gold was piled high.

And I'd nearly missed it in the mad rush of life.

Soon these same trees will stand bare when I drive past, overtaken by another winter of temporary death. As the miles rolled by I was reminded by God's inner voice that change, and even death, are only that – temporary. Praise, on the other hand, is something that should permanently be on my lips.

Lord, I choose to praise You today, whatever life's season. Amen.

18 September

'Oh, that I knew where I might find Him,
That I might come to His seat!'
Job 23:3

Reading: Job 23:8–10

There are times when God seems absent. We long to feel His presence or to hear His voice. Instead we wait, disappointed with the silence: unsure of where He is leading, keenly aware of the wilderness around us. Job knew exactly how that felt, and it caused him great distress.

'Look, I go forward, but He is not there,' he said, 'and backward, but I cannot perceive Him; when He works on the left hand, I cannot behold Him; when He turns to the right hand, I cannot see Him' (Job 23:8, 9).

It seemed that wherever Job looked he could neither see God's purposes nor feel His presence. But God didn't need to be visible for Job to trust Him or to believe that his life was safe in God's hands. In spite of his very human response to searching for God in his own particular wilderness, Job knew enough about His character not to allow doubt to fuel his disappointment. After pouring out his heart over God's apparent absence, he added a big 'BUT' to his statement, changing the perspective completely.

'But', Job adds, 'He knows the way that I take; when He has tested me, I shall come forth as gold' (Job 23:10).

One day it will all come to an end. In the meantime it's important to remember that God knows exactly where all of this is heading. Not only that, but when it's all over we will be changed for the better. For now, we may not feel Him near . . . but He is. We may not understand His plan . . . but He has it all under His control. The future might look bleak . . . but He promises the complete opposite.

When we can't see God's hand, we can trust His heart.

Thank You, Lord, that You know the way that I take – You've written the road map! You know the end from the beginning, so I can trust You completely. Amen.

19 September

For the LORD will go before you,
And the God of Israel will be your rear guard.
Isaiah 52:12

Reading: Psalm 32:8–11

It's a foolish climber who sets out to climb Everest without a Sherpa, an unwise trekker who heads into the wilderness without a guide.

Yet many difficult life-journeys are unplanned. Sickness, sorrow and disappointment aren't what we'd scheduled. We have no desire to wade through waters of difficulty, or to traverse rough desert terrain. Neither are we looking for thrills in the hard places, nor seeking recognition for surviving what we would never have chosen to do in the first place. Yet, remarkably, God's Word instructs us not to be afraid. How so, when circumstances dictate otherwise?

Isaiah provides the answer: God is both our vanguard and our rear guard in every journey we take.

A vanguard is the guide who goes ahead – he shows the way. Our Vanguard has already walked the route and discovered the pitfalls. He knows the places we might stumble, the climbs that will trouble us, and He plans the best possible route. And He gets there first, in order to be our welcoming party at journey's end.

A rear guard is the one who provides protection from behind. Our Rear Guard has our back! He deals with the Enemy's accusations and his attempts to discourage us. Rear guard also means 'to gather up'. Imagine, as He comes behind us, our Heavenly Father picks up our failures and despondencies and deals with them in love! He understands how difficult this journey is.

But more than this ... He also walks with us as we travel (Isaiah 43:2). We are never alone, whether on mountain track or desert path.

Before, behind, and all the way in between, God makes wilderness-walking safe and arrival possible, at the destination He has planned.

Lord, You are ahead of me, behind me, and willing to cross every difficult step with me. Thank You that You are omnipresent. Amen.

285

20 September

But when they looked up, they saw that the stone had
been rolled away – for it was very large.

Mark 16:4

Reading: Mark 16:1–7

Getting old is no fun. Dad always loved his walks in the nearby park, but with reduced mobility, getting out and about was becoming increasingly difficult. When researching walking aids for him I was advised to choose something that would enable him to lift his head up and look ahead. There's no enjoyment in seeing only your feet when you walk.

When the three women arrived at the garden tomb that first Easter morning, they were sad and discouraged. Jesus was dead. Joy had been stolen from their lives at Calvary. With heads bowed and hearts dismayed, they made their way to the tomb, wondering how they would move the huge stone door aside to enable them to anoint Jesus' body. But when they looked up . . . they witnessed a miracle! The stone had been rolled away. The thing that could've kept them from Jesus had been removed. Better still – Jesus was alive! The future now looked completely different.

What if they hadn't come that morning? What if their circumstances had prevented them? What if they'd allowed their grief to tie their feet to home? What if they hadn't looked up, but had turned back when they remembered the size of that gravestone? They've have missed the wonderful sight God had for them. They'd have missed the opportunity to spread the good news the angel gave them: 'He is risen! He is not here' (Mark 16:6).

Pain bows our heads and causes our steps to shuffle, but there comes a time when we must to look up – 'looking unto Jesus, the author and finisher of our faith' (Hebrews 12:2). Fixing on eyes on Him restores our joy, strengthens our hearts, renews our hope and enables us to move on.

Lord Jesus, there is nothing too large in my life that You cannot roll away. Help me to lift my eyes away from my circumstances and look up! Amen.

286

21 September

'Incline your ear, and come to Me.
Hear and your soul shall live.'
Isaiah 55:3

Reading: Isaiah 55:1–3

When trouble strikes we want quick answers, good advice and someone to tell us how to fix it. We'll take all the help we can get to remedy the situation, going wherever, and to whomever, we think might make the problem disappear. Too often God's Word is our place of last resort. Perhaps we reckon subconsciously that God might not give us what we want. While we make every attempt to sort out what we are experiencing and feeling in the here and now, God works on that part of us that will not end with the grave – our souls.

Yes, there are times when God is silent. Yes, there are times when He asks us to wait for answers. Neither is easy, but He will speak to us, if we quieten ourselves long enough to listen. And when He speaks, it is invariably through His Word. Oh, what we miss when we neglect to open the Book. For then we fail both to hear those necessary words of life and to experience His calm for our troubled souls.

'Lean in and listen,' God says to Israel's suffering exiles. 'Come closer; hear what I have to say . . . and I promise you life beyond the burdens of your pain. Life for your soul' (my paraphrase of Isaiah 55:3).

God's invitation to meet with us is deeply personal. He wants us to be close enough to lean in and listen, because what He has to give us is more than information. He wants us to feel His heart in what He says. And that is possible, for 'His way is perfect; the word of the LORD is proven; He is a shield to all who trust in Him' (Psalm 18:30).

That's something we don't want to miss . . . so lean in.

Lord, thank You that You desire to speak to me. May I be willing to listen to Your heart as well as to Your words. Amen.

287

22 September

A PASSAGE TO PONDER

Therefore we do not lose heart.

Even though our outward man is perishing,

yet the inward man is being renewed day by day.

For our light affliction, which is but for a moment,

is working for us a far more exceeding and eternal weight of glory,

while we do not look at the things which are seen,

but at the things which are not seen.

For the things which are seen are temporary,

but the things which are not seen are eternal.

2 Corinthians 4:16–18

Read through the passage slowly and let the Author speak to you. As you ponder, ask yourself these questions:

- What does it say?
- What does it mean?
- What is God saying to me?
- How will I respond?

23 September

'So do not fear, for I am with you;
do not be dismayed, for I am your God.
I will strengthen you and help you;
I will uphold you with my righteous right hand.'

Isaiah 41:10, NIV

Reading: Isaiah 41:9–13

Piles of dilapidated rubber flip-flops lay discarded at either side of the orphanage door. If they could speak, each pair could have told us how they got their holes and tears over many miles of forest walking. They belonged to young feet that had fled their homes when the Burmese army came to their villages to dispense mutilation, murder and rape. The wearers of this footwear were the lucky ones, we were told . . . not something you'd recognize in their sad eyes, or when you wrapped your arms around those who hadn't spoken since the dreadful day when they'd lost everything. Now, they didn't even have a country to call their own.

Isaiah 41:10 was the memory verse we taught the children as we moved between orphanages and refugee camps on the Thai–Burma border. So deeply moving was their plight that I welled up every time we repeated that verse – one that had been such a comfort in my own life. *'So do not fear'* . . . how afraid they must have been as they ran for their lives, leaving dead fathers and burning homes behind them. *'Do not be dismayed'* . . . how could they not be, for their futures were uncertain, their safety not assured, with only a few hundred yards separating them from the nearest Burmese army post just across the river.

Exchanging their old flip-flops for new ones brought some excitement, but the children couldn't discard their pain as easily as the worn footwear. The treats, food and flip-flops we left with them wouldn't last, but we prayed that these promises would stay with them for ever. To the hurting God says, *'I am with you . . . I will strengthen and help you . . . I will uphold you.'*

Caring God, grant Your healing love to those who hurt today because of man's inhumanity to man, and give them Your peace. Amen.

289

24 September

When my spirit was overwhelmed within me,
Then You knew my path.

Psalm 142:3

Reading: Psalm 142

I've tried many times to learn to swim. If I could do it with my feet firmly placed on the ground, then I'd have no problem. My fear that the water won't hold me up is overwhelming.

As a teenager, I was doing okay at teaching myself to swim. I'd got as far as managing to complete a width of the local pool without flotation aids. I loved it, and was looking forward to the day I'd move on to lengths. Until one evening, when someone jumped in and landed on top of me, pushing me under. The shock quickly morphed into fear, causing me to thrash about in the water, sinking and rising numerous times. The water overwhelmed me. I genuinely thought I was going to die. Eventually the lifeguard jumped in and pulled me out. His excuse for waiting so long was that he thought I was fooling around – he'd previously watched me swim across, so was surprised by what he witnessed.

'If that happens again,' he said, 'don't panic. Relax – the water will hold you up.'

As far as I was concerned there wouldn't be a next time. Years passed before I tried again, but each and every time fear has stopped me from trusting the water . . . and think what I've missed.

Thankfully, in spite of more serious life-circumstances that also threatened to overwhelm me, I have discovered that God will hold me up. Yes, I've splashed around in the waters of doubt and disappointment from time to time, but God has kept His promise . . . I haven't drowned. And it's been more than mere survival. He has taught me over the years to relax in His sovereignty, to trust His Word, and to remember that He knows this path I'm on.

With God by our side, panic need not be our immediate response.

Lord, when life seeks to overwhelm me, I choose to trust You. Amen.

290

25 September

But may the God of all grace, who called us to His eternal glory by Christ Jesus, after you have suffered a while, perfect, establish, strengthen, and settle you.

1 Peter 5:10

Reading: Psalm 73:23–26

One little phrase in God's Word can stop us in our tracks. Words that contain the power to 'wow': the ability to wash over our souls, leaving contentment in their wake. The 'God of all grace' is one such phrase.

Who is this who Peter says will perfect us in such a way 'after [we] have suffered a while'? He is the 'God of all grace'.

He's not simply the God of grace, or of some grace. He's not even merely the God of past grace, who called us to Himself through salvation and has forgiven our sin – amazing though that is. But this God chooses not to stop there, because He is also the God of future grace. When our time in these earthly bodies is over, when pain and sorrow have done their worst, He promises perfection. One day we will leave it all behind. Our suffering here is temporary, Peter explains. God's future grace promises a different life ahead, free from pain, and full of joy and peace.

Yet there's more, because Peter calls God 'the God of *all* grace'. And what a difference those three letters make. Too often our gospel is a two-thirds variety – we're saved from hell and on our way to heaven. But what about the big section in between – the 'now' we walk through? He is the God of *all* grace. He meets today's need for strength and peace, perfecting us through Christ and establishing trust through His living Word. He leaves nothing out.

God says to us as He said to Paul, 'My grace is sufficient for you, for My strength is made perfect in weakness' (2 Corinthians 12:9).

God of all grace, thank You for blessings past and future, but thank You especially that Your grace is available for what I will face today. Amen.

291

26 September

For I consider that the sufferings of this present time
are not worthy to be compared with the glory
which shall be revealed in us.
Romans 8:18

Reading: Romans 8:18–23a

Perspective is the vital lens through which we look at life.

Can we really understand what a person is saying unless we are able to determine what lies behind their words? It's helpful to listen by looking beyond the words. What is that person really trying to say? Can we sense their heart as they speak? One of the downsides of digital communication is that neither tone nor intent is available to us. Messages, often abbreviated, flash on to empty screens and we have no perspective through which to view them. Some things should only ever be said face to face.

Similarly, are we ever likely to understand God's plan in our pain without viewing it through the lens of the perspective of His grace? The more we examine God's loving character, and His willingness to walk with us day by day, the more we begin to see things differently. The shortsighted 'sufferings of this present time' lose their blurriness when the bigger picture comes into view.

Yet here Paul is adding another lens to our spiritual glasses, which allows our focus to take on an even sharper edge. For when the lens of the perspective of future glory is added, our long-distance vision also becomes clearer. What lies ahead for us will completely overshadow what we are going through now. Paul reminds us that 'our present troubles are quite small and won't last very long', 'yet they produce for us an immeasurably great glory that will last forever!' (2 Corinthians 4:17, NLT).

Need to see more clearly? Time to put the specs on!

Thank You, Lord, that You make it possible for me to see a little more clearly through life's fog. Help me to look through the correct lens to see the way ahead. Amen.

292

27 September

And we know that all things work together for good
to those who love God, to those who are the called
according to His purpose.

Romans 8:28

Reading: Romans 8:23–28

Even now my heart misses a beat when I type out these words. At one time they brought no encouragement to my soul. Regrettably, I would even go as far as to say I strongly disliked this verse.

I was deeply distressed after the paediatrician told us that our baby daughter would 'never be normal'. It left a deep scar on my soul and a multitude of questions in my heart, none of which was helped by those well-meaning people who chose Romans 8:28 as the verse they thought might comfort us best at that time. They couldn't have been more wrong.

Yes, I loved God. Yes, I knew I was called according to His purpose. But no, I couldn't see any good coming from our situation. Instead of bringing comfort, I felt like I'd been stood against a wall in front of a firing squad. Each and every bullet fired contained the words of Romans 8:28. I was deeply wounded. But it wasn't the words of Romans 8:28 that wounded me; it was my unwillingness to accept what God was so desperately trying to tell me.

He was promising to turn the situation around for my good, while I was wasting precious energy fighting His plan. I didn't want what He had given, so I couldn't see the point of Him working it together for my good. I stubbornly refused to put on my spiritual specs. It took weeks before I donned the lens of the perspective of present grace and future glory. When I did, I started to see things more clearly. And even Romans 8:28 eventually became a healing balm.

Don't be like me. Stop fighting God. He's on our side, and one day we'll see Him work together all things for good.

Forgive me, Lord, for the time I've wasted fighting Your purposes for my life. Thank You for Romans 8:28. Amen.

293

28 September

And God will wipe away every tear from their eyes;
there shall be no more death, nor sorrow, nor crying.
There shall be no more pain, for the former things
have passed away.

Revelation 21:4

Reading: Revelation 21:3–6

Some Scripture verses we associate with specific life events, or times in the church year – births, marriages, Christmas, Easter and so on. Rarely do we hear them used outside of their particular context.

Today's verse is often read at funerals, and undoubtedly brings comfort to the sorrowing. However, it's my opinion that these words are so profound in the theology of suffering that they ought to be considered more often than at funerals. They give us both the richness of future perspective and a tender picture of God as we think of Him wiping away our tears. Apart from the cross, is there any sweeter picture of God's love towards us than this?

On days when I'm particularly missing our two daughters, I like to go into my study and close the door. Then I open the Bible at these words and read them out loud. Reading aloud is so satisfying, for we not only see what's written but we hear it also, giving the thought a double opportunity to impact our hearts and soothe our souls. Then afterwards I meditate on what God has promised.

Imagine – never again will I have to visit the girls' graves. Never again will the tsunami of sorrow roll over my life. Their pain is already gone, and my sorrow will one day be completely transformed into joy. Not one tear will ever again roll down my cheek and drip from my chin, for the final wiping of them all will be completed by the One who loves me best. 'The former things [will] have passed away' and our Heavenly Father will 'make all things new' (Revelation 21:5).

Heavenly Father, thank You for Your constant kindness towards me. I look forward to the day when You will wipe the final tear from my eyes. Amen.

29 September

A PASSAGE TO PONDER

A thorn in the flesh was given to me . . .

Concerning this thing I pleaded with the Lord three times

that it might depart from me.

And He said to me, 'My grace is sufficient for you,

for My strength is made perfect in weakness.'

Therefore most gladly I will rather boast in my infirmities,

that the power of Christ may rest upon me.

Therefore I take pleasure in infirmities,

in reproaches, in needs, in persecutions,

in distresses, for Christ's sake.

For when I am weak, then I am strong.

2 Corinthians 12:7–10

Read through the passage slowly and let the Author speak to you. As you ponder, ask yourself these questions:

- What does it say?
- What does it mean?
- What is God saying to me?
- How will I respond?

30 September

He has made everything beautiful in its time.
Also He has put eternity in their hearts.
Ecclesiastes 3:11

Reading: Ecclesiastes 3

How can God make everything beautiful? How can the brokenness we experience – the sorrow we go through, the suffering that tortures mind and body – be transformed into something beautiful? I don't know. But I know it has happened. I've watched bitter, angry souls transformed by God's working in their lives. I've seen grieving widows infused with a peace that literally glowed. Demoralized men have found their way again. Bullied kids have discovered their identity in Christ. I've even felt my own anger dissipate, and experienced for myself the tender hand of God mend my broken heart.

When God touches our lives He never leaves us the same. He's in the transformation business (Revelation 21:5).

The Preacher in Ecclesiastes 3 drops a hint as to the how, when he explains that God has put eternity in our hearts. We are hardwired with something that pain can cloud – now is not all there is! There is more planned for our lives, more for us to live for, than the now. We are blessed throughout our days on earth with much to enjoy. For that we should be thankful. But it is our painful journeys that come most quickly to mind. Yet even these can be made beautiful – if not here, then we can be sure that eternity will beautify them permanently.

Joshua had lived through forty years of wilderness wanderings and had seen much bloodshed in the battles he'd fought, yet in the end he said, 'Deep in your hearts you know that every promise of the Lord your God has come true. Not a single one has failed!' (Joshua 23:14, NLT).

How will God make beautiful what is ugly in our lives? I can't answer that, but I know He will – He always keeps His promises.

Take all the broken pieces of my life, Lord, and make them beautiful for Your glory. Amen.

October

1 October

And He said to me, 'Son of man, can these bones live?'
Ezekiel 37:3

Reading: Ezekiel 37:1–3

Ezekiel was around twenty-five years old when the Babylonians invaded Jerusalem. He witnessed the decimation of his nation before being carried away as a slave to Babylon. He lost his home and his job, and then his wife died in that most dreadful of years. Everything that could go wrong did. But every time his name was voiced, the young trainee priest, now prophet, was reminded that he was 'Strengthened by God'. When all seemed lost, Ezekiel's name declared otherwise.

When the young prophet lived with the ten thousand other slaves in Tel Abib, God used Ezekiel to speak words of judgment, but also encouragement, to His captive people. And what could have been more encouraging in their desolation than the vision recorded in Ezekiel 37?

In his dream, Ezekiel was transported to a valley filled with dry bones. The scene was reminiscent of the human debris of battle. The number of casualties had been huge; the sight, one of hopelessness. Then God asked Ezekiel a preposterous question: 'Can these bones live?'

Ezekiel's answer was suitably wise: 'O LORD GOD, You know' (verse 3).

Dead things live again? Surely not?

In context, this vision was God's promise that the nation of Israel would return from exile – come back from the 'dead' (verse 12), while also hinting at the final resurrection. But there is also much here for those of us who feel withered, dry or even dead in our own souls. What brought us to this state? How did we arrive in our spiritual desert? Did we lose our way, or listen to error? Or did life's struggles, disappointment, or even rejecting our first love (Revelation 2:4) cause us to give up on God?

Perhaps, like Ezekiel, all seems lost, but he was not so foolish as to forget that God is sovereign. Only He is able to make the dead live again.

Lord, You who know all things, who bring life to what is dead, or dying, minister to those who need Your touch today, I pray. Amen.

2 October

'O dry bones, hear the word of the Lord!'
Ezekiel 37:4

Reading: Ezekiel 37:4–8

Dry hearts and dead souls require God's miraculous intervention if they are to live again. But we have our part to play before God plays His.

Ezekiel was commanded to speak to the bones: to tell them to listen to God's word and to believe His promise. What was God promising? He was promising life! All that was lying dead in the valley would be re-created by its original Maker. Bone by bone He would first put together the skeleton, then sinews and flesh would be added, with a final covering of skin. Israel's exile would one day end, but only after they heard the word of the Lord, including God's promise (verses 5–6). The One who had originally made them a nation was promising to make them great again.

Order is essential for restoration. What is broken needs to be assembled in a specific sequence before success is achieved. Paul confirms what Ezekiel is saying: 'Faith comes by hearing, and hearing by the word of God' (Romans 10:17). It's only when we determine to listen to what God is saying to us that we will be able to recognize again the first signs of spiritual life.

Then, even if the damage seems irreversible, we need to admit that only God can fix it. 'I acknowledged my sin to You . . . I said, "I will confess my transgressions to the Lord"' (Psalm 32:5). That's when God's restoration work really begins, for He promises, 'If we confess our sins, He is faithful and just to forgive us our sins and to cleanse us from all unrighteousness' (1 John 1:9).

Watch what happens when we hear the word of the Lord and believe His promises? We get to hear the rattling, as the bones come together, bone to bone (Ezekiel 37:7). The miracle of restoration has begun.

Lord, Your word is the light that I need to get me back on the right path. Help me to listen. Amen.

3 October

'Thus says the Lord God: "Come from the four winds,
O breath, and breathe on these slain,
that they may live."'
Ezekiel 37:9

Reading: Ezekiel 37:9–14

As Ezekiel surveyed the scene, no longer was the valley full of dry bones. It was now full of corpses. They were still dead! But they certainly held more potential than in their former state. Just one more thing was needed for them to be fully restored to life: they needed breath. No oxygen meant no life, and no functioning organs. So Ezekiel did what God commanded him, summoning 'breath' from the four winds, 'and breath came into them, and they lived, and stood upon their feet, an exceedingly great army' (verse 10). What a sight that must have been!

God is still the God of restoration. His ability to breathe life into the 'dead' is just as real today. In fact, the Hebrew word used in this chapter for 'breath' is the same word used in Scripture for the 'Spirit'. The same word is also used for the coming of the Holy Spirit in Acts 2:2–4. And look what happened to the followers of Jesus, who had been hiding away, when the breath of God's Spirit came upon them. They were transformed! Filled with life. Ready to tell the world about Jesus. Equipped to face whatever lay ahead.

That very same 'breath' is available to breathe new life into dry souls today. In fact, Paul says, 'But if the Spirit of Him who raised Jesus from the dead dwells in you, He who raised Christ from the dead will also give life to your mortal bodies through His Spirit who dwells in you' (Romans 8:11).

Resuscitation can happen in any soul who will 'Call upon Me in the day of trouble', says the Lord, who promises deliverance (Psalm 50:15).

Life or death? Time to make that call!

Lord, You alone are the giver of life. Pour Your Spirit into my heart – renew and restore my soul that I might live in Your fullness. Amen.

4 October

My soul thirsts for You;
My flesh longs for You
In a dry and thirsty land
Where there is no water.
Psalm 63:1

Reading: Psalm 63:1–8

Spells of spiritual dryness are common. If we're honest, we've all at times felt lost, discouraged or weary. Dearth is easy to identify. God seems distant. Corporate worship doesn't thrill as it should. Personal worship is as regular as the times of prayer that haven't materialized. The preached word sounds boring, and our Bible has begun to gather dust. Yet, in spite of all this, there remains a longing in our souls for things to be different. We're hardwired that way.

As David trudged through the dry land, desperate for his physical and spiritual thirst to be assuaged, he continued to express hope, recognizing that God's 'lovingkindness is better than life' (verse 3). Therefore he chose to voice praise because he knew with his head that God loved him still. There are times when we need to let our head lead, and we'll discover that our heart will follow. We are sentient beings, and while we have a need to feel and to respond with emotion, our feelings can't always be trusted. That's when we need to act on what we know rather than on how we feel.

- **Fact:** God loves me, and that cannot change: 'I have loved you with an everlasting love' (Jeremiah 31:3).
- **Fact:** God has not moved. He has promised, 'I am with you always, even to the end of the age' (Matthew 28:20).
- **Fact:** God cares about our sorrow: 'You have collected all my tears in your bottle. You have recorded each one in your book' (Psalm 56:8, NLT).

And that's only three to get us started! Surely it's enough to get the praise-wagon rolling, even if we don't feel like it.

Lord, make me thirsty for You. Help me to focus on what I know about You, and let it fire my praise on the days when I don't feel like it. Amen.

302

5 October

'But the water that I shall give him will become in him
a fountain of water springing up into everlasting life.'
John 4:14

Reading: John 4:1–13

Stand in the drinks aisle of any supermarket and you will be faced with row upon row of bottled and canned liquids, all marketed to quench our thirst. So much choice, but when it comes down to it, nothing quenches our thirst like pure, clear water. There are no rivals.

Water is essential to life. Two-thirds of our body is made up of water. It's required to help our body work at every level, from keeping joints supple to balancing the salts and chemicals essential for the heart and kidneys to function correctly. Reduce your fluid intake sufficiently and dry skin won't be the only problem that results. So important is it that the body has a clever early-warning system to tell us when we need to replenish: thirst. When we are lacking what is essential, thirst should be enough to send us for a drink.

Thankfully, our souls have a similar system in place. When we need spiritual rejuvenation, we are made aware that something is missing. We might think it's God, or peace, or satisfaction, when all the time we are being prompted to go for a 'drink' – of the kind that only Jesus can give.

Kidney failure makes you feel very ill – rotten in every way. The main culprits for this condition are a build-up of waste in the body and lack of fluid in the right places to make things better. In simple terms, extract the waste, correct the fluid imbalance, and soon the patient will begin to feel human again.

Soul-dryness is exactly the same. We feel empty and joyless. But when we deal with the waste – sin, laziness, anger or whatever – and drink deeply from the water Jesus gives, we soon begin to feel spiritually infused . . . satisfied once more. For our soul's sake, we need to obey our thirst!

Lord Jesus, give me the water of life, and make me thirsty for more. Amen.

6 October

A PASSAGE TO PONDER

As the deer pants for streams of water,

so my soul pants for you, O God.

My soul thirsts for God, for the living God.

When can I go and meet with God?

My tears have been my food day and night,

while men say to me all day long,

'Where is your God?'

Psalm 42:1–3, NIV

Read through the passage slowly and let the Author speak to you. As you ponder, ask yourself these questions:

- What does it say?
- What does it mean?
- What is God saying to me?
- How will I respond?

7 October

He turns a wilderness into pools of water,
And dry land into watersprings.

Psalm 107:35

Reading: Psalm 107:35–38

The River Lagan originates in the Mourne Mountains and travels fifty-three miles before flowing through Northern Ireland's capital city into Belfast Lough. Land hugs the lough on either side, forming a beautiful landscape. However, at one time, the lough was larger than it is today, owing to land reclamation in the areas closest to the city. What is this reclaimed land made of? Waste! Remarkably, the waters of the lough were deliberately pushed back, and a substantial portion of useable and beautiful land was created with the rubbish from thousands of households!

What appears ugly and even harmful can be made beautiful again. And no-one can make that happen better than the Creator Himself. Lives that once were vibrant, praise that at one time rang true, hearts that used to seek after God: all can be reclaimed and redesigned. We may find ourselves right in the middle of a desert experience, but God can transform it 'into pools of water' – into a place where life can begin again.

> I've learned that the desert itself is not a tragedy. The tragedy would be not to hear what God was saying to me there. How amazing that God does speak to us – but it takes courage and willingness to listen.[23]

Heavenly Father, give me the courage and willingness to listen to what You are saying to me when I find myself in the desert. Amen.

305

8 October

'Stand at the crossroads and look;
ask for the ancient paths,
ask where a good way is, and walk in it,
and you will find rest for your souls.'
Jeremiah 6:16, NIV

Reading: Psalm 25:1–5

My dad always says that if you've a tongue in your head you'll never stay lost. Jeremiah agrees. The prophet advises us to seek out routes that have already been tested. Not only that, he tells us also to ask for the best way. No point in complicating the issue. If we're going on a journey we might as well go on good roads. Unfortunately, pride produces the biggest hindrance to reaching our destination safely. Few of us like to ask for directions!

Thankfully, God knows all about our stubborn nature, and He often pre-empts our enquiries with questions of His own. What He asks invariably takes us back to the crossroads, where we'll see clearly the direction we need to take.

'Where are you?' He asks. Strange question, since God is all-seeing and all-knowing. But God isn't looking for information; rather, He's asking the very question we should be asking of ourselves. We can't move forward until we know where we are now.

God asked Adam this question after he and Eve had sinned in the Garden of Eden (Genesis 3:9). Of course, God knew where they were, but He wanted them to own up to their wrongdoing . . . to take that first step towards Him.

Finding ourselves in a spiritual desert rarely happens that quickly. Usually it happens one step at a time. Busy lives, broken hearts, lazy attitudes, selfish plans all contribute to a journey we hadn't initially planned to make. Sometimes we don't even realize we are there, until we hear a still, small voice inside whisper, 'Where are you?' An honest answer might surprise us, but at least now we can ask God to show us the way out . . . and we will 'find rest for [our] souls'.

Lord, I didn't realize I'd walked so far in the wrong direction. Show me the way back to the cross. My soul needs that promised rest. Amen.

9 October

And He said, 'Hagar, Sarai's maid, where have you
come from, and where are you going?'

Genesis 16:8

Reading: Genesis 16:6–16

Hagar had had enough. She was tired of Sarai's attitude towards her. It wasn't her fault that her mistress couldn't have children, but Hagar's smug contempt over carrying Abram's child proved the breaking point for Sarai, evoking a cruel response that made the young servant flee. Egypt was Hagar's destination – home. She was tired of the loveless mess she found herself in, but crossing the wilderness was no easy journey. Her swollen abdomen combined with the desert heat forced her to stop at the watering hole on the way to Shur.

A voice surprised Hagar as she rested in the shade. The unusual figure knew her. He addressed her as 'Sarai's maid', so she listened nervously. 'Where have you come from?' he asked. She quivered, remembering how her master had heard God speak directly to him. But God couldn't be interested in her, could He? So she blurted out that she'd run away from her cruel mistress, not bothering to mention her own misdemeanours. And the Angel of the Lord, in His graciousness, didn't mention them either, for in the desert He had found a broken woman who had been crushed by the circumstances of life.

Sometimes we find ourselves in a desert place because of what life throws at us. We might even be trying to run away from someone, or something, hoping that distancing ourselves might bring us peace. It didn't work for Hagar, and it won't work for us. She was all alone when God found her, and in the most inhospitable of places.

However, looking back and identifying what brought us to this difficult place, even if it wasn't our fault, is vitally important. For in our remembering we can hear the voice of the One who sees our broken hearts and is able to bring healing.

Help me, Lord, to visit past hurts, and to place them in Your hands for healing. Amen.

10 October

'I know your works. See, I have set before you
an open door, and no one can shut it.'
Revelation 3:8

Reading: Revelation 3:7–9

Hagar didn't know how to answer the stranger's second question: 'And where are you going?' (Genesis 16:8). He'd found her on the way to Shur, on the road to Egypt, where Abram had acquired her after his debacle with Pharaoh (Genesis 12:1–20). It seemed logical to run for home, but she didn't know if any of her family were still alive, or even if they'd take her back. In essence, Hagar hadn't a clue where she was going. But this messenger seemed to know all about her and exactly what she needed to do.

She was going to have a son, he told her – and many other descendants (Genesis 16:10), but first she had to return to her mistress. That was certainly not what Hagar wanted to hear, but when she heard the Angel of the Lord say, 'the Lord has heard your affliction' (verse 11), she knew that the God of Heaven would protect her. He'd promised: something that would reassure her in the days ahead.

When the way ahead looks unclear, or even bleak, and God whispers, 'And where are you going?' to us, it's good to remember that He is 'El Roi' – the God who sees me. He also knows what's best for us when we leave the wilderness. Perhaps it's time to re-examine the promises He gives of His love and His presence with us, and of His future plans for us.

> The Lord your God in your midst,
> The Mighty One, will save;
> He will rejoice over you with gladness,
> He will quiet you with His love.
> (Zephaniah 3:17)

> The Lord will guide you continually,
> And satisfy your soul in drought,
> And strengthen your bones;
> You shall be like a watered garden,
> And like a spring of water, whose waters do not fail.
> (Isaiah 58:11)

El Roi, thank You that I am never hidden from Your sight. I trust You to take me wherever You have planned. Amen.

11 October

Delight yourself also in the LORD,
And He shall give you the desires of your heart.

Psalm 37:4

Reading: Mark 10:35–40

James and John had a big answer to Jesus' question, 'What do you want Me to do for you?' They wanted a privileged place beside Christ in the next life. A big ask? A cheeky request? Perhaps both, but Jesus cautioned them that they didn't understand what they were asking for, or the personal cost involved should He have been able to grant it (Mark 10:39–40).

My guess is that most of us have a whole list of things that we want the Lord to do for us! But do we really understand what it is we're asking for? Are we aware of what could be involved if He were to answer our requests exactly as we wish?

The psalmist tells us that we will receive the desires of our hearts – wow, what a promise – but wait, there's a condition. We have first of all to delight ourselves in the Lord. What does that mean? The dictionary defines delight as receiving joy from someone, or giving joy to someone. Our fulfilment in life, including peace in each and every circumstance, is to be found in Him. He is our joy giver. When we make God our delight, we begin to see His heart for us and for those we love. Soon our desires will reflect His, and we will find it harder to ask amiss – selfish desires won't be what we're looking for.

Jesus clarifies it for us in Matthew 6:33: 'But seek first the kingdom of God and His righteousness, and all these things shall be added to you.'

The challenge is not getting God to answer our prayers, but rather to get to know more deeply the One who knows what we should be praying for. It's a win-win!

Show me Your heart, Heavenly Father, that my desires might mirror Yours, for that is where true fulfilment lies. Amen.

12 October

'Who do men say that I, the Son of Man, am?'
Matthew 16:13

Reading: Matthew 16:13–20

Caesarea Philippi was twenty-five miles north of the Sea of Galilee. As the centre of pagan worship in the region, it was spiritually alien territory. Carvings of the god Pan still decorated the streets – a chilling reminder of the many child sacrifices made to this monster, worshipped by multitudes. Now they were somewhat overshadowed by the temple built for the worship of Augustus Caesar. It was in these dark surroundings that Jesus asked this searching question.

The disciples answered that some people looked on Him as a prophet, even naming a few. Not an unusual answer, as Jewish expectations were that the Messiah would be a great prophet (Malachi 4:5). Then Jesus made the question personal: 'But who do you say that I am?' (verse 15).

Peter answered like a shot: 'You are the Christ, the Son of the living God' (verse 16). My paraphrase: 'You are the Messiah – the Anointed One! You are the Son of the living God – not like all these dead ones around us!'

Peter got it in one! Recognizing Jesus as the Messiah – not merely a new or a returning prophet – and as the Son of the only true and living God was vital for all that lay ahead of them, and for the church that would soon be formed. Their Messiah-God was not going to be overshadowed by any false deity in the future. God had come to earth.

Jesus always makes His questions personal. He asks us as pointedly as He did the disciples, 'But who do you say that I am?' We live in a world that wants to dilute who Jesus is, a world that calls us foolish for believing what the Bible says about Him. But if He is not Messiah then He is not worth worshipping, and He can't meet our need.

I'm with Peter . . . let's say it like it is, and declare Jesus as Messiah – Son of the living God!

Messiah-God, make me fearless like Peter in declaring who You are to a needy world. Amen.

310

13 October

A PASSAGE TO PONDER

When they walk through the Valley of Weeping,

it will become a place of refreshing springs.

The autumn rains will clothe it with blessings.

They will continue to grow stronger,

and each of them will appear before God in Jerusalem . . .

A single day in your courts is better than a thousand anywhere else!

I would rather be a doorkeeper in the house of my God

than live the good life in the homes of the wicked.

For the Lord God is our sun and shield.

He gives us grace and glory.

The Lord will withhold no good thing

from those who do what is right.

O Lord of Heaven's Armies,

what joy for those who trust in you.

Psalm 84:6–7, 10–12, NLT

Read through the passage slowly and let the Author speak to you. As you ponder, ask yourself these questions:

- What does it say?
- What does it mean?
- What is God saying to me?
- How will I respond?

14 October

To everything there is a season,
A time for every purpose under heaven.
Ecclesiastes 3:1

Reading: Job 14:7–9

'Why do the leaves fall off, Granny?'

'Because it's autumn.'

Phew! I breathed a sigh of relief that my inadequate reply satisfied our granddaughter . . . for now! Her other granny undoubtedly would've answered her question more accurately. I had homework to do, and in the learning God taught me more than about trees.

In the Northern Hemisphere, deciduous trees are in a race to survive the winter, so they rid themselves of what isn't necessary for life in the cold – their leaves. This way, all the energy they require as the days shorten and the temperature drops is conserved to ensure they can burst into life again once spring returns. Conversely, evergreens have smaller leaves coated in wax to protect them from the cold – coats that will withstand winter's blasts.

Shedding leaves has other benefits for the deciduous trees. It's said to reduce damage by the absence of insects, while lack of foliage may also allow for better pollination. Once stripped of last year's grandeur, the tree is ready to face whatever winter throws at it, and ready for new, healthy growth come spring.

The shedding of the autumn leaves is God's annual illustration of the importance of letting go. While there is such comfort in holding on to what we have and know, there comes a time when we have to let go of what stunts our growth in Christ. Harder still are the times when we have to let go of what we believe is good, or even best, in our lives. It difficult to imagine that it is only for a season . . . but spring will return and deliver joy once more.

Job thought a felled tree to be better off than he was – it could at least sprout again (Job 14:7), but he hadn't reckoned on God's restorative powers (Job 42:12–13). Spring blossomed once more for the man who had had to let go of so much.

Teach me to let go, Lord, in order that spring might come. Amen.

15 October

Yea, though I walk through the valley
of the shadow of death,
I will fear no evil;
For You are with me;
Your rod and Your staff, they comfort me.

Psalm 23:4

Reading: 1 John 3:2–3

Letting go is rarely easy, generally because it produces change – something few of us welcome. Undoubtedly, death brings about the biggest change of all. It takes so much, and appears to give back very little.

I thought I was prepared for the death of our first child. It wasn't unexpected, and I knew that heaven held far more for Cheryl than remaining here in her weak body. But I was her mother, and she was our firstborn – the one who filled our home with love, and whom God had used to teach me so much about Himself. Sickness and death meant that I couldn't keep her with me, or hold her in my arms, or stroke her soft skin. But neither could I let her go. Grief was all I had left of her, and so I held it close, not believing that God could bring me into a new season of happiness.

I had misunderstood what the psalmist had said about 'the valley of the shadow of death'. I hadn't recognized that I was to 'walk through' this valley, not live in it. The 'walk through' was to be a season of sadness that held the promise of an end. Only after I chose to let go of the depth of my grief, handing it over to the One who knew all about sorrow, did I receive the peace that added the energy to enable me to 'walk through'. Everyone grieves differently, and some stay longer in the 'valley' than others, but in the midst of our greatest losses we need to remind ourselves that God has more ahead for us. Now is not all there is.

Winter will one day turn into spring, but it requires the autumn of letting go in order for it to blossom as it should.

Lord, thank You that sadness is for a season, and seasons change. Amen.

313

16 October

But one thing I do, forgetting those things which are
behind and reaching forward to those things which
are ahead, I press toward the goal for the prize
of the upward call of God in Christ Jesus.
Philippians 3:13–14

Reading: Philippians 3:7–14

'Vindy, Ganny!' our nearly two-year-old grandson exclaimed, trying resolutely to hold on to his favourite hat.

He'd got it in one. In fact, 'vindy' was an understatement. He made a bolt for the front door across the lawn, now thickly carpeted with autumn's glorious cast-offs. Stopping to kick at a pile of leaves, something suddenly caught his eye. One bright red leaf stood out from all the rest. That was the one he wanted! The chase was on.

His little legs propelled him towards the leaf, but every time he stooped to pick it up a gust of wind took it from his reach and planted it somewhere else. The poor little man ran all over the garden trying to catch this one leaf, in spite of the fact that he was surrounded by hundreds of others. I began to feel sorry for him, thinking his chase futile. So I attempted distraction by pointing out a few other beautiful leaves he could pick up instead. But he wouldn't be sidetracked. There was only one for him!

And – eventually – he caught it! Such excitement!

'I got it!' he shouted, holding on tightly to his treasure. Determination had paid off. The most beautiful leaf in the garden was now his.

In Philippians 3, the apostle Paul declared himself a 'one thing' man. He could so easily have been distracted by the needs of the young church: the necessity to put false teachers right, the squabbles over circumcision, the persecution of new believers. Instead, Paul chose to focus on 'one thing' – his personal commitment to Jesus Christ.

It's easy to become distracted, but we'll never experience God's best unless we determine to become people of 'one thing', with Christ as the prize.

Lord, give me the determination to run after only what really matters! Amen.

314

17 October

'Do not marvel that I said to you,
"You must be born again."'

John 3:7

Reading: John 19:38–42

The dimly lit room was in stark contrast to where Nicodemus normally met to discuss religious matters, but what he had to ask Jesus wouldn't keep until morning. So when the Sanhedrin had exited the Chamber of Hewn Stone earlier, this particular Pharisee had made a beeline for the small house where the new rabbi was lodging for the night. Anyway, it was better for him not to attract the criticism of his peers before he found out for himself what Jesus of Nazareth was teaching.

Arriving in darkness suited the educated teacher and ruler of the Jews. The crowds had gone home – he had the privacy to ask what he wanted. But it was Jesus who led the conversation, confusing Nicodemus with talk of needing to be born again as a prerequisite to seeing the kingdom of God. *Impossible*, he thought. But the light began to dawn as Jesus continued. The Rabbi wasn't talking about physical rebirth, but of being born from above – made new on the inside – by God Himself!

Nicodemus' rule of life had been to make himself right with God by keeping the Law. He'd never heard anything like this before, or that God loved him … and everyone else in the world. How could it be? He headed home with as many questions as answers, and determined to keep an eye on Jesus. Not a difficult task, as barely a day passed without word reaching the Sanhedrin about the miracles Jesus had performed, as well as the insults He was throwing the Pharisees' way. But no-one wanted to listen to Nicodemus when eventually he was brave enough to stand up for Jesus.

Then, one Friday, the blood of the crucified One soaked into Nicodemus' cloak, as he and his friend Joseph gently lifted the Saviour from the cross. He no longer cared what others thought … he now understood what Jesus had told him that night in the darkness.

Lord Jesus, thank You that I am born again by Your Spirit. Amen.

315

18 October

If you confess with your mouth the Lord Jesus
and believe in your heart that God has
raised Him from the dead, you will be saved.

Romans 10:9

Reading: Romans 10:6–11

The news of Nicodemus' defection would have reached the Chamber of Hewn Stone at the speed of light. He had chosen to side with the blasphemer against his self-righteous colleagues who had pushed for the crucifixion of Jesus. The highest council in all of Judaism, who believed they were ridding themselves of a trouble-maker while holding fast to the Law, would have been horrified by the action of one of their own. For the Pharisees, Nicodemus' involvement in handling the corpse of Jesus was as demeaning as it was defiling. The wealthy 'ruler of the Jews' (John 3:1) hadn't just gone a step too far – he'd run a full mile from all he'd stood for previously.

I wonder whether Jesus' words, 'You must be born again', had kept Nicodemus awake at night . . . until he felt compelled to choose Jesus' way above his own. All those years of ritual, of laying on himself and others more burden than even the Law required. All that time believing and teaching that what he did made him right with God. Perhaps he concluded that Solomon was right: 'here is a way that seems right to a man, but its end is the way of death' (Proverbs 14:12). We are not told what brought Nicodemus to make his declaration of faith so public.

The Bible is silent about what happened to him after that weekend that shook Jerusalem and the world beyond, but it was a decision that changed his life for ever. History fills in a little of the story. Nicodemus lost his position as a Pharisee, and with it his honoured position on the Sanhedrin. Eventually he was forced to leave Jerusalem, hounded by the very religious Jews he once counted as friends.

Following Jesus today is costly, but the eternal rewards are great (Matthew 16:24–27).

Lord, may my lips confess to others what my heart believes. Amen.

19 October

'For whoever is ashamed of Me and My words in this adulterous and sinful generation, of him the Son of Man also will be ashamed when He comes in the glory of His Father with the holy angels.'

Mark 8:38

Reading: Mark 8:34–38

Jesus is standing in Pilate's hall,
Friendless, forsaken, betrayed by all;
Hearken! What meaneth the sudden call?
What will you do with Jesus?

What will you do with Jesus?
Neutral you cannot be;
Some day your heart will be asking,
'What will He do with me?'

Will you evade Him as Pilate tried?
Or will you choose Him, whate'er betide?
Vainly you struggle from Him to hide?
What will you do with Jesus?

Will you, like Peter, your Lord deny?
Or will you scorn from His foes to fly,
Daring for Jesus to live or die?
What will you do with Jesus?

'Jesus, I give Thee my heart today,
Jesus, I'll follow Thee all the way,
Gladly obeying Thee!' will you say:
'This I will do with Jesus!'[24]

Lord, I'm taking sides – Yours! Neutral I will not be. Amen.

317

20 October

A PASSAGE TO PONDER

Nothing in all creation can hide from him.

Everything is naked and exposed before his eyes.

This is the God to whom we must explain all we have done.

That is why we have a great High Priest who has gone to heaven,

Jesus the Son of God.

Let us cling to him and never stop trusting him.

This High Priest of ours understands our weaknesses,

for he faced all of the same temptations as we do,

yet he did not sin.

So let us come boldly to the throne of our gracious God.

There we will receive his mercy,

and we will find grace to help us when we need it.

Hebrews 4:13–16, NLT

Read through the passage slowly and let the Author speak to you. As you ponder, ask yourself these questions:

- What does it say?
- What does it mean?
- What is God saying to me?
- How will I respond?

21 October

'Do not be afraid of their faces,
For I am with you to deliver you,' says the LORD.
Jeremiah 1:8

Reading: Jeremiah 1:4–8

Rarely had I seen terror etched on a face so intensely as I did that morning. It was clearly the young man's first public solo appearance. He was under scrutiny, and not coping with the experience very well. Watching him struggle over constructing a mushroom and tomato omelette quickly became unbearable, so I opted for bacon and scrambled egg from the buffet instead.

Fear had made the young trainee chef completely lose it over something as simple as beaten egg, chopped mushrooms, a diced tomato and a hot skillet! The result was almost as painful to observe as it was for him to perform. The cold, critical stares of hungry guests fuelled the fear, resulting in a total mess-up.

Fear has a way of doing that. It starts with a little doubt that can quickly morph into panic. It can present a huge stumbling block to any task we wish to attempt, or communication we want to make. It's especially true when we're trying to address what the Bible has to say on important issues. Fear of sticking our heads above the parapet and of being shot down, especially on social media, can cause us to back down when we should be presenting truth with grace.

The young prophet Jeremiah understood this kind of fear back in his day too. He was terrified that the people wouldn't listen to him because he was so young. In fact, fear followed the young man around, but he decided to deliver God's message in spite of the threats made against him. After all, God told him not to be afraid of their faces – He would be right there with him . . . and He was!

That promise still stands, and at times silence isn't golden, as someone has said – it's just plain yellow!

Dear Lord, help me to push down the fear that wants to overwhelm me when I should be speaking up for You. Amen.

319

22 October

And the LORD said to him, 'Surely I will be with you,
and you shall defeat the Midianites as one man.'

Judges 6:16

Reading: Judges 6:11–16

Was there ever a story of a man more fearful than Gideon?

Remarkably, the Angel of the Lord addressed him as a 'mighty man of valor' (verse 12)! This quality was not evident at first glance, for Gideon was hiding from his enemies in a hole in the ground, trying to do a job that needed elevated, flat ground with access to a winnowing wind. He even went as far as to suggest to the divine Visitor that the Lord had forsaken them, declaring that his experience of God was certainly not that of the Deliverer from Egypt he heard of as a child (verse 13).

But God was patient with His fearful servant, and met each of his fears with a response that eventually assured the young man that God would be with him, and that he would 'defeat the Midianites as one man' (verse 16).

Eventually we see fear transformed into courage as Gideon led the small army of three hundred men, armed only with a flaming torch concealed in a pot and a ram's horn, against the 135,000 fighting men of Midian, Amalek and the people of the East. All it took was for Gideon to shout, 'The sword of the LORD and of Gideon!', wave his torch, blow his trumpet and watch – watch as God kept His promise. The battle was God's, just as He said (Judges 7:9). Victory occurred without a drop of Hebrew blood being shed!

What happened to transform the shaking servant into a gallant general? Little by little, Gideon handed his fears over to God, and eventually he saw God as bigger than what terrified him.

Fear can cause us to freeze, or help us to focus on the truth that when we can't, God can. It's promised – Philippians 4:13!

Lord Jesus, when fear comes, help me to pass it over to You, for 'with God nothing shall be impossible' (Luke 1:37). Amen.

320

23 October

What then shall we say to these things?
If God is for us, who can be against us?

Romans 8:31

Reading: Judges 7:9–15

Ask any military leader to list the challenges to victory in battle, and fear among his own men will be at the top. Fear is contagious and can become destructive when it goes unchecked. Its negativity is also problematic in our spiritual lives, a fact not lost on the enemy of our souls.

Thankfully, courage is every bit as catching.

Eventually, an army of sorts from the neighbouring tribes gathered around Gideon. Bit of a motley crew, really. As farmers and shepherds they knew nothing of warfare. Their bravery went as far as showing up. While defeating the advancing enemy was imperative, God also had important lessons to teach His own people in the process. So the 32,000 gathered forces were whittled down to 10,000, simply by sending home those who were afraid (Judges 7:3). God knew that Gideon didn't need the contagion of fear to spread. Eventually, Gideon's army numbered a mere three hundred men . . . plus God.

Then, hours before battle, God gave Gideon the most extraordinary picture of victory (Judges 7:13–15), and His general had his fear finally exchanged for courage. Such was the rampant spread of that courage on Gideon's farming-force that a military impossibility was the result. Three hundred men plus God put a trained army of 135,000 to flight!

Courage grows when we recognize that 'If God is for us, who can be against us?' (Romans 8:31).

God of the Heavenly Hosts, thank You that with You by my side I have the majority needed to face down any foe in my life. Amen.

321

24 October

'But I have prayed for you, that your faith should not fail.'
Luke 22:32

Reading: Romans 8:26–27

Some of us are natural risk-takers, relishing a new challenge, dependent on the adrenaline rush to take us on to the next thing. Others, like myself, are more conservative about trying new things, yet able to tolerate a little fear to face the challenge of moving out of our comfort zones. However, a few of us are literally terrified of our own shadow; held captive by unreasonable levels of fear that make faith difficult and even daily life problematic.

I am deeply encouraged by these words spoken to Peter by Jesus. Even though the Saviour knew exactly how badly Peter was going to react when put under pressure, He didn't see him as a lost cause. In fact, Jesus told Peter that He had already prayed for him – not that he'd be saved from the test, but that Peter's faith would not fail through the experience. And He went on to confirm that He still had a plan for the big fisherman to strengthen his brethren after he returned to the Lord (verse 32).

There will always be days when our faith in God is challenged, particularly over standing up for Him in the public square. That is a scary experience that doesn't always turn out the way we'd like. All of us have a 'Peter streak' running through us, because fear is a favourite weapon used by the enemy of our souls. But take heart . . . Jesus is praying for us, that our faith might not fail. He still has plans for us. He's the God of the second chance.

So when our heart races and our palms are sweaty, let's call to mind that powerful picture of Jesus praying for us – an image sure to rout any foe, even the enemy of our souls.

Lord, thank You for praying for me. Please don't let my faith fail, but rather may I daily choose to trust You rather than to give in to fear. Amen.

25 October

He shall cover you with His feathers,
And under His wings you shall take refuge.
Psalm 91:4

Reading: Psalm 91:1–6

Sometimes you just need to run for cover!

Fear may rise, courage might fail and exhaustion overtake us, but there is always a way out. God has promised a way of escape: 'but God is faithful, [and] will not allow you to be tempted beyond what you are able, but with the temptation will also make the way of escape, that you may be able to bear it' (1 Corinthians 10:13).

God is tender towards His children. He recognizes our struggles and longs to draw us to His heart, protecting us with the gentle covering of His Fatherly love. Too often we live under punitive law, when He has given us the gentleness of His grace to keep us safe – spreading his wings in invitation to seek His refuge.

'O Jerusalem, Jerusalem,' Jesus lamented over the Holy City, 'the one who kills the prophets and stones those who are sent to her! How often I wanted to gather your children together, as a hen gathers her chicks under her wings, but you were not willing!' (Matthew 23:37). Past failure didn't stop Jesus wanting to gather Jerusalem's children in His tender embrace, but sadly they were having none of it. They rejected the kindness of God – a response that broke the Saviour's heart.

So whatever burdens our hearts today, let's not reject His invitation. And if you need to, run for cover! His welcoming wings are already outstretched.

Heavenly Father, there are some days when the sound of Your heart is what I need to hear. Thank You that even this is possible. Amen.

26 October

And so, since God in his mercy has given us this
wonderful ministry, we never give up.
2 Corinthians 4:1, NLT

Reading: 2 Corinthians 4:5–10

Speaking to the boys and young men of his former prep school in Harrow, Sir Winston Churchill said, 'Never give in, never give in, never, never, never, never – in nothing, great or small, large or petty – never give in, except in circumstances of honour and good sense.'

Churchill's strong leadership and motivational words were undoubtedly influential in Britain, and with her allies, in the winning of the Second World War. He never gave in – even when victory seemed impossible. His attitude of heart and will was contagious.

The apostle Paul encourages Christ's followers to do the same – never give up. In this difficult passage in his letter to the Corinthian church, he makes it clear that following Jesus will involve hardship (verse 8), but God never abandons us (verse 9). Speaking of 'this wonderful ministry' (verse 1, NLT) that we should never give up, Paul reminds us that 'this precious treasure – this light and power that now shine within us – is held in perishable containers, that is, our weak bodies. So that everyone can see that our glorious power is from God and is not our own' (verse 7, NLT).

Imagine. The glorious light of the gospel message has been entrusted to us – 'jars of clay' (NIV), 'perishable containers' (NLT). We are breakable! But then those who need the good news we carry don't need powerful people to tell them how to live, but ordinary people who show them an all-powerful God. He is the reason we should never give up 'this wonderful ministry' (verse 1), 'so that the life of Jesus may also be seen in our bodies' (verse 10, NLT).

So, never, never, never . . . you get the point!

Thank You, Lord, that You never gave up on me. May I determine to serve You with the same passion. Amen.

324

27 October

A PASSAGE TO PONDER

The Lord will guide you continually,

watering your life when you are dry and keeping you healthy, too.

You will be like a well-watered garden,

like an ever-flowing spring.

Your children will rebuild the deserted ruins of your cities.

Then you will be known as the people

who rebuild their walls and cities.

Keep the Sabbath day holy.

Don't pursue your own interests on that day,

but enjoy the Sabbath and

speak of it with delight as the Lord's holy day.

Honour the Lord in everything you do,

And don't follow your own desires or talk idly.

If you do this, the Lord will be your delight.

Isaiah 58:11–14, NLT

Read the passage slowly, and let the Author speak to you. As you ponder, ask yourself these questions:

- What does it say?
- What does it mean?
- What is God saying to me?
- How will I respond?

28 October

For God has not given us a spirit of fear and timidity,
but of power, love and self-discipline.

2 Timothy 1:7, NLT

Reading: 2 Timothy 1:6–12

I love the fact that our God is the God of the great exchange.

- He exchanges our sin with His forgiveness (Romans 5:8).
- He exchanges the judgment we deserve with the freedom of His mercy (Romans 8:1).
- He exchanges our pain with His peace (Philippians 4:7).
- He exchanges the rejection of others with His acceptance (Ephesians 1:6).
- He exchanges our imperfections with His perfection (Hebrews 10:14).
- He exchanges the ashes of our lives with His beauty, replacing our sorrow with His joy (Isaiah 61:3).
- He exchanges my selfish dreams with His plans (Jeremiah 29:11).
- He exchanges my loneliness with His presence (Deuteronomy 31:6).

In today's scripture, Paul is reminding us, through the advice he gives to the young Timothy, that God will exchange our fear with power, love and self-discipline. Power: to face what we know we cannot handle by ourselves. Love: to remind us that we are not merely disciples, but God's own children. Self-discipline: to help us make the godly decisions along the way that will prevent fear from forming in the first place.

God waits to make an everlasting swap with us on a daily basis. All it takes on our part is a willingness to surrender what isn't working into His hands: to give up 'me' in exchange for Him.

Loving Father, I gladly give up the inferior in order that I might utilize Your best in my life. Amen.

326

29 October

A merry heart does good, like medicine,
But a broken spirit dries the bones.
Proverbs 17:22

Reading: Ecclesiastes 9:7–10

The Bible contains more wisdom than all the self-help books ever written. Who would ever have thought that the psychology of laughter was right in there too? For laughter is indeed good medicine, just as the Bible says. It reduces tension, and at the same time releases endorphins – the body's 'feel-good' chemicals – into the bloodstream. According to research, these endorphins produce a sense of well-being, even stretching temporarily to relieve pain. It's hard to feel tense when you're laughing! And even if it is only temporary, it can cause enough of a diversion to help you think straight again.

I'd had a tough week. Disappointment and hurt had rolled in faster than a tropical storm, with resultant damage. I'd tried to hide how I felt, and to sort out the problem before it became even more out of control. Then, while feeling both tired and discouraged, God sent me some medicine. It came in the guise of a WhatsApp chat with my daughter-in-law. She'd had a hard week too, but of a different kind.

Before long, silly conversations travelled the fifty miles back and forward between us, rapidly visualized by even sillier emojis, leaving me literally rolling in the aisles! It was one of those occasions when exhaustion fuels inane, harmless laughter that makes no sense to anyone else, and not even to yourself the following day! But oh, it did feel good to laugh. It's exactly what my broken spirit needed – just what the Great Physician ordered. Try a dose of it yourself today – engage in something that will make you laugh. It's unlikely to fix the problem, but it will lighten your heart, and perhaps even help to add perspective to the mix.

Thank You, Lord, for creating me with the ability to laugh. May I display a cheerful heart to bless others today. Amen.

327

30 October

Great peace have those who love Your law,
And nothing causes them to stumble.

Psalm 119:165

Reading: Psalm 119:161–168

One definition of a classic is 'a book everyone has heard of, but nobody reads'. I could certainly rattle off the names of some very famous books I have never read! But would that make me knowledgeable about the classics?

In our consideration of fear, we discover that where peace resides, fear might dare to knock at the door, but will find it hard to obtain houseroom. But how do we 'fill up' our heart-space with such quantities of peace to be able to refuse entry to fear? By getting to know – and love – the world's best-known classic!

How sad if the Bible were to gather dust alongside Dickens and Tolstoy on our bookshelves, with, at best, an occasional cursory glance at a few verses – especially when the psalmist explains that the knowledge and love of God's Word fills us with *great* peace. And even more than that, minds and hearts filled with God's Word won't stumble like those of us do who don't know what God says on the difficult issues of life. The importance of hiding God's Word in our hearts (Psalm 119:11) can hardly be made any clearer.

We are always the beneficiaries when it comes to getting stuck into this particular classic. If you're still in doubt, then slowly read through the longest psalm in the Bible, for every one of Psalm 119's 176 verses explains what God's Word is about and the benefits it brings to our lives. That's a lot of evidence! Surely, the Bible is one classic we don't want to miss out on?

Thank You, Lord, that the antidote to fear is found in Your Word, which is available to me in so many formats. Give success to those who are working hard to make the Bible accessible to every tribe and tongue and nation. Amen.

31 October

They searched the Scriptures day after day
to check up on Paul and Silas, to see if they were
really teaching the truth.
Acts 17:11, NLT

Reading: Ephesians 2:4–10

You can't have lived through 2017 and not heard mention of the Reformation, and especially the name of one man in particular – Martin Luther. More than 500 years ago, on this day in 1517, the German monk nailed his '95 Theses' to the door of the church in Wittenberg in an attempt to open debate about the corrupt practices that had seeped into the Catholic Church.

Martin Luther had no intention of starting a new church, but meant rather to call the church to account for straying from the primacy of the Bible and the truth that only God could grant salvation. Like the Bereans spoken about in Acts 17, Martin Luther had been checking out what God's Word said on these important matters. He was particularly distressed about the selling of 'indulgences' by the church to absolve sin – a practice Luther couldn't find in Holy Scripture.

Emerging from the Reformation that followed Luther's brave stand came the five 'Solas': five biblical statements of faith for all believers to follow, and which became the foundation of the Protestant Church.

- **Sola Scriptura**: 'Scripture Alone' (2 Timothy 3:16–17). The Bible is the only source of authority for Christians.
- **Sola Fide**: 'Faith Alone' (Ephesians 2:8–9). Salvation is God's free gift through faith in Him. It cannot be bought.
- **Sola Gratia**: 'Grace Alone' (Ephesians 2:8–9). Salvation is by God's grace – unmerited favour – alone, and not by our works.
- **Sola Christus**: 'Christ Alone' (Hebrews 4:15). Jesus provides the only access to God.
- **Sola Deo Gloria**: 'God's Glory Alone' (1 Corinthians 10:31). God's glory is to be the goal of our lives.

Lord Jesus, help me to test what others say by what's written in Your Word, that I might keep to the right path. Amen.

329

November

1 November

Praise be to the Lord, to God our Saviour, who daily bears our burdens.

Psalm 68:19, NIV

Reading: Psalm 68:32–35

Sometimes it's just one word that hits you between the eyes when you read the Bible. Today's verse would still read well without this word. It's not essential to make the sentence structure correct. But oh, what a powerful message we would miss if it had been left out.

Jesus is our burden bearer! Our sin He has willingly carried on the cross, taking with it the punishment we deserve, exchanging it for forgiveness and new life.

Jesus also carries the burdens of life for us, lightening our load of heartache, sorrow and pain. He enables us to continue when we feel that we cannot face another day, granting us strength when our own is used up. The carrying of heavy hearts is no challenge to Him, for He 'is close to the broken-hearted and saves those who are crushed in spirit' (Psalm 34:18, NIV).

Yes, the Bible is crammed with evidence that Jesus is indeed our burden bearer, but this verse reminds us that He *daily* bears our burdens'. How wonderful to have that extra word! *Daily!* Each and every day the Saviour is willing to take every single thing that weighs us down and carry it for us. He doesn't expect us to carry it for a time, until He's ready to take it on. No. Every day He waits for us to release it into His care, 'for his compassions never fail. They are new every morning; great is your faithfulness' (Lamentations 3:22–23, NIV).

Lord Jesus, I am so thankful for that extra word! That, daily, You are willing to bear my burdens, however difficult they may be. Faithful is Your name. Amen.

2 November

Our purpose is to please God, not people.
He is the One who examines the motives of our hearts.

1 Thessalonians 2:4, NLT

Reading: 1 Thessalonians 2:4–8

Already the seasonal aisles in the supermarkets have been changed from Halloween (a non-event in our home) to Christmas. And as I hurried by I allowed a sigh to escape.

Christmas. It's only November but already I feel my pulse rate increase, and my inner self reminds me of last year's promise not to stress so much. I love Christmas, but the 'busy meter' seems to rise beyond where I want it to go. That's true for most people, especially women, but for those involved in church life it adds an extra dimension.

Choir practices, nativity plays, fellowship dinners, carol services, extra visiting, and special Advent, Christmas and watchnight services. Phew! I'm tired just thinking about it! I doubt we were ever meant to greet the season with such frenzied activity, or that the Lord was the inventor of these backbreaking schedules. In all of our busyness to encourage others to see the true meaning of Christmas, it can be easy to miss the joy ourselves. Perish the thought that we might ever get to the stage where we resent this season of celebration because we are too involved in pleasing other people.

Yes, it is important to make the most of Christmas – we have so much to celebrate, and to share with others. But let's be careful not to lose our focus. 'Our purpose is to please God, not people' (verse 4, NLT). Neither should we forget to plan in refreshment and rest for our own souls. It's not selfish – it's sensible. Let's look at those Christmas schedules now: plan early, cut back on what is not essential, and strive this year to focus on what is important ... preparing our own hearts to worship the newborn King.

Lord, busyness is a human trait. But You are never in a hurry. Help me work on that which brings You honour, something a stressed heart cannot do. Amen.

334

3 November

A PASSAGE TO PONDER

It is the same with my word.

I send it out, and it always produces fruit.

It will accomplish all I want it to,

and it will prosper everywhere I send it.

You will live in joy and peace.

The mountains and hills will burst into song,

and the trees of the field will clap their hands!

Where once there were thorns, cypress trees will grow.

Where briers grew, myrtles will sprout up.

This miracle will bring great honour to the Lord's name;

it will be an everlasting sign of his power and love.

Isaiah 55:11–13, NLT

Read the passage slowly and let the Author speak to you. As you ponder, ask yourself these questions:

- What does it say?
- What does it mean?
- What is God saying to me?
- How will I respond?

335

4 November

The LORD has done great things for us,
And we are glad.

Psalm 126:3

Reading: 2 Corinthians 9:10–15

When the *Mayflower* finally reached the New World in 1620, after five months at sea, the Pilgrims were totally unprepared for the harsh winter that decimated many of those who had survived that long journey to religious freedom. In spite of the grace of God, and the help of the native Indians, only 51 souls remained alive of the 102 who had disembarked at Plymouth Rock.

Yet, having suffered such great loss, these men and women treasured their freedom to worship God above all else. Following their first harvest in America, they hosted a three-day feast of thanksgiving to Almighty God in celebration. Eventually it became an annual one-day event, declared as a day of thanksgiving across the USA in 1771, and finally written into law as a national holiday in 1941!

To this day, Thanksgiving is observed as a day for families to come together to give thanks to Almighty God for His goodness. Enjoying special food together and praying around the table is seen as part of the celebration – even for those who do not pray at any other time of the year. There is no exchange of gifts so that the focus is directed appropriately, and no Christmas preparations until Thanksgiving comes to an end.

We may not sit at a 'Thanksgiving' table today, but that doesn't mean we shouldn't take time to thank God for His blessings in our lives: for the food we eat, the home we live in, the clothes we wear, the friendships we enjoy, the job we work at, the people who love us . . . and the God who sent His Son to bring us salvation – we say thank You, Lord, from the bottom of our hearts!

Lord, I'm not thankful enough for the blessings You shower on my life. Help me to develop a gratitude attitude every day of the year. Amen.

5 November

'Well done, good and faithful servant . . .
enter into the joy of your lord.'
Matthew 25:21

Reading: 1 Peter 4:9–11

After serving the Lord in evangelism for more than two decades, my husband accepted the call to pastor a church. I don't know how many hands we shook the night of his installation, but there is one in particular I will never forget. As with most people at the service, we'd never met this man before. He was small in stature but he had a surprisingly strong grip. I thought he was never going to let go of my hand, so excited was he that God had answered his prayers that my husband would come to the church. And for the seventeen years that have passed since that night, neither his enthusiasm nor his smile has ever dimmed.

We were to learn that Eddie Norris was one of God's encouragers. There isn't one person in our church that this godly man hasn't prayed for, and often encouraged in other ways too. He had the ability to bear the burdens of others like few I have known, while his fervent love for the Saviour often put me to shame.

For many years God blessed our lives, and those in our congregation, through His servant, but earlier this morning Eddie entered into the joy of his Lord. His work here has finally ended. Imagine the smile on his face now! Eddie may have left us, but the challenge of his life lives on. You see, serving the Master was no chore to Eddie. God's love so overwhelmed him that he couldn't keep it to himself – it burst out in service – he leaked!

We might be tempted to ask God for more 'Eddies' in our churches, but actually any faithful 'name' will do. That's all God requires. He'll do the rest.

Lord Jesus, thank You for using Your faithful servant to bless my life. Make me part of the next generation who leak the love of God to all those we meet. Amen.

6 November

The rain and snow come down from the heavens and stay
on the ground to water the earth. They cause the grain
to grow, producing seed for the farmer and bread for the
hungry. It is the same with my word. I send it out,
and it always produces fruit.

Isaiah 55:10–11, NLT

Reading: Isaiah 55:8–11

God's Word, the Bible, compares itself with a number of things, including a refining fire and a hammer to break hardened hearts (Jeremiah 23:29), a lamp to guide us (Psalm 119:105), a mirror to reflect our true selves (James 1:22–25) and food to nourish our spiritual lives (1 Peter 2:2).

But I love that God's Word also likens itself to the rain that falls on parched ground, something that Isaiah, living in the Middle East, would have known all about. Initially the rain would bounce off the hard ground, but the promise here is that the rain would 'stay on the ground to water the earth' (verse 10, NLT). Eventually the showers would soften the soil, then seep through it, refreshing it and making it possible for the seeds to germinate and the crops to grow. The bread that ultimately satisfied the hungry was made possible because of the rain that fell.

Refreshing rain. The most precious promise a dry and thirsty soul can receive. God says, 'I will send showers, showers of blessings, which will come just when they are needed' (Ezekiel 34:26, NLT). Wonderful news for those times when we feel the cracks of hurt and disappointment forming, and no rain clouds can be seen on the horizon. Yet Isaiah reminds us that the very refreshment we need – those showers of blessing – are found in God's Word. As we open the Book, 'Then he will respond to us as surely as the arrival of dawn or the coming of rains in early spring' (Hosea 6:3, NLT).

Lord God, thank You that Your Word is living and powerful. Help me to open the Book regularly to receive the refreshment my soul needs. Amen.

338

7 November

Avoid all perverse talk;
stay far from corrupt speech.
Proverbs 4:24, NLT

Reading: Proverbs 4:20–24

The BBC was once a paragon of virtue with regard to how its presenters spoke and the language they used. However, listening back to old recordings, it's easy to see that the life experience of its very posh speakers was a million miles distant from that of the average listener.

Today things are very different, with regional accents now widespread on television and radio. But on the flipside, the language and innuendo used by presenters can at times be shocking. Standards have fallen, and the sad thing is that most people don't even notice it.

We are encouraged in Ephesians 4:1, 17 'to walk worthy of the calling with which you were called', and to 'no longer walk as the rest of the Gentiles walk'. We are meant to be different from those around us. That includes what comes out of our mouths.

Yet sometimes it is not what we say that challenges people's lives, but what we don't say. At conversion we become a new creation in Christ Jesus (2 Corinthians 5:17) – that includes our speech. Is our conversation devoid of bad language? Do others know we won't listen to office gossip? Are we speaking about, and to, others with kindness and grace 'as a representative of the Lord Jesus' (Colossians 3:17, NLT)?

In this digital age, 'perverse talk' comes at us from all directions. But we can be ambassadors for change – the kind of change that is good for all of us.

Heavenly Father, may my conversation be pure and full of encouragement. May my ears close quickly to words that damage others, and may my influence instigate change in my home, workplace and community. For Your glory, Amen.

8 November

Being confident of this very thing,
that He who has begun a good work in you
will complete it until the day of Jesus Christ.
Philippians 1:6

Reading: Philippians 1:3–11

God never stops working on us. He never gives up. He never decides that He's tired of trying to make us what we're meant to be. And certainly He never reaches the place where He concludes that we are a lost cause – not worth any more effort.

God always finishes the job He starts.

Once He has begun that good work of salvation in our lives, He will keep on going with us until it is complete. As He chips away at our imperfections, we are reminded that His 'grace is sufficient' (2 Corinthians 12:9) – when we feel inadequate, discouraged or even rebellious. Sometimes it takes the gentle touch of a kind Father to make the necessary changes, especially when the image is painfully crushed. On other occasions it's the firm hand of correction that is required to keep us on course, like when resentment attempts to stop essential maintenance. But whatever we need in these 'work-in-progress' lives of ours, the Master Builder faithfully sticks at it.

The cost of our construction has been too great for the Father ever to give up: 'For by one sacrifice [– the death of His Son –] He has made perfect for ever those who are being made holy' (Hebrews 10:14, NIV). This same Jesus will one day 'present [us] holy, and blameless' (Colossians 1:22). The work will finally be finished! Made possible by God's grace and love, our final robing in Christ's righteousness – for we 'are complete in Him' (Colossians 2:10).

And God has a completion date. A date that can neither be changed nor delayed, for on that day when Christ Jesus comes back again (Philippians 1:6, NLT), the Master will put down His tools and we will be presented 'faultless' before His throne (Jude 24).

You are still working on me, Creator God. May I wait patiently until the work is complete. Amen.

9 November

For wherever there is jealousy and selfish ambition,
there you will find disorder and every kind of evil.

James 3:16, NLT

Reading: James 3:13–18

Pixar Animation has made a fortune out of monsters. I remember watching the first *Monsters, Inc.* film with my granddaughter, concerned that some of the monsters were really quite scary for one so young. But the filmmakers were clever enough to make the main character, Sully, so adorable and cuddly, and his one-eyed friend Mike so cute, that the baddies were totally overshadowed by this winsome pair. So much so that Sully and Mike are taken to bed every night by a multitude of children worldwide.

If only the monsters we meet in real life were so easily house-trained!

As with the scary kind we used to get our parents to check for under our beds when we were growing up, most of the monsters we encounter today are of our own making. The green-eyed version James speaks about here can, if left unchecked, cause enormous damage to ourselves, and to those on whom we inflict it. There's nothing cuddly nor adorable about 'jealousy'. And its companion 'selfish ambition' is no better. Instead, James attributes 'disorder and every kind of evil' to the presence of these two monsters in our lives. Wow! That's tough talk.

Maybe it's time to search under the bed, throw open the cupboard doors, pull back the curtains and rid ourselves of such monsters before they cause any further damage? Or better still, don't let them gain entrance in the first place. Instead, let's be 'peace loving, gentle at all times, and willing to yield to others' (James 3:17, NLT).

Forgive me, Lord, for the times I've coveted what others have and have pushed my own agenda to gain recognition. Help me to give praise where it is due, and to seek good for others. Amen.

10 November

A PASSAGE TO PONDER

Anyone who lives on milk, being still an infant,

is not acquainted with the teaching about righteousness.

But solid food is for the mature,

who by constant use have trained themselves

to distinguish good from evil.

Therefore let us leave the elementary

teachings about Christ

and go on to maturity.

Hebrews 5:13 – 6:1, NIV

Read the passage slowly and let the Author speak to you. As you ponder, ask yourself these questions:

- What does it say?
- What does it mean?
- What is God saying to me?
- How will I respond?

11 November

Looking steadfastly at him, [all] saw his face as the face of an angel.
Acts 6:15

Reading: Acts 6:8–15

Stephen had been chosen – along with six others – to do the rather menial job of overseeing the practical needs of the growing number of converts, particularly the widows among them. Stephen did his job well and was also gifted in other ways. 'And Stephen, full of faith and power, did great wonders and signs among the people' (Acts 6:8).

In spite of the good Stephen did, there were those who feared the downfall of Judaism more than the miraculous workings of God, so they set about concocting false charges of blasphemy against this man of God. It wasn't long before Stephen was dragged before the Jewish high court. Such was the power they wielded, the Sanhedrin usually struck terror into those brought before them.

They were doggedly trying to keep control of the 'rabble' that was causing havoc in synagogues across the land with their message of a risen Messiah. They saw in Stephen an opportunity to put a stop to that by making an example of him. Except that there was a problem they hadn't reckoned on: as the seventy-one members of council looked at Stephen, they 'saw his face as the face of an angel' (verse 15).

This man was more than a dissenter. This man had the manifestation of God written on His face. His very presence in their religious court challenged their own spirituality. I wonder whether Stephen made these experts in the Law think about Moses, whose face shone when he left God's presence to speak to the people (Exodus 34:29)?

What does my face say when I enter a room, or return to work on Monday morning? Do I bring the presence of Jesus with me, or am I just like everyone else, muttering about the weather, my workload and whatever else is current news? Or could it be that someone will notice that I have been with Jesus (Acts 4:13)?

Lord Jesus, may someone see Your presence manifested in me today. Amen.

12 November

After this I saw a vast crowd, too great to count,
from every nation and tribe and people and language,
standing in front of the throne and before the Lamb.
Revelation 7:9, NLT

Reading: Revelation 14:6–7

My first involvement in a truly international Christian conference was deeply moving. More than 300 Christian workers from all over Europe had made their way to the five-day event in Germany, by train, plane, car and bus. While I had only to step on a plane, many had travelled for days in clapped-out cars. They came together for fellowship and Bible teaching, and to report on how their work was progressing back at home.

My involvement was within the seminar programme and counselling team. It was the first time I had spoken through an interpreter, which was fun, except during those personal counselling appointments when those baring their souls had to do so through someone else's lips.

However, the highlight for me was the presentation of the national flags on the opening evening. Men and women who willingly presented the gospel to boys and girls across Europe proudly carried dozens of flags on to the platform. Many of them worked in countries hostile to the Christian message, and they were greeted with much applause and many tears as they mounted the platform steps. Mention was made, and prayers were offered, for those who had been refused exit visas to attend the conference. Their flags were proudly lifted by substitutes.

In a small way, I caught a glimpse of John's vision recorded here in Revelation. And I couldn't help wondering what it would be like to hear the roll call in Heaven, not only for those from Europe, but also for believers from 'every nation and tribe and people and language' (verse 9, NLT), believers who today need our prayers as they carry on serving God in tough places.

Lord, please bless Your children today who labour in the dangerous places of this world. Grant them strength and peace, laced with joy. Amen.

13 November

And if one member suffers, all the members suffer with it.
1 Corinthians 12:26

Reading: 2 Corinthians 1:7–9

'**Nigeria: Ambush**' 'A Christian woman and her two children killed in north-central Nigeria.'

'**Egypt: church attack**' 'More than 50 Islamists attacked the church of Anba Moussa in Ezbet al-Qeshri.'

'**Sudan: arrests**' 'Police arrested five SCOC church leaders after they refused to comply with an order to refrain from worship.'

'**Malaysia: no news**' 'There was still no news about the pastor almost nine months after his abduction.'

'**India: attack after conversions**' 'Weeks after a pastor led five families to faith in Christ in southern India, masked men on motorbikes intercepted him on his way home from worship and tried to kill him.'[25]

You could be forgiven if you thought these quotes came from a publication specializing in news of the persecuted church, but you'd be wrong. These are headlines taken directly from a general Christian newspaper that reports on matters of interest to the Christian church. And these five headlines are only a small number taken from one edition of said publication.

Where is the response from those of us whom Paul says are all part of one body (1 Corinthians 12:20)? Does God hear me cry for the plight of my brothers and sisters across the world who suffer for believing in Jesus? Sadly, if I'm honest, not nearly often enough. Let's join forces to pray for those under persecution today, praying that God will strengthen them, grant them protection and give them peace. Only let's not stop at today.

Heavenly Father, forgive my neglect of those parts of the 'body' who are suffering because of their faith in You. Surround them with an outpouring of Your love, assuring them of Your presence through it all. Amen.

345

14 November

When He opened the fifth seal, I saw under the altar
the souls of those who had been slain for the word of God
and for the testimony which they held.

Revelation 6:9

Reading: Revelation 6:9–11

We listened to the Indian pastor with great interest as he recounted his journey from devoted Hinduism, while serving as a high-ranking officer in the Indian army, to trusting in Christ.

The PowerPoint presentation of his current ministry all over India was both exciting and deeply challenging. Hundreds of evangelists now spread the gospel message in small villages and great cities alike, while dozens of orphanages and schools have been established to care for poverty-stricken children. In addition, a Bible college now trains young men and women who hear God's call on their lives to Christian service.

The last slide was of a happy group of graduates, beaming from ear to ear, on what was obviously a very proud day for them. The pastor cleared his throat in an attempt to control his emotion at the sight. I thought it was 'fatherly' pride causing the tears, but what he said next is indelibly written on my heart: 'When I look at their faces, I can't help but wonder which of them will join the martyrs' roll.'

In spite of its claim to religious freedom, India rates 'very high' on the Open Doors Persecution Index. Christians are killed for their belief in Jesus Christ, churches are burnt to the ground, individuals are excluded from families and employment, and physical and verbal abuse are regular occurrences. As the pastor looked at the slide, he knew that some of those young people would be added to those mentioned in Revelation 6:9. It had happened before. Yet each of those smiling faces had already counted the cost, deciding that Jesus was worth the ultimate sacrifice, should they be called upon to make it.

Lord Jesus, one day the last martyr will die, and You will avenge their blood. Until then, visit them with strength, and me with a willingness to pray. Amen.

15 November

'The LORD has blessed me because of you.'
Genesis 30:27, NIV

Reading: Genesis 39:1–5

Who came to mind when you read those words? Whose face pops up and makes you smile while you think of a reply? Whose life has impacted you greatly, so much so that you know God was behind it?

I'm sure we all have lists of favourite teachers and friends who have indeed been a blessing in our lives. But the people I am particularly thankful for are those who are not the 'big names' but the 'little' people – the ones who couldn't mount a platform or stand under a spotlight. They are the encouragers, the prayers, the kind, the considerate – the people who see my heart in spite of what my face says.

They don't pressure me with advice or opinions, but rather provide a shoulder to cry on and a listening ear. They don't tell me how to do it right, or judge me when I'm wrong, but remind me that we all make mistakes. They don't comment on the condition of my house, but are quick to bring a pot of soup when life gets tough.

I'm so thankful for people like this whom God has put across my path. Some have visited my life for only a short time, and that's okay. Others are stayers, continually adding quiet blessing to the others they've left before. And what's remarkable is that they don't even realize they are doing it. Often what they do is not monumental, but rather a precious reminder of the tender mercies of God that have helped to mould and shape my life.

Of such dear friends I can honestly say, 'The LORD has blessed me because of you' – and I am deeply grateful.

Lord, thank You from the bottom of my heart for those whom You have used to bless my life. Please use me to bless others who need to experience Your loving touch today. Amen.

16 November

They desired only that we should remember the poor,
the very thing which I also was eager to do.
Galatians 2:10

Reading: Acts 9:36–43

Peter hadn't long arrived in Joppa before he discovered who was caring for the poor, and especially for the widows in the area. Joppa was a busy port city, the sea providing much employment for the men of the district. Unfortunately, such employment also rendered Joppa successful at producing widows. Stormy weather, wooden ships, untrained labour and no safety regulations often defeated those who tried to make a living at sea for their families. Wives and children were often left destitute.

It seemed that there wasn't a widow in the district who didn't thank Dorcas (Aramaic: Tabitha) for her kindness. 'The LORD has blessed me because of you' (Genesis 30:27, NIV) would have fallen easily from many lips in respect of her. Many widowed shoulders were covered by the beautiful work donated by seamstress Dorcas, while her hand also clothed their children. Dorcas had a heart for the suffering, and a gift that she used well for the Master (Acts 9:36).

But Dorcas was not immune from nature's ravages on the body, and when she became ill and died, her loss was greatly mourned. So much so that when the believers heard Peter was at nearby Lydda, they sent for him. And seeing what this great loss meant to the poorest in the community, Peter prayed and Dorcas was raised from the dead! It seems that the lady with the big heart had more blessings to pour into the lives of others, while what God had done for her was used to bring many to the Saviour (Acts 9:42).

Dorcas had a consecrated needle; my friend has a consecrated car; another has a consecrated soup-pot. What we consecrate to Him, He uses to bless others.

Lord Jesus, take my gift and use it to bless others, and in the doing may some discover that You are the generous One. Amen.

17 November

A PASSAGE TO PONDER

So then, since Christ suffered physical pain,

you must arm yourself with the same attitude He had,

and be ready to suffer, too.

For if you are willing to suffer for Christ,

you have decided to stop sinning.

And you won't spend the rest of your life

chasing after evil desires,

but you will be anxious to do the will of God.

1 Peter 4:1–2, NLT

Read the passage slowly and let the Author speak to you. As you ponder, ask yourself these questions:

- What does it say?
- What does it mean?
- What is God saying to me?
- How will I respond?

18 November

But the LORD your God turned the curse into a blessing
for you, because the LORD your God loves you.

Deuteronomy 23:5

Reading: Genesis 50:15–21

Some situations have the look and feel of God's curse or judgment about them. We look on in horror, believing that nothing good could ever come from this. Critics of the goodness of God love to sow doubt in our minds when disaster strikes, and especially when it touches us personally. I've fielded the 'How can you trust God when He lets this happen to you?' comments. Perhaps that's why I love the story of Joseph so much.

Sold into slavery at the age of seventeen, by his own brothers, Joseph's life is one catalogue of disaster after another. Transported to Egypt, with no hope of ever seeing his father again, he is wrongly accused of adultery, and then imprisoned for years. How could God say that He loves His people and let all this happen to one of them?

Eventually, after a broken promise is made right, Joseph not only is freed but also becomes the second most powerful man in all of Egypt. You can imagine the terror his brothers experience when they come face to face with the brother they threw in a pit all those years earlier! But Joseph has had a long time to glimpse God's big picture, and has experienced God transforming his curse into blessing.

So when his big moment comes, Joseph says to his brothers, 'Don't be afraid. Am I in the place of God? You intended to harm me, but God intended it for good to accomplish what is now being done, the saving of many lives' (Genesis 50:20, NIV).

'God intended it for good.' He turned the curse into blessing in Joseph's life, eventually impacting a nation. Whatever we are facing – however disastrous it seems – let's remember the most important part of Deuteronomy 23:5: 'the LORD your God loves you'.

Some stories never cease to thrill me, Lord, no matter how often I hear them. Your intentions are for my good. That gives me peace. Amen.

350

19 November

But Jonah got up and went in the opposite direction
to get away from the Lord.
Jonah 1:3, NLT

Reading: Jonah 1:1–12

Perhaps some of us are trying to do a Jonah right now!

What is it that we are running away from? We might think it's only a job or a task that we don't want to do, but if God has asked us to do it, then it's far bigger than we're trying to fool ourselves into believing. Is it a relationship we've left behind, or one that we're planning to end in the near future? Yet when that relationship started, we were absolutely convinced that God was in it. Perish the thought, but could it be a 'real' Jonah moment and we think that God's got it wrong this time, and we want no part in it?

While some of us might actually try to 'board a ship' and physically remove ourselves from a situation, it's more likely that the 'running away' is an internal battle, and we're finding stubborn resistance to God's will an uncomfortable place to live.

Like Jonah, we eventually discover that we cannot run away from God. Rebellion offers no prospect of peaceful success.

Yes, God may give what He has asked of us to someone else to complete, but there are times when He doggedly pursues us until obedience becomes the only satisfactory response. Because He knows that nothing settles our heart like being in the centre of His will. And we need to learn the important lesson of who is Master. While we might not land ourselves in deep water like Jonah (sorry, couldn't resist!), this is one lesson that will be painful in the learning.

If Jonah were here, I think he might argue the case for talking with God rather than taking to our heels!

Forgive me, Lord, for trying to run away from Your plans for me, and from what You have asked me to do. Your will is best. Amen.

20 November

'When I had lost all hope, I turned my thoughts once more to the Lord. And my earnest prayer went out to you in your holy Temple.'

Jonah 2:7, NLT

Reading: Jonah 2

Sometimes life puts us in circumstances where the only way left to look is up. At other times we find ourselves in exactly the same position by our own doing!

Let's face it – and it might come as a shock to some of us – we don't always get it right. We don't always make the best decisions, or use the right words, or treat people the way we should. There are even times when we think that we know better than God, and dare to fight our corner over it with the Creator of the universe. Jonah knew that only too well, but the rebellious prophet had one saving grace: when he thought all was lost, in every sense of the word, Jonah allowed his thoughts to change direction and to focus on the Lord. That was enough to turn his heart to prayer.

Interestingly, Jonah didn't pray for rescue. He already viewed the 'fish-swallowing' as rescue from sure death in the turbulent sea (Jonah 2:6). Although uncertain of permanent rescue, while undoubtedly suffering pain, Jonah used his prayer time in the belly of the great fish to praise God, and to promise to fulfil his vows (2:9a). And for the first time since he had left the port of Joppa, Jonah recognized his need for repentance and for God's mercy.

'For my salvation comes from God alone,' Jonah declared (verse 9, NLT). 'Then the Lord ordered the fish to spit up Jonah on the beach, and it did' (verse 10, NLT).

Rebellion doesn't stop God from loving us. Mercy missions are what God does best – especially for repentant hearts.

Thank You, Lord, that mercy is always on Your heart. In the deep, dark places, help me to look up, for there I will find You. Amen.

21 November

'I knew that you were a gracious and compassionate God,
slow to get angry and filled with unfailing love.'

Jonah 4:2, NLT

Reading: Jonah 3

We can only imagine how Jonah looked when he had completed the long cross-country journey of more than 500 miles to reach Nineveh. Time would have healed his damaged skin, but it's my guess that the runaway prophet had visible scars that marked his rebellion.

His visage couldn't hide the fact that Jonah hated the Assyrians. He would happily yell, 'Forty days from now Nineveh will be destroyed!' (Jonah 3:4, NLT). Delivering the message of God's judgment was right up his street, except for one thing: Jonah knew God was merciful. All these Ninevites had to do was show genuine repentance and God would forgive them. So what was the point of his prophecy if God was going to let them get away with the evil they'd dealt the Israelites? That's why he'd run away in the first place. Jonah didn't want God to forgive them – he wanted them wiped off the face of the earth!

How ironic that the very man to whom God had shown forgiveness, had rescued from the very jaws of death and given a second chance, couldn't understand how God wanted to do the same for the repentant Assyrians. Somewhere in Jonah's heart lurked the lie that only certain people deserve the mercy of God – and the Assyrians were not included in Jonah's list. Thankfully, God saw it differently, for 'When God saw that they had put a stop to their evil ways, he had mercy on them and didn't carry out the destruction he had threatened' (Jonah 3:10, NLT).

I wonder which of the two hearts best reflects our own. Do we have an unwritten 'Jonah' list in our hearts? Are there those to whom we think God should never show mercy? Or is mercy our default with the repentant that we previously deemed unworthy?

Lord, You have forgiven me much. Teach me to do the same, and to mirror Your mercy in my daily life. Amen.

22 November

'Even to your old age, I am He,
And even to gray hairs I will carry you!
I have made, and I will bear;
Even I will carry, and will deliver you.'
Isaiah 46:4

Reading: Psalm 71:17–21

Yesterday was my dad's birthday and, at the time of writing, he is eighty-eight years old. Way back in 1929 he wasn't expected to survive his first night. He was born prematurely at home, weighing only 2lb, and his grandmother put him in an old cardboard shoebox and placed him in the bread-proving hole at the side of the fireplace in their tiny Belfast home. But God had other plans for William John Fraser, incorporating those that would bless the lives of many people, including my own.

His life is not remarkable by today's measurement of greatness: he was only ever employed as a labouring man throughout his working life. However, the impact he has made on those who know him has been immense. Dad's life has been one of unfailing kindness and generosity. His huge heart for others, combined with devoted love for the Saviour, has been the benchmark of his long life. However, disease and the aging process are now taking their toll in ways that are difficult for him to endure, and for his family to watch. As my father-in-law used to say, 'Growing old isn't for the fainthearted!'

Many of his conversations these days centre around what lies ahead. He is looking forward to heaven more than any other person I know! Yet for Dad, and Mum too, they gratefully rejoice in all the Lord has done for them until now. But what excites them more is that God's promise continues – combing through the grey hairs reminds them of that, each and every day!

Thank You, Lord, that there is never a time in our lives that You are not with us. Whether in the days of youthful exuberance, or the difficulties of old age, You carry us through . . . and will deliver us. Amen.

23 November

'He is a liar, and the father of it.'
John 8:44

Reading: Isaiah 41:8–10

There are some days when Satan's lies deeply wound with their relentless message of how worthless and pathetic we are. It's time to switch channels. Instead, let's listen to what is good and wholesome – words that build up and give strength to our weary souls – words from the Father's heart to His children, and confirmed to us today in Jesus.

> 'But you . . . are My servant . . .
> whom I have chosen . . .
> whom I have loved . . .
> whom I have taken from the ends of the earth . . .
> called from its farthest regions.
> Remember, I have chosen you . . .
> And I have not, nor will not, forsake you.'
> (My adaptation of Isaiah 41:8–9)

Sometimes, Lord, I don't need to say any more. It's enough to be reminded of who I am in Christ. Thank You that I don't have to listen to the devil's lies. I'd rather hear of Your great love. Amen.

355

24 November

A PASSAGE TO PONDER

I will sing of the mercies of the LORD forever;

With my mouth will I make known Your faithfulness

to all generations.

For I have said, 'Mercy shall be built up forever;

Your faithfulness You shall establish in the very heavens' . . .

And the heavens will praise Your wonders, O LORD;

Your faithfulness also in the assembly of the saints.

For who in the heavens can be compared to the LORD?

Who among the sons of the mighty can be likened to the LORD?

Psalm 89:1–2, 5–6

Read the passage slowly and let the Author speaker to you. As you ponder, ask yourself these questions:

- What does it say?
- What does it mean?
- What is God saying to me?
- How will I respond?

25 November

So then, my beloved brethren, let every man be swift
to hear, slow to speak, slow to wrath.

James 1:19

Reading: James 1:19–21

My aunt used to have a little ornament, a set of three brass monkeys, that fascinated me as a child. Cast in a squatting position, one covered its eyes, one covered its ears and one covered its mouth. She called them, 'See no evil', 'Hear no evil' and 'Speak no evil'. Certainly good advice for life.

James writes here about qualities that we need to develop as children of God, which demonstrate the Spirit's presence in our lives.

The apostle's mandate is:

- **'Be swift to hear . . .'** We are to take time to listen carefully before we react to what is being said. Get all the facts as soon as possible, as heartache often results from half-heard conversations. When correcting his children on this as we were growing up, my dad used to say, 'Bad hearing makes bad rehearsing!'
- **'. . . slow to speak . . .'** James reminds us that unrestrained speech shows an undisciplined life that can lead to irresponsible actions. If we don't need to say it – don't!
- **'. . . slow to wrath.'** Anger rarely wins any battles. And if it is of the quick-tempered selfish variety, then everyone is a loser, and recovery from the fallout can be very difficult. Love is not visible in any angry outburst.

But James is trying to teach us about more than some good attitudes to acquire along the way. He's not trying simply to make us nice people, like the message of the three brass monkeys. The progression he's pointing out here – not listening carefully, jumping in with careless talk and responding with a quick temper – leads to sinful behaviour, which does not reflect 'the righteous life that God desires' (James 1:20, NIV).

Lord, forgive me if my behaviour reflects my 'old nature' rather than Your righteousness. Help me to listen in, and put a button on my tongue. Amen.

357

26 November

But be doers of the word, and not hearers only, deceiving yourselves.
James 1:22

Reading: James 1:22–26

James' writing is effectively descriptive. He paints vivid pictures with his words, helping his readers to understand his practical teaching on living out their faith. While addressing mainly Jewish believers – people who had spent a lifetime listening to the Law and the prophets, including the extraneous teachings of the Pharisees – James points to the importance of not only listening to God's Word, but also acting on what is heard. And he cleverly uses a mirror to drive home what he's saying (James 1:23f).

After all, he quips, it's pretty foolish to look closely at yourself in a mirror and do nothing about what you see the minute you step away from it. Why bother looking in the first place? If you see in the mirror a dirty mark at the end of your nose, but make no attempt to remove it, then looking has proved meaningless.

God's Word is likened to a mirror, because it shows us who we are and what we're like. James says that a 'man who looks intently into the perfect law that gives freedom, and continues to do this, not forgetting what he has heard but doing it – he will be blessed in what he does' (James 1:25, NIV).

Listening to God's Word is a good place to start, but doing what it says is what brings life and maturity. Action is the best reaction!

So then, how often do you look in the mirror? A recent survey in the UK said that men look in the mirror twenty-three times every day, while women only do so sixteen times daily. You might be keen to dispute that figure, but hold on ... if a survey were carried out asking how many times a week we looked into 'God's Mirror', I wonder how we would answer. And question two in the survey? How often do we do what it says? The results might be rather embarrassing!

Heavenly Father, I want to be a doer as well as a hearer. Amen.

358

27 November

'You will know them by their fruits.'
Matthew 7:16

Reading: James 2:14–26

Luther had a real problem with James' words: faith without works is dead (James 2:17). The father of the Protestant Reformation had spent so much time trying to convince people that salvation is by faith alone through Christ alone (Ephesians 2:8–10) that he balked at James' teaching combining both faith and works as necessary to salvation. But he was a clever man and soon worked it out.

In the most famous sermon ever given, Jesus put it more simply than his brother did years later: 'A good tree cannot bear bad fruit,' Jesus said, 'nor can a bad tree bear good fruit … Therefore by their fruits you will know them' (Matthew 7:18, 20). The evidence for who we are comes from what we produce. You can't harvest grapes from thornbushes, Jesus explained (Matthew 7:16).

Throughout James' practical missive, he attempts to move us from mere biblical head knowledge to living out our faith visibly. He put it bluntly – 'faith without works is dead' (James 2:26). You can't have one without the other. We can shout all we like about having 'faith' in Jesus, but if there's no visible evidence of Jesus working through us then the 'faith' we proclaim is seriously in doubt … or absent altogether.

Therefore, both Jesus and James teach us that genuine faith is measured not by how much Bible we know, but rather by how much Bible radiates from our lives to others. In recent decades, dissension has occurred in the church between those seen as merely providing a social gospel and those who major on Bible teaching without social action. Let's do what James suggested earlier, and listen carefully to what the Bible says. The truth of Scripture balances the two. Both Jesus and His brother teach us that faith ought always be translated into works. There is no either/or, only both together.

Lord, I want my life to speak of You in both words and action. Make me real. Amen.

359

28 November

Therefore, as the elect of God, holy and beloved,
put on tender mercies, kindness, humility,
meekness, longsuffering.
Colossians 3:12

Reading: Colossians 3:12–15

Paul and James often sang from the same hymn sheet. Both were keen to teach new believers what this new life in Jesus that they had embraced was all about. So they took time to be as practical as possible about what God expected from those who were now part of His family. In his letter to the Colossians, Paul explained the characteristics with which they were to 'clothe' themselves – behaviour that had been completely alien to most of them.

I wonder whether another list of 'things to do' put them off. Was this new religion they'd embraced beginning to look more like a catalogue of dos and don'ts? Where was the freedom they'd been promised? Was the One-True-God just the same as the others they'd previously given their allegiance to? But wait a minute. Had they even got as far as hearing the list, or were they aghast at how they were described at the start of Paul's instruction?

'Elect'. 'Holy'. 'Beloved'.

Was that really how God saw them?

No other god had ever spoken of them in that way. All the deities they'd worshipped in the past only ever made demands of them, taking everything from them and giving nothing in return.

Jesus was different. They meant something to Him. They were members of His family: a family built on love, peace and joy. Allowing the Holy Spirit to strengthen them to live as they should wasn't a chore once they recognized who they were in God's eyes.

And me? When I want to protest and shout 'legalism', I remember that I am God's 'beloved', and then following His commands is no longer tedious.

Heavenly Father, catching a glimpse of Your love for me puts everything else in perspective. Clothe me, Lord, in Your righteousness. Amen.

29 November

They are abundantly satisfied with the fullness
of Your house,
And You give them drink from the rivers
of Your pleasures.

Psalm 36:8

Reading: Psalm 36

'Abundantly satisfied'. What a beautiful thought!

Such copious satisfaction means that we do not need to go elsewhere for fulfilment. The psalmist declares that 'the children of men put their trust under the shadow of [His] wings' (verse 7), and the Father's protection lavishly provides for all of their needs. He even lets those who trust 'drink from the rivers of [His] pleasures' (verse 8). God is no killjoy – He delights to give us pleasure (Psalm 16:11). Neither does He ration His gifts to His children. He is a generous Father. This fact was not lost on David, the author of this psalm, who confirms the generosity of our Heavenly Father with these words:

> Your mercy, O Lord, is in the heavens;
> Your faithfulness reaches to the clouds.
> Your righteousness is like the great mountains;
> Your judgements are a great deep.
> (verses 5–6)

In need of mercy? The Lord's mercy is higher than any other.

Feeling let down by others? God's faithfulness is incomparable . . . reaching further than we can imagine.

Need to be made righteous? There's only One who can do that for us . . . and He is more than willing.

Unfairly treated? God's justice is unfathomable.

Whatever our need, He will abundantly satisfy . . . 'For His mercy endures forever' (Psalm 136:1).

Thank You, Lord, for Your unfailing kindness and abundant love. Amen.

30 November

But for you who fear my name,
the Sun of Righteousness will rise
with healing in his wings.

Malachi 4:2, NLT

Reading: Malachi 3:1–3

As November ends, the high streets of our nation are already bedecked with coloured lights and Christmas trees. Their presence brings light back into the short, dark days of winter, and hope for retailers that cash registers will ring more loudly than the Christmas music playing on a persistent loop. The hype is already in full swing, and the run-up to the great day is underway. But what great day are we preparing for in our 'tinseltown'?

Back in Malachi's day, the prophet was warning the people to get ready: 'For behold, the day is coming . . .' (Malachi 4:1). What day? So many messengers had come before Malachi. Many pronounced the same message from God. The people were to prepare for . . . judgment . . . healing . . . restoration . . . deliverance. So many messages, so often! Little did the people know then that Malachi was to be God's final Old Testament prophet. The message he brought from a patient and merciful God was the last of its kind until the messenger Malachi foretold (Malachi 3:1) would arrive – a messenger whose life would overlap with that of Messiah.

For 450 years God would remain silent. He had said enough. He had left them plenty to consider and obey. It was time to get ready – Messiah was on His way.

Today, it's our turn to wait. We wait for the 'Sun of Righteousness [who] shall arise with healing in his wings' (Malachi 4:2). Malachi's prophecy pointed forward to the Day of the Lord, when Christ will come again in glorious manifestation with healing and righteousness for His people, and just judgment for the unrighteous.

I can't help but wonder if we are busying ourselves with frivolity and missing the message of what lies ahead, like the many today who have forgotten why Jesus came in the first place. Messiah is on His way!

Lord Jesus, thank You for all that Your first coming accomplished. May I recognize the importance of readying myself for Your glorious return. Amen.

362

December

1 December

A PASSAGE TO PONDER

'The day will come,' says the Lord,

'when I will do for Israel and Judah

all the good I have promised them.

At that time I will bring to the throne of David

a righteous descendant,

and he will do what is just and right throughout the land.

In that day Judah will be saved, and Jerusalem will live in safety.

And their motto will be

"The Lord is our righteousness!"'

Jeremiah 33:14–16, NLT

Read the passage slowly and let the Author speak to you. As you ponder, ask yourself these questions:

- What does it say?
- What does it mean?
- What is God saying to me?
- How will I respond?

365

2 December

And beginning at Moses and all the Prophets,
He expounded to them in all the Scriptures
the things concerning Himself.
Luke 24:27

Reading: John 5:39, 46

Wherever the Roman army went, they built roads. Their push for world domination was greatly enhanced by a civil engineering genius unknown until that time. And suddenly the world was accessible to more than advancing armies. Travel was possible where it had once been unthinkable. But, for the Romans, there was only one reason behind the construction: 'all roads led to Rome'.

The Bible is a bit like Roman roads. Its message takes us in the same direction to the one destination. Throughout the Old Testament – wherever we read – we find a path running through it. It weaves its way through the history books, the Psalms and the Prophets, ultimately leading to Jesus, Messiah. The Bible is more than a collection of sixty-six books of wisdom and commands on how God wants us to live our lives. The Bible is a record of God's plan of salvation for mankind. It provides confirmation of His love for us, which was fulfilled by the coming of the Saviour. God spent a long time repeating Himself, preparing His people for the coming Messiah. Right from Adam's rebellion in Genesis 3, redemption's plan was set in motion, pointing to the day when the seed of the woman would deliver a blow to Satan's head (Genesis 3:15). Over time, and little by little, God revealed through Moses and all the Prophets who that seed would be.

He promised that one day He would walk with us as He had done with Adam and Eve in the Garden of Eden (Genesis 3:8). God would come near. No, more than that – God would come and live with us in human form. It was all promised before any of it happened. And our God always keeps His promises.

God of Heaven, thank You for Your Word, where, within its pages, You have revealed Your plan for mankind . . . and for me. Thank You for coming to live among us. Amen.

3 December

That it might be fulfilled which was spoken by Isaiah the prophet.
Matthew 8:17

Reading: Micah 5:2

Twelve times in his gospel writings Matthew uses the words 'that it might be fulfilled which was spoken by the prophet' in reference to Jesus.

Before Jesus was born, Messiah 'declarations' were commonplace. Such claims were short-lived. In spite of imposters, Messiah-watchers were everywhere. God's silence, along with the Roman occupation, had made the Jews restless. They longed that God would send the Messiah to defeat the Romans, and purify their religion once more. Even John the Baptist had to make it clear that he wasn't the 'Promised One', but that he was there to prepare the way for His coming (John 3:28). Little wonder then that Matthew made a point of providing scriptural evidence that Jesus was indeed the Messiah.

Sceptics abounded back then, just as they do today. Some claim Matthew's 'fulfilled' passages have been manipulated to 'fit' an occurrence, or that relevant Old Testament passages have been taken out of context and given an application not originally intended. If that's true, then isn't it remarkable how the baby Jesus arranged to be born in Bethlehem as prophesied in Micah 5:2? And that He managed to arrange to be buried in a rich man's grave (Mark 15:43) as prophesied in Isaiah 53:9?

Biblical scholars affirm that some texts are not exclusively Messianic, but that they do contain a deeper meaning pointing forward to Jesus. The matter is clarified by the meaning of the word 'fulfilled' that Matthew uses. The translation of 'fulfilled' in Greek, 'pleroo', reflects the Hebrew meaning of 'mala'. Both are interpreted 'to fill' or 'to be filled', with the Hebrew adding an extra layer – 'to bring to an end'. What had been predicted concerning the Messiah in the Old Testament was completed in Jesus Christ! The speculation had been brought to an end ... and evidence abounds. Jesus is the Messiah!

Promised Messiah, thank You that You came for the whole world, including me. Amen.

367

4 December

For all the promises of God in Him are Yes, and in Him Amen, to the glory of God through us.
2 Corinthians 1:20

Reading: John 1:1–5

Jesus didn't come into existence at Bethlehem. The baby born that night in the unusual circumstances of a stable was no stranger to planet earth. His birth may have temporarily contracted Him into human form, but His divinity did not change. He is the unchangeable, eternal One (Hebrews 13:8).

John describes Jesus beautifully in the opening chapter of his Gospel as being 'in the beginning with God' (John 1:2), yet also as 'the Word [*who*] became flesh and dwelt among us' (John 1:14). Jesus was the Word who spoke the earth into being. He was also the fulfilment of 'all the promises of God' in God's written Word (2 Corinthians 1:20). Jesus the Word, present at creation, and Jesus the man, born as a baby, cannot be separated. Wow! What a combination! Yet it was the only permutation that could bring about our salvation. And with His coming, everything changed.

- The regular blood sacrifices required for the forgiveness of sin were no longer needed, for 'with His own blood He entered the Most Holy Place once for all, having obtained eternal redemption' (Hebrews 9:12).
- The priesthood became obsolete. Jesus is our High Priest 'for there is one Mediator between God and men, the Man Christ Jesus' (1 Timothy 2:5).
- The temple building was rendered surplus to requirements, for 'God is Spirit, and those who worship Him must worship in spirit and truth' (John 4:24).
- The keeping of the Law to make one righteous is no longer a prerequisite, for 'if you confess with your mouth the Lord Jesus and believe in your heart that God has raised Him from the dead, you will be saved' (Romans 10:9).

Word made flesh, You are the One who brings me close to God. You alone make perfect the imperfections of my heart, mind and spirit. I worship You. Amen.

5 December

Surely the LORD GOD does nothing,
Unless He reveals His secret to His servants the prophets.
Amos 3:7

Reading: Acts 2:29–32

God doesn't need to tell us anything. Yet throughout Scripture He chose to reveal to the prophets many of the plans He had, both for the Children of Israel and for us who are now His children. Much of that revelation concerned messages of judgment, to provide motivation and opportunity for repentance. Some included prophecies on deliverance, both for a specific time and for the coming of the final Deliverer – the Messiah.

Today we have the privilege of examining these Messianic prophecies, and of revelling further in the delight of knowing that Jesus is indeed the Promised One.

- **Born of a virgin:** 'Behold, the virgin shall conceive and bear a Son, and shall call His name Immanuel' (Isaiah 7:14).

Fulfilled: 'After His mother Mary was betrothed to Joseph, before they came together, she was found with child of the Holy Spirit' (Matthew 1:18).

- **Born in Bethlehem:** 'But you, Bethlehem Ephrathah, though you are little among the thousands of Judah, yet out of you shall come forth to Me the One to be Ruler in Israel' (Micah 5:2).

Fulfilled: 'Now after Jesus was born in Bethlehem of Judea . . .' (Matthew 2:1).

- **Brought back from Egypt:** 'And out of Egypt I called my Son' (Hosea 11:1).

Fulfilled: In a dream to Joseph in Egypt: 'Arise and take the young Child and His mother, and go to the land of Israel' (Matthew 2:19–20).

- **Murder of the innocents:** 'A voice was heard in Ramah, lamentation and bitter weeping, Rachel weeping for her children' (Jeremiah 31:15).

Fulfilled: 'Then Herod . . . put to death all the male children who were in Bethlehem . . . from two years old and under' (Matthew 2:16).

Holy Child of Bethlehem, You alone are worthy of my praise. Amen.

6 December

He is the image of the invisible God,
the firstborn over all creation.

Colossians 1:15

Reading: Colossians 1:15–20

There has never been anyone like Jesus. Prophecy concerning Him did not stop with His unique birth. The Old Testament writers also predicted details of his matchless life. While little is written about the early years of his boyhood and youth in Nazareth, that is not the case concerning His adult ministry.

- **Ministry began in Galilee:** 'The land of Zebulun and the land of Naphtali . . . In Galilee of the Gentiles. The people who walked in darkness have seen a great light' (Isaiah 9:1–2).

Fulfilled: 'And leaving Nazareth, He came and dwelt in Capernaum, which is by the sea, in the regions of Zebulun and Naphtali' (Matthew 4:13).

- **Worker of miracles:** 'Then the eyes of the blind shall be opened, and the ears of the deaf shall be unstopped. Then the lame shall leap like a deer, and the tongue of the dumb sing' (Isaiah 35:5–6).

Fulfilled: 'Then Jesus went about all the cities and villages . . . healing every sickness and every disease among the people' (Matthew 9:35).

- **Spoke in parables:** 'I will open my mouth in a parable; I will utter dark sayings of old' (Psalm 78:2).

Fulfilled: 'All these things Jesus spoke to the multitude in parables; and without a parable He did not speak to them' (Matthew 13:34).

- **The temple cleansed:** 'For my house shall be called a house of prayer for all nations' (Isaiah 56:7).

Fulfilled: 'Then Jesus went into the temple of God and drove out all those who bought and sold in the temple . . . And He said to them, "It is written, 'My house shall be called a house of prayer,' but you have made it a 'den of thieves'"' (Matthew 21:12–13).

Matchless Saviour, there is nothing You cannot do. May my life display Your love and grace to those who need it today. Amen.

7 December

For it pleased the Father that in Him all the fullness
should dwell, and by Him to reconcile all things
to Himself . . . through the blood of His cross.

Colossians 1:19–20

Reading: Ephesians 2:13–18

'Give me proof and I'll believe,' people say, yet none is more plentiful than the
evidence for our Saviour's death. Vivid descriptive passages about Christ's crucifixion – a form of execution unheard of at the time – are numerous in the Old
Testament. Those same words now confirm the completion of God's redemptive
plan for mankind.

- **Suffered a humiliating death:** 'They divide My garments among them,
  and for My clothing they cast lots' (Psalm 22:18).

Fulfilled: 'Then they crucified Him, and divided His garments, casting lots'
(Matthew 27:35).

- **Wounded and bruised:** 'He was wounded for our transgressions, He was
  bruised for iniquities' (Isaiah 53:5).

Fulfilled: 'When he had scourged Jesus, he delivered Him to be crucified'
(Matthew 27:26).

- **'I thirst':** 'And for my thirst they gave me vinegar to drink' (Psalm 69:21).

Fulfilled: 'They filled a sponge with sour wine, put it on hyssop, and put it to His
mouth' (John 19:29).

- **Silent before His accusers:** 'And as a sheep before its shearers is silent,
  so He opened not His mouth' (Isaiah 53:7).

Fulfilled: 'And while He was being accused by the chief priests and elders, He
answered nothing' (Matthew 27:12).

- **Crucified with thieves:** 'And He was numbered with the transgressors'
  (Isaiah 53:12).

Fulfilled: 'Then two robbers were crucified with Him' (Matthew 27:38).

Thank You, Saviour, for dying in my place. Amen.

371

8 December

A PASSAGE TO PONDER

There was a man sent from God, whose name was John.

This man came for a witness, to bear witness of the Light,

that all through him might believe.

He was not that Light,

But was sent to bear witness of that Light.

That was the true Light

which gives light to every man coming into the world.

He was in the world, and the world was made through Him,

and the world did not know Him.

He came to His own, and His own did not receive Him.

But as many as received Him,

to them He gave the right to become the children of God,

to those who believe in His name:

who were born, not of blood, nor of the will of the flesh,

nor of the will of man, but of God.

John 1:6–13

Read the passage slowly and let the Author speak to you. As you ponder, ask yourself these questions:
- What does it say?
- What does it mean?
- What is God saying to me?
- How will I respond?

9 December

'Now indeed, Elizabeth your relative has conceived
a son in her old age; and this is now the sixth month
for her who was called barren.'
Luke 1:36

Reading: Luke 1:13–16

I just love how God adds the finishing touches: how He understands when we need that little something extra when we are finding life confusing.

A visit from an angel. A message from God. A very unexpected pregnancy – miraculous, in fact! Chosen by God to carry His Son . . . to give birth to the Saviour of the world. And still only a teenager!

How could it happen? Who would believe it? What will Joseph say? How will Father react? Me? Really? Is it true? Could it really happen? Honestly?

Then, with a touch as gentle as that of the One who had sent him, Gabriel spoke into all the unspoken questions of the nervous young woman standing before him. His message seemed impossible, yet she wanted to believe. So Gabriel informed her that hers was not the only miraculous conception to have occurred. Elizabeth, an elderly relative of Mary's, was also pregnant – now into her sixth month. She and her husband had never been able to have children, but now, amazingly, God was making it possible for them to have a son.

That was all Mary needed. In faith she responded, 'Let it be to me according to your word' (Luke 1:38). If God could do it for Elizabeth and Zacharias, then He could do for her as the angel had said.

Soon after Gabriel's visit, Mary saw Elizabeth for herself, witnessing with her own eyes that God is the God of the inexplicable. And in Elizabeth He had given her someone who would believe her story: someone who was well acquainted with angelic messages and the miraculous touch of God.

And the words 'For with God nothing shall be impossible' (Luke 1:37) rang in the ears of the pregnant virgin, and brought her peace.

God of the impossible, forgive me when I find it hard to believe . . . Teach me to be full of faith, like Mary. Amen.

10 December

'Joseph, son of David, do not be afraid to take to you
Mary your wife, for that which is conceived in her
is of the Holy Spirit.'

Matthew 1:20

Reading: Matthew 1:18–21

Joseph was not normally an angry man. But his earlier conversation with Mary was bringing out a very emotional response in him. Had his future wife gone mad? Where did such a preposterous story come from? They'd promised to stay pure – to wait for the wedding night. The marriage contract had already been signed! He was working all hours to build that little room on to his parents' home. He wanted it to be just right – for her. For Mary. What had she done?

With head in hands, Joseph tried to work out what he could do with a pregnant promised-wife. All the legal stuff had been completed. But now? What would people say? There'd be no happy singing from her house to his now. Doubtful anyone would want to carry him along the street, cheering, to his marriage room! Everything was spoiled. And now Mary had taken herself down south to visit some relative, leaving him to face the music.

One thing Joseph was sure about: he hadn't touched Mary. Maybe she'd been assaulted by one of those soldiers from the nearby garrison? What self-respecting Jew would dare touch the promised-wife of another man? Yet Nazareth's carpenter still had feelings for Mary. He had every right to turn her in to the religious leaders. But they would stone her as an adulteress! He wrestled with his tormented thoughts, finally deciding to send her away with as little fuss as possible.

But there was a redemptive streak in Joseph. He was a good man . . . no, Joseph was a godly man. One to whom God could speak. One who would listen, believe and trust God when He said, 'That which is conceived in her is of the Holy Spirit' (Matthew 1:20).

And as another day dawned, the faithful carpenter was ready to become the surrogate father to God's son.

God, give me the faith to trust You with the difficult things in my life. Amen.

374

11 December

And behold, an angel of the Lord stood before them,
and the glory of the Lord shone around them,
and they were greatly afraid.
Luke 2:9

Reading: Galatians 4:3–7

'Granny, I'm an angel in the school Christmas play.' Our little granddaughter could barely sit still as she blurted out her news. 'And Dad says I have the best words in the whole play!'

A speaking part. Such excitement!

Watching the junior-school nativity production was such fun, and we had been warned that Bethany wouldn't actually make an appearance until near the end. Finally, with the whole cast squeezed on to the small stage, a little angel, replete with silver garland in her hair, stepped forward and passionately announced, 'This is Jesus – the Son of God!'

Her daddy was right. She did have the best words in the whole play. She delivered God's message as the angels have done for millennia – and introduced the gathered throng to Jesus . . . Son of God, Messiah.

Angels are mentioned in thirty-four books of the Bible – 196 times in the Old Testament and ninety-three times in the New Testament. They are created spiritual beings whose roles include the worship of God (Isaiah 6:3), delivering God's specific messages to individuals (Daniel 8:15f), dispensing God's judgment (2 Chronicles 32:21) and involvement in spiritual combat (Revelation 12:7).

But I love what the writer to the Hebrews says of angels: 'Are not all angels ministering spirits sent to serve those who will inherit salvation?' (Hebrews 1:14, NIV). Perhaps one day we will be told of the times the angels of God have protected us, diverted us or led us in the right way. For now, I simply thrill to consider those messages given to Zacharias, Mary, Joseph and the shepherds by the angels, declaring that the 'fullness of time had [*finally*] come' (Galatians 4:4).

Heavenly Father, I am truly grateful for Your unseen care over me. But my heart is full of thanks, not only for the message delivered by the angels, but for the reality of Messiah living in my heart. Amen.

12 December

And because Joseph was a descendant of King David, he had to go to Bethlehem.

Luke 2:4, NLT

Reading: Matthew 2:13–18

The real Christmas story was nothing like the one we roll out every year, or sing about in the annual carol-fest. Bethlehem was far from still when the exhausted Mary and Joseph arrived in town. The census had made sure of that. A cacophony of noise greeted the newly-weds; the narrow streets heaved with people. Market traders bartered noisily with travellers seeking goods for their stay in the town they'd left years earlier.

Rome was counting heads; collecting the tax of a reluctant nation was their game. Even the little town of Bethlehem was overrun with soldiers.

The beautifully carved figurines that grace our homes elegantly tell a story distant from reality. There was nothing sanitary about Christ's birthplace, nothing cute about animals too close to a woman giving birth. Dusty travel clothes and the lack of washing facilities are a far cry from the Christmas-card pictures of the 'holy' family. Hopefully, Joseph, who had never known Mary intimately, had help from local midwives during the long, traumatic birth of the Son that God was placing into his care.

The rogue of Christ's birth was hardly the innkeeper, whom we love to berate, in spite of the fact that his place was indeed probably overcrowded. No, Judea's king was the real monster of the piece. Already a murderer of his wife, sons and mother-in-law, Herod felt so threatened by the young child that he ordered the death of all the little boys under two years old in Bethlehem.

Not much tinsel in this story. No glamour for the King of kings. Instead, Jesus was born into the mess of poverty, family difficulties and political instability. He experienced life in the raw. He understands our pain. He didn't look down on us. He lived among us. And when the time came for the Baby in the manger to become the Christ on the cross, He didn't hold back there either.

Babe of Bethlehem, there is room in my heart for You. Amen.

13 December

For unto us a Child is born,
Unto us a Son is given.
Isaiah 9:6

Reading: Revelation 1:4–7

'Save the date' notifications have become extremely popular. They are an early announcement that there's an invitation on the way, usually for a wedding or another very special celebration. The important thing is that the sender wants you to know that on a specific date in the future something very special is going to happen, and they'd like you to be present. You need to save the date in order not to miss out! You don't want to double-book on that day! So you'd be wise to put it in your diary. Mark it on the calendar. Something big is on its way!

God peppered the Old Testament with 'save the date' notifications. While He didn't give us the exact day or year, He made it clear that one day He would send His Son to earth. And He wanted to make sure we'd participate in the event, not merely by bedecking the tree, but by personally welcoming the 'Sent One' into our lives. God gave us plenty of notice about Christ's first coming, and daily we have the opportunity to respond to it.

And 'save the date' information for when the Saviour will return to earth again has already been posted in God's Word. One day Christ will come to take His bride, the church, home to Himself, and He will finally judge mankind. We need to ensure that our lives are not so cluttered with other things that we misuse the time He has given for us to prepare for an event that should not be missed – in fact, cannot be missed!

At His first coming, the world slept, but that will not be the case when Jesus returns, for, 'Behold, He is coming with clouds, and every eye will see Him' (Revelation 1:7, emphasis added). 'Save the date.' He will return!

Lord, while I thank You for Your coming, I look forward to the day when You will return again. Make me ready, Father. Prepare my heart. Amen.

377

14 December

Now after Jesus was born in Bethlehem of Judea in the
days of Herod the king, behold, wise men from the East
came to Jerusalem, saying, 'Where is He who
has been born King of the Jews?'
Matthew 2:1–2

Reading: Matthew 2:1–12

My friend had enjoyed a lovely meal with a family who had recently joined the church. The children had regaled her with excited conversation about Christmas, then only a few days away. A lovely nativity scene was on display, giving opportunity to speak with the children about 'Jesus' birthday' – something these particular children were only too aware of.

On a trip to the bathroom she discovered the three wise men from the nativity set sitting on one of the stairs. 'So who's been playing with the Three Wise Men?' she joked on returning to the sitting room.

A rather indignant little boy replied, 'We're not playing with them! They are making their way to Bethlehem to find Jesus – they travelled a long way, you know!' Early December sees the wise men start their journey on the upstairs landing, and every day the children get to move the figures a few inches until they arrive downstairs in Bethlehem on Christmas morning! While we don't know the exact date of the wise men's arrival, these precious children were being taught the importance of making a journey to meet with Jesus.

Mary and Joseph were the first to meet the tiny child who would one day become their Saviour. Theirs was a journey of acceptance and obedience. The shepherds took only a brisk walk in from the fields to find the Christ-child lying in the manger. The wise men's journey was undoubtedly the longest both in distance and the time it took to complete. Geography was the biggest obstacle in their reaching Jesus, yet the journey was worth it.

I can't help but wonder if something might be impeding our journey to meet with Jesus. Yet if we take that first step, we'll meet Him at the cross – not in the stable. Let's not keep Him waiting.

No journey is too great, Lord, if it ends in You. Amen.

15 December

A PASSAGE TO PONDER

And the Word became flesh and dwelt among us,

and we beheld His glory,

the glory as of the only begotten of the Father,

full of grace and truth . . .

And of His fullness we have all received,

and grace for grace.

For the law was given through Moses,

but grace and truth came through Jesus Christ.

No one has seen God at any time.

The only begotten Son, who is in the bosom of the Father,

He has declared Him.

John 1:14, 16–18

Read the passage slowly and let the Author speak to you. As you ponder, ask yourself these questions:

- What does it say?
- What does it mean?
- What is God saying to me?
- How will I respond?

16 December

So let each one give as he purposes in his heart,
not grudgingly or of necessity;
for God loves a cheerful giver.

2 Corinthians 9:7

Reading: 2 Corinthians 9:5–8

Christmas is like a magnifying glass.

It magnifies all that is good about humankind in a way that no other season does.

- More is given to charity than at any other time of the year. Cheerful bag-packers help move the shopping queues along while taking a little of your change for their particular good cause. Christmas appeals and the rattling of collection boxes in the streets encourage us to open our wallets. The food-bank trolleys are filled more quickly as we add a little something to ease another person's Christmas.
- It reminds us of how fortunate we are to have friends and family as people head home for Christmas; families make the effort to get together; friends meet up or communicate in some way, even if it is just once a year.
- Christmas highlights the things that are important in communities: getting together for fun and festive events; putting smiles on faces at school nativities and local functions.

More importantly, Christmas magnifies the goodness of God by putting the spotlight on Jesus as the reason for the season. At what other time of the year do you hear Christian songs played through loudspeakers in the town square, or as you push a trolley down the supermarket aisle?

There is no greater example of generosity than that of God. The Father gave us His one and only Son (John 3:16) . . . and the Son, Jesus, gave Himself willingly for our redemption (John 10:18).

Heavenly Father, may my heart reflect something of Your generosity in the way I give to those in need this Christmas. Amen.

380

17 December

Surely He has borne our griefs
And carried our sorrows.
Isaiah 53:4

Reading: Isaiah 53:4–6

Christmas not only magnifies what is good; it can also magnify the difficulties in our lives.

- The annual get-together over turkey is approached with dread by some, as not all families mirror those screened in the afternoon Christmas movies. Family problems are easily heightened under the spotlight of the 'perfect' family of our dreams.
- Loneliness raises an even larger ugly head with those who wish they had a family of any kind to share the festivities.
- Financial difficulties loom large as the shopping gets under way, and you wonder how you will manage the extra expense. Or perhaps you might even struggle to put gifts under the tree for your children.
- Perhaps worst of all, grief has robbed you of a loved one, and the 'vacant' place at the table has taken away your joy, replacing it with an ever-deepening sadness. Perhaps this even causes you to question this God who is shown to be good and kind, especially at this time of the year?

The pain of grief is certainly something I understand. I also have a grave to visit. Every year I buy wreaths instead of other more pleasant gifts for our two daughters. Not a year passes without missing their presence as our family gathers to celebrate. Yet while I understand the sentiment 'Christmas isn't the same any more', I have chosen to celebrate it passionately. For if it weren't for Christmas, what hope would we have? Therefore I choose to concentrate on God's great love for us. I choose to make much of the coming of the Saviour to this sick, sad world – and especially to my own soul. Rejoicing this Christmas is not to deny our grief, but it does remind us that because Christ came, there will be a day when pain will be gone for ever.

That is something to celebrate ... with exuberance!

Precious Saviour, thank You that Your coming gives me hope for the future. Amen.

18 December

And he will be called Wonderful Counsellor.

Isaiah 9:6, NIV

Reading: Colossians 2:1–10

Elizabeth Alexandra Mary of the House of Windsor is the Queen of the United Kingdom, Canada, Australia and New Zealand, and Head of the Commonwealth of Fifty-two Nations. She was named after her mother, King George V's mother and her paternal grandmother. Those three names reflect her royal blood.

Seven hundred years before Christ's birth, Isaiah foretold the 'royal' names of the King of kings. He wasn't named after anyone, for while His human lineage was kingly of itself – through David's ancestry – Jesus' divinity was what marked His naming. The names given by the Father to Isaiah were those describing Christ's attributes rather than His family tree.

'Wonderful Counsellor' is a single assignation with powerful meaning when both words are combined.

Jesus is simply, yet remarkably, 'full of wonder'. His wisdom is so great it is beyond our limited comprehension. For in Christ 'are hidden all the treasures of wisdom and knowledge' (Colossians 2:3). All the knowledge we need is found in Him; all of our questions are answered in the One called 'Wonderful'.

Back in Isaiah's day, the term 'counsellor' would be used of a wise king, one who gave advice and guidance to his people, influencing the direction they should take. Yet even they could get it wrong, however hard they tried. King Jesus, however, is the 'Counsellor' who, because of His complete wisdom, can never advise us incorrectly or take us down the wrong path. And what is even more amazing is that He is always available and always willing to help. In fact, this 'Wonderful Counsellor' has no complicated appointment system or exorbitant fees. He simply waits for us to experience Him through the name given to Him centuries earlier.

Wonderful Counsellor, You who see all and know all, accept my praise today. Lead me in the ways of truth and righteousness, for Your glory. Amen.

19 December

His name will be called . . .
Mighty God.
Isaiah 9:6

Reading: Isaiah 40:29–31

The incarnation is a tough concept to grasp. God became a man, but He didn't burst on to the scene without anyone knowing where He came from. His earthly life is traceable right back to His birth. 'Is not this the carpenter, the Son of Mary, and brother of James, Joses, Judas, and Simon?' (Mark 6:3). His critics denounced His teaching and miracles because they figured they knew where He came from – Jesus was only a lad from Nazareth. They'd got it so wrong. Jesus was not *merely* a lad from Nazareth; He was the 'Mighty God' spoken of by the great prophet Isaiah.

A fifty–fifty Saviour? Some kind of a superhero with supernatural powers? Absolutely not! Jesus was 100% human and 100% divine – two complete natures dwelling in one human frame for a specific time span. Jesus didn't leave His deity behind for thirty-three years, planning to pick it up again after He returned to heaven. No. He was the 'Mighty God' from before time began, as well as for those years He spent on earth.

Isaiah's words simply confirmed the deity of God's Son centuries before Jesus' feet walked Nazareth's dusty streets.

As part of the Trinity, Jesus not only displays the divine nature; He is God. He is omnipotent, omniscient and omnipresent, while all the time working in us, through us and for us with care and compassion. By His great strength, this 'Mighty God' answers our innate weakness, replacing it with the power to face life's difficulties, all the while empowering us to live a life pleasing to God.

And when our strength is gone, He has promised that 'those who wait on the LORD shall renew their strength; they shall mount up with wings like eagles, they shall run and not be weary, they shall walk and not faint' (Isaiah 40:31).

Mighty God, there are times when I feel weak, powerless to face another day. Thank You that in You I will find all that I need, if I but take time to 'wait'. Amen.

20 December

His name will be called . . .
Everlasting Father.
Isaiah 9:6

Reading: Hebrews 1:1–4

How is it that Isaiah prophesies that the coming Messiah would be known as the Everlasting Father? Is He not the second person of the Trinity – the Son?

Thankfully, Jesus explains what Isaiah pronounced: 'He who has seen Me has seen the Father . . . I am *in* the Father and the Father *in* Me' (John 14:9, 11, emphasis mine). Jesus is not the Father, but in the mystery that is the Trinity, Jesus is able to display Fatherlike characteristics towards us. He also made it clear that if we want to see the Father, then we merely need to look at Jesus Himself.

The term 'Father' is also frequently used in the sense of being the source of something. There is no doubt that Messiah-Jesus is the source of the gospel, the church and the Father of Christianity, through whom we are loved, cared for and protected. Isaiah has made no mistake, but rather has reminded us that all that we need is found in Him.

The prefix 'Everlasting' adds an overwhelming note of confidence to this designation of Jesus. For He was and is and ever will be the same; even 'If we are faithless, He remains faithful; He cannot deny Himself' (2 Timothy 2:13). Nothing can separate us from His love.

> His forever, only His,
> Who the Lord and me shall part?
> Ah, with what a rest of bliss
> Christ can fill the loving heart!
> Heaven and earth may fade and flee,
> First-born light in gloom decline;
> But, while God and I shall be,
> I am His and He is mine.[26]

Everlasting Father, You who sees all and is in all, I lay my life at Your feet in thankful adoration. Amen.

21 December

His name will be called . . .
Prince of Peace.
Isaiah 9:6

Reading: Luke 2:13–16

In a generation that chases fulfilment and tranquillity through money and achievement, peace is often as elusive as the pot of gold at the end of the rainbow.

The word 'peace' conjures up different images. More commonly it is seen as a cessation of violence, particularly in relation to war, which is one reason why the Jews found it difficult to accept Jesus as Messiah. They interpreted Isaiah's prophecy that, as 'Prince of Peace', the Messiah would rid them of their enemies and bring a military peace to the nation. But while the peace of Jerusalem has a special place in His heart (Psalm 122:6), God's interest was in expunging the enemy of sin from within the individual hearts that would one day make up His eternal kingdom.

Paul said, 'Therefore, having been justified by faith, we have peace with God through our Lord Jesus Christ' (Romans 5:1). The enmity between us and God, caused by our sin, would indeed end when the promised 'Prince of Peace' comes to dwell in us. It is Jesus who dispenses peace to our souls – that calm tranquillity that ends the spiritual conflict within us (John 14:27). And the peace of God then enables us to be at peace with ourselves, which eventually overflows to others as we follow Paul's directive to 'live peaceably with all men' (Romans 12:18).

The salutation of the angels to the shepherds outside Bethlehem spoke of God's glory, and peace on earth to those on whom God's favour rests (Luke 2:14, NIV). It is precisely because of God's glory that we can find rest for our souls. After all, only the One who sees the end from the beginning can speak peace to our hearts in this mixed-up world.

Thank You, Prince of Peace, that You can do for my heart what no-one else can. You can bring calm where confusion once reigned, and tranquillity in exchange for tears. Amen.

22 December

A PASSAGE TO PONDER

For unto us a Child is born,

Unto us a Son is given;

And the government will be upon His shoulder.

And His name will be called

Wonderful, Counselor, Mighty God,

Everlasting Father, Prince of Peace.

Of the increase of His government and peace

There will be no end,

Upon the throne of David and over His kingdom,

To order it and establish it with judgment and justice

From that time forward, even forever.

The zeal of the LORD of hosts will perform this.

Isaiah 9:6–7

Read the passage slowly and let the Author speak to you. As you ponder, ask yourself these questions:

- What does it say?
- What does it mean?
- What is God saying to me?
- How will I respond?

386

23 December

Thanks be to God for His indescribable gift!
2 Corinthians 9:15

Reading: 2 Corinthians 8:1–5

Today is the busiest shopping day of the year in the UK. That's especially true for the men of our nation as they rush out to purchase the one and only gift they are solely responsible for!

We spend considerable amounts of time and money each year seeking out those special, yet appropriate, gifts for friends and loved ones. Yet for some, the process has become a huge burden in every way. We seem to have forgotten that exchanging gifts is to help us remember God's gift to us in sending Jesus. Christmas has become yet one more opportunity for us to compare ourselves with each other (who buys the best gifts?), rather than pointing us to the One whose gift is 'indescribable'.

The Saviour gave up everything in order that we might know the kind of riches you can't buy in the shops – even in Harrods!

'For you know the grace of our Lord Jesus Christ, that though He was rich, yet for your sakes He became poor, that you through His poverty might become rich' (2 Corinthians 8:9). Jesus' thoughts were not about Himself when He willingly left the glory of heaven to live in abject poverty on earth. Rather, we were the motivation behind His self-sacrificial generosity. Wrapped in a baby-sized package, God gifted the very best of His love, grace, mercy and forgiveness to anyone willing to receive it.

The lavish generosity of our God ought to be remembered every time we give or receive a gift . . . however small it appears, and especially as we are urged to share what we have with the household of faith (Galatians 6:10). 'Support the weak. And remember the words of the Lord Jesus, that He said, "It is more blessed to give than to receive"' (Acts 20:35).

Lord Jesus, Indescribable Gift of the Father, I thank You for this expression of Your generosity. May I mirror Your generosity this Christmas to those in need. Amen.

387

24 December

The heavens declare the glory of God.
Psalm 19:1

Reading: Luke 2:8–17

Picture the scene with me. The sheep had been gathered into the makeshift pen for the night, and the shepherd on first watch lay across the entrance. He was close enough to hear the jovial banter around the fire, as his friends joked about escaping from relatives they hadn't seen for years: happy to stretch out under the inky sky while distant family members lay comfortably in their beds. Sleep didn't come easily as talk was directed skyward. These shepherds knew every inch of that sky; they could name the constellations as easily as the sheep they grazed in the fields around them. But there was something different about it that night.

Suddenly, the darkness fled, and the noise from the sheep pen was enough to wake the dead! 'And behold, an angel of the Lord stood before them, and the glory of the Lord shone around them' (Luke 2:9)! The shepherds sat bolt upright in absolute terror! What was going on?

The men shook. The heavenly being spoke – to them! Surely not? He told of good news; joy; a baby – no, not just any baby – a Saviour. The Christ! The men barely drew breath for fear of missing anything. They would find the baby in the town nestling below them, lying in a manger. Unbelievable! Wonderful! Amazing! There weren't enough words to form a reply, but that didn't matter, because as the 'visitor' finished speaking, the sky filled with what could only be described as a heavenly host. A choir in the sky! They sang and praised God: 'Glory to God in the highest, and on earth peace, goodwill toward men' (Luke 2:14).

Their majestic presence momentarily obliterated the stars! Their message blew these simple men away! Was there ever a night that declared the glory of God like this one? The shepherds didn't think so as they hurried off to find the Christ-child.

Heavenly Father, the One before whom angels bow, accept my praise for that night of all nights, when heaven came to earth. Amen.

25 December

And she brought forth her firstborn Son, and wrapped
Him in swaddling cloths, and laid Him in a manger,
because there was no room for them in the inn.

Luke 2:7

Reading: Luke 2:1–7

Mary was no different from any other mother who had just given birth.

Amazement would have dismissed the pain of childbirth, while love and wonder immediately filled the empty space her baby had occupied for the previous nine months.

I'm absolutely sure that Mary wouldn't have been able to take her eyes off her little son. Several pounds of human flesh captivating both heart and mind. I wonder what questions filled her mind about all the years that stretched ahead. Had the angel's words morphed the sense of responsibility she and Joseph suddenly felt as they tried out His name for the first time? *Jesus. Saviour.* Or was it simply a mother's love that overwhelmed Mary as she felt his little mouth tug at her breast?

And as she counted his toes before wrapping Him in those ribbons of cloth, could she ever have imagined that they would one day miraculously hold Him atop the stormy waves of Galilee's rough sea? Or that the sticky little hand grasping her finger so tightly now would one day touch a leper, making him whole again, or take the lifeless hand of a young girl and raise her back to life? Could that young mother ever have dreamt, as sleep finally visited Bethlehem's stable, that her infant son had walked with angels before He came to visit her world, never mind that He had created it in the first place?

When His eyes caught hers, did Mary know that in the future her baby boy would rule the nations without a sword in His hand? Or that one day she would stand beneath His cross and finally understand what the title the angel gave her son really meant for her and all mankind. *Jesus. Saviour!*

Thank You, 'heaven's perfect Lamb', that You came to earth to be my Saviour. In everything else that happens today, I choose to celebrate Your coming, Lord Jesus. Amen.

389

26 December

And when eight days were completed for the circumcision of the Child, His name was called Jesus, the name given by the angel before He was conceived in the womb.
Luke 2:21

Reading: Romans 15:7–10

God's people were always meant to be distinctive. The Jewish males were even to have a physical mark that distinguished them from the Gentiles – the religious rite of circumcision. God's covenant with Abraham and his descendants – to make them a great nation, and to be their God (Genesis 17:7) – was affirmed by circumcising baby boys at eight days old.

This act of obedience was both a sign of faith and a willingness to put away evil – an outward sign of an inward act (Deuteronomy 10:16). Therefore, when Jesus was eight days old, Joseph sought out the Mohel to circumcise the child he would bring up as his own. The Law demanded it, and Joseph was a godly man. Remarkably, the Mohel who skilfully removed this baby boy's foreskin had no idea that this Child would one day be the One to remove evil from *his* own heart.

In Christ, all the promises made to Abraham were fulfilled. 'And if you are Christ's, then you are Abraham's seed, and heirs according to the promise' (Galatians 3:29). We, whose hearts have been 'circumcised by Christ' – that is, our evil nature has been removed – are now God's special people. This is something that is also confirmed in the name given to Mary's child. Jesus in Hebrew is 'Yeshua', the same name Moses gave to Joshua (Yeshua), who would one day lead Israel into freedom. Only this little boy was destined to deliver more than a nation out of physical bondage. His task was to 'redeem those who were under the law, that we might receive the adoption of sons' (Galatians 4:5).

The bloody, painful act of Jesus' circumcision satisfied the Law. His next bloody, painful act would fulfil the Law completely.

Lord Jesus, Your willingness to suffer in my place means that I am a redeemed inheritor of the promises of God. Thank You. Amen.

27 December

Now when the days of her purification according
to the law of Moses were completed, they brought Him
to Jerusalem to present Him to the Lord.

Luke 2:22

Reading: Leviticus 12:1–8

Jesus was born into a deeply devout Jewish home. Joseph and Mary both followed the Law of Moses as best they could, and keeping the requirements concerning the birth of a child was no different.

'The firstborn of your sons you shall give to Me,' God had commanded the Israelites through Moses in Exodus 22:29. Even before then, the firstborn son was seen as special within God's covenant race. This was reinforced when the Jewish firstborns were saved from the angel of death in Egypt by applying the blood of a sacrificial lamb on the doorposts of their homes (Exodus 12:12–13).

Mary and Joseph had already demonstrated their obedience in circumcision, and now they followed that by bringing Jesus to the temple forty days after His birth to present Him to the Lord, while also fulfilling the sacrificial obligation for Mary's purification (Leviticus 12). They already knew Jesus would be special, but I doubt they were prepared for a visit to the temple they would never forget, eventually returning to Nazareth with Simeon and Anna's prophecies ringing in their ears. No wonder they 'marveled at those things which were spoken of Him' (Luke 2:33).

But the words spoken were not all sweet. Undoubtedly, Mary thought long and often on Simeon's words: 'a sword will pierce through your own soul also' (Luke 2:35). But for now they had a son to raise, and that could only be done well if they continued to do what God had instructed. The fact that Jesus was 'the firstborn over all creation ... before all things ... the head of the body, the church ... the firstborn from the dead ...' (Colossians 1:15–18) was lost on them at that time. Mary and Joseph simply and powerfully remained faithful in what they knew, and God blessed them.

You've told us Lord, that 'to obey is better than sacrifice' (1 Samuel 15:22). May I be obedient in all You ask of me. Amen.

391

28 December

And the Child grew and became strong in spirit,
filled with wisdom; and the grace of God was upon Him.
Luke 2:40

Reading: Luke 2:39–50

The New Testament writers give us virtually no information on Jesus' childhood and adolescence. Such wisdom was obviously Spirit-given, for much unsubstantiated nonsense is written outside of Scripture. Documents describing some sort of 'wunderkind' are unreliable, unhelpful and disrespectful. But the little information we have from Luke perfectly matches the Jesus we find throughout the Scriptures, and can therefore be trusted.

What we do know is that 'He was obedient to them' (speaking of His mother Mary and Joseph; Luke 2:51, NLT), and that 'He grew in wisdom and in stature and in favour with God and all the people' (Luke 2:52, NLT). The only other information we have is of the incident when Mary and Joseph have to go looking for Jesus when He is twelve years old, only to find Him engaging with rabbinical teachers in the temple (Luke 2:43–46). It's a very important incident for, on the cusp of full participation in religious life, the adolescent Jesus informs His earthly 'parents' that He knows exactly who He is and what His life's mission is to be.

'I must be about My Father's business,' Jesus told them (Luke 2:49) – something He took very seriously, as His engagement with men of spiritual wisdom confirms. How challenging to think that if Christ sought wisdom and learning, then we ought also to strive to know God better, both through His Word and from wise spiritual teachers. Mary and Joseph remained somewhat puzzled by Jesus' response, but Mary 'stored all these things in her heart' (Luke 2:51, NLT). A very wise thing to do, for even with historical hindsight, who among us will not benefit from pausing to reflect on who Jesus really is?

Jesus, Son of God, Messiah, Friend of Sinners, Lover of my soul, I cannot grasp the enormity of who You are, but I am thankful that Your 'Father's business' included my salvation! Amen.